The History of Deptford, in the counties of Kent and Surrey, compiled from authentic records.

Nathan Dews

The History of Deptford, in the counties of Kent and Surrey, compiled from authentic records.

Dews, Nathan
British Library, Historical Print Editions
British Library
1883
266 p. ; 8°.
10352.bb.30.

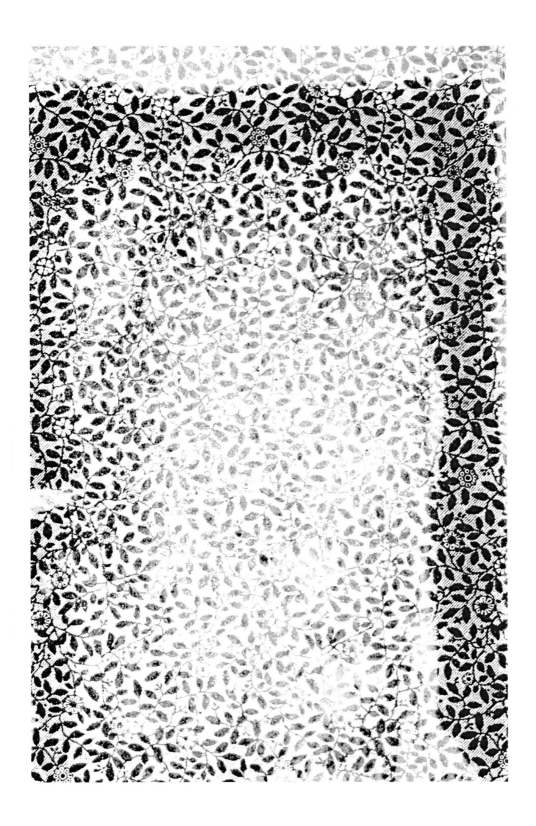

Yours very Truly.
W. I. Evelyn.

THE
HISTORY OF DEPTFORD,

IN THE COUNTIES OF KENT AND SURREY,

COMPILED

FROM AUTHENTIC RECORDS,

BY

NATHAN DEWS,

Author of the "History of Somersham," &c.

"Such place hath Deptford, navy-building Town."—*Pope.*

PRICE FIVE SHILLINGS.

LONDON:
PUBLISHED BY J. D. SMITH, BOOKSELLER, &c., THE BROADWAY,
DEPTFORD.

PRINTED AT THE "GREENWICH OBSERVER" STEAM PRINTING
WORKS, STOCKWELL STREET, GREENWICH.

1883.

London :
' Greenwich Observer " Steam Printing Works.
18 & 19, Stockwell Street.
Greenwich, S.E.

TO

WILLIAM JOHN EVELYN,

OF WOTTON, SURREY, ESQUIRE,

THE REPRESENTATIVE

OF AN ANCIENT FAMILY

LONG AND HONOURABLY CONNECTED

WITH THE

TOWN OF DEPTFORD,

THIS WORK IS

BY PERMISSION

RESPECTFULLY DEDICATED

BY THE COMPILER.

CONTENTS.

PREFACE.

———

It seems somewhat surprising that the History of so important a town as Deptford is, and has been,—in a portable book form—should have remained so long unpublished. That such a work was needed is evident from the readiness of old parishioners and others to become subscribers.

The task of compiling this work was undertaken eighteen months ago, at the suggestion of the Rev. S. A. Dougherty, a native of the town.

I beg here to tender my humble thanks to the clergy and others for supplying me with much valuable information which could not otherwise have been obtained.

N. D.

HISTORY of DEPTFORD.

ROMAN AND SAXON PERIOD.

"It is opportune to look back on Old Times and contemplate our
fathers."   *Sir Thomas Browne.*

"Sunt lachrymæ rerum ; et mentem mortalia tangunt."
                                              Æneid Lib. I., 462.

THE Parish (*a*) of Deptford is situated on the banks of
the River Thames, about four miles from London,
in the north-west corner of the County of Kent (*b*) and
partly in Surrey.   It is in the Lath of Sutton-at-Hone ;
Hundred of Blackheath (called in Domesday Book, the
hundred of Grenviz) ; Diocese of Rochester ; Archdea-
conry of Rochester, and Rural Deanery of Deptford.

a The word Parish is derived from an old Anglo-Saxon term mean-
ing "priestshire"—the division or jurisdiction of a priest. Kent was
ecclesiastically divided into parishes by Archbishop Honorius, about
A.D. 630 ; but it was not until the reign of Queen Elizabeth that the
ecclesiastical divisions, previously existing, assumed their great lay
importance, through being made the area of the district, which, by
rates, was to maintain its own poor.

b Kent is the only county in England retaining its Celtic name, all
the others being of Saxon origin.   The Celtic term of which Kent is
a corrupted form, signifies a head or termination, and was, therefore, a
very appropriate designation for the part of this island projecting
towards the opposite continent, by whose inhabitants it was in all
probability bestowed.

B

In shape, it is an irregular oblong, two-and-a-quarter miles from north to south, and one-and-a-half from east to west. Its boundary has five unequal sides ; that on the north-north-west is formed by the Earl sewer ; on the north-east, by the river Thames ; on the east, by the river Ravensbourne and Deptford Creek ; on the south, by an irregular arbitrary line, marked by stones, running along the summit of Deptford Common ; on the west-ward, by a line running northward from a point on the high land, near Nunhead Cemetery, along the White Post Lane sewer, to its junction with the Earl sewer.

It is not very surprising that few facts of historical importance are to be found in the voluminous chronicles of our early British annalists, connected with the origin, progress, and establishment of so inconsiderable a village as West Greenwich or Deptford-le-Stronde must have been prior to the reign of Henry VIII. ; but notwith-standing the absence of written authorities to prove its high antiquity, there is good inferential evidence to sup-port an opinion that the site of it was originally occupied by Roman settlers. It might be a work of supererogation to establish the existence of a Grenovicus in the ichno-graphy of Roman Britain, or to attach any higher import-ance to the origin of Deptford than is to be derived from the positive testimony of authentic history ; but there are various coincidences of name, site, and local indica-tions, which, to the mind of a learned antiquary, would present strong presumptive features in support of an hypothesis that the Saxons, who conferred the names Meretone and Depeford, succeeded a settlement of Roman adventurers.

Roman remains are known to exist at some thirty feet below the roadway, at the top of High Street, near the New Cross Road : a portion of tessellated pavement and massive brickwork—which Mr. Liddiard says was unques-tionably Roman—having been discovered there during the construction of the sewer, about eighteen years ago. The Romans had a camp at the corner of St. George's Fields, with a chain of forts and bastions extending east- *wes* ward to the Thames, at Lambeth, and westward to the *East*

Ravensbourne, at Deptford Bridge. "It is hardly to be questioned" that these Lines "were cast up to prevent the incursion of the Britons into Kent." Two pillars of a gate, with a Janus' Head (c) on each, were found in 1685, at the end of Kent Street (Old Kent Road), together with many stone foundations, Roman bricks, &c., and some fifty years later, in a garden, near to the road, at New Cross, a simpulum, two urns, and five or six of those viols, usually called lachrymatories (d) were unearthed. On the 8th of May, 1868, some workmen engaged in constructing a sewer in Nelson Street, New Town, Deptford, discovered a stone coffin (e), such as used by the early British Christians, containing the skeleton of a man of great size ; and quite recently, in digging the foundation of a new public house, on the Gravel Pit Estate, in Church Street (near the Broadway), there was discovered, what is supposed to be a Druid's Head.

The deflection of the old Watling Street, after it had crossed the Ravensbourne, was, probably, owing to the riverside portion of the parish being swampy, wooded marshland, subject to periodical inundations of the tide ; indeed, as will be presently seen, it is called Meretun and Meretone, i.e, the "Town in the Marshes," in the Anglo-Saxon Chronicle and Domesday Book.

c
>"Now by two headed Janus,
>Nature hath fram'd strange fellows in her time :
>Some that will evermore peep through their eyes,
>And laugh, like parrots, at a bagpiper ;
>And others of such vinegar aspect,
>That they'll not show their teeth in way of smile,
>Though Nestor swear the jest be laughable.

Merchant of Venice, Act I, Scene I.

In 1690, one of these Janus Heads was purchased by the learned Dr. Woodward of Gresham College ; and it would be interesting to know what has become of it.

Hasted, in his History of Kent, gives an illustration of this Roman antiquity, and seems to have fallen into an error, in supposing it to have been found within the confines of the parish of Deptford.

d Hasted.

e Mr. Baker, potato merchant, of Deptford Bridge, a native of the parish, is in possession of a tooth taken from the skull of this skeleton.

The first recorded event connected with the parish occurs in the Anglo-Saxon Chronicle, A.D. 871, when "King Aethered and Aelfred (afterwards King Alfred the Great) his brother fought against the army (the Danes) at Meretun ; and they were in two bodies, and they put both to flight, and during a great part of the day were victorious ; and there was great slaughter on either hand ; but the Danes had possession of the place of carnage ; and there Bishop Headmund (of Sherborne) was slain, and many good men." Deptford Creek was evidently much frequented by the Danish fleet, as it had probably been by that of the Anglo-Saxons in earlier times, for we find them here again in the beginning of the eleventh century.

"A.D. 1011. And then in this year, between the Nativity of St. Mary and St. Michael's Mass, (f) they besieged Canterbury, and got into it through treachery, because Aelmaer betrayed it, whose life the Archbishop Aelfeah (Alphege) had before saved. And there they took the Archbishop Aelfeah, and Aelfweard the king's steward, and the Abbess Leofrune (g) and Bishop Godwin. And Abbot Aelfmar they let go away. And they took there within all the men in orders, and men and women : it is not to be told to any man how many of the people were there. And they remained within the city afterwards as long as they would. And when they had thoroughly searched the city, then went they to their ships, and led the Archbishop with them.

"He was then captive
who erewhile was
the head of the English race
and of Christendom.
There might then be seen
misery, where men oft
erewhile had seen bliss,
in that hapless city,
whence to us came first
Christendom and bliss,
for God, and for the world.

"And they kept the Archbishop with them so long as until the time that they martyred him.

f That is, between the 8th and 29th of September.

g Leofrune was abbess of St. Mildred's in the Isle of Thanet ; Godwin was Bishop of Rochester ; and Aelfmaer was abbot of St. Augustine's at Canterbury.

"A.D. 1012. In this year came Eadric the ealdorman, and all the chief witan, clergy and laity, of the English people to London, before Easter ; Easter-day was then on the date, the ides of April (13th April) ; and they were there then so long as until all the tribute was paid, after Easter ; that was eight and forty thousand pounds (h). Then on the Saturday (19th April) was the army greatly excited against the Bishop, because he would not promise them any money ; but he forbade that anything should be given for him. They had also drunk deeply, for wine had been brought there from the south. Then took they the Bishop, led him to their husting on the eve of Sunday, the octaves of Easter, which was on the 13th of the Kalends of May (19th April) ; and there they then shamefully slaughtered him ; they cast upon him bones and the horns of oxen, and then one of them struck him with an axe-iron on the head, so that with the blow he sank down ; and his holy blood fell on the earth, and his holy soul he sent forth to God's kingdom. And on the morrow the body was carried to London, and the bishops, Eadnoth (of Dorchester) and Aelfun (of London), and the townsmen, received it with all reverence, and buried it in St. Paul's minster ; and there God now manifesteth the miraculous powers of the holy martyr" (i).

St. Alphege was martyred where Greenwich Parish Church now stands, which is dedicated to him. His body was removed from St. Paul's minster to Canterbury, in 1023.

The Domesday Survey, relating to Deptford, is somewhat perplexing, " Hi duo Solini (in Grenviz) tempore regis Edvardi fuerunt duo maneria. Unum tenuit Heraldus Comes et aliud Brixi et modo sunt in uno."

Translation. These two sowlings (in Greenwich) in the time of King Edward, were two manors. One held by Count Harold (afterwards King) ; the other by Brixi. And now (temp. Domesday Survey) they are one.

h The Bodleian and Cottonian MSS. state the sum to have been " viii thousand pounds."

The Anglo-Saxon Chronicle. Stevenson 1853.

The manor held by Brixi is supposed to have been in Deptford.

Again, Episcopus Lisoiensis tenet in Chent (in Meretone in Brixistan Hundred in Comitatu de Sudrie) duos solinos qui huic manerio (Meretone) adjacuerunt tempore Regis Edvardi et Regis Willelmi sicut testantur homines de hundred. Ipse reclamat advocatorem episcopum Baiocensem, et prœpositus suus inde noluit placitare.

Translation. The Bishop of Lisieux holds in Kent (in Mereton in Brixton Hundred in the County of Surrey), two sowlings, which lay to this manor in the time of King Edward and King William, as the men of the hundred testify. He rejecteth as a voucher the Bishop of Bayeux, and the bailiff would not thenceforth enter his plea.

Henshall says " The hundred of Greenwich comprehended seven distinct hamlets in the reign of Edward, under more numerous jurisdiction, for the place, whence the name was assumed, was divided into two manors, analagous to our East and West Greenwich," and " to Greenwich occupied by the Bishop of Liseux, as subtenant of the Conqueror, two sowlings adjoining to Deptford, then denominated Meretone or the town in the marshes, in the Hundred of Brixton, and included under its manorial jurisdiction as part of the county of Surrey, in the days of the Confessor and early part of William's reign, were annexed by the Earl (Odo) to his principality of Kent. This fact was clearly proved by the testimony of the impannelled evidence of the jury of the district. When this military retainer was summoned to account for this infringement, or invasion, on the royal demesne, he appealed to his feudal chieftain as his protector, who had guaranteed the position to him. The Commissioners then cited the bailiff of the Bishop of Baieux to prove by what title, such lands were seized by him, and conveyed to his lord's vassal ; but so great was the independent power and authority of Odo, and the general peers of the monarch, that his deputy refused to plead before this court and considered himself superior to their control. William probably overlooked this encroachment, and deemed such a trifling possession of too inconsiderable importance, for which to cite Odo before the high national council. Hence probably the knight of this Norman noble continued to enjoy the district without farther molestation."

The king's settlement of the matter in favour of his half-brother proved a bone of contention between the officials of the two counties for centuries; official documents at one time stating the parish to be within the boundary of the county of Surrey and at other times in Kent.

Philipot (1796) in his "Villare Cantianum" speaking of Hatcham says "The manor was formerly considered as part of the county of Kent, and its appropriation to either county became a matter of contest until the year 1636, when it was decided judicially to be subject to assessments as belonging to Surrey. This determination was made on the petition of Mr. Randolph Crew, a London merchant, probably lessee of the manor, who, on a levy of ship money, was taxed for his property here, by the assessors of both counties. He did not (like Hampden) question the legality of the tax, but merely objected to the hardship of being compelled to make a double payment, and petitioned the Lords of the Council for redress; when being referred to the Judges of Assize for Kent and Surrey, they, after inquisition and examination of witnesses, on the 31st of May, 1636, certified the Lords that the petitioner's manor of Hatcham lies in Surrey and not in Kent. The certificate was signed by Francis Crawley, Justice of the Common-Pleas; and Richard Weston, Baron of the Exchequer."

At what time the parish adopted its present name is not certain, but it could scarcely have been before the Norman Conquest, for, as has already been seen, in the Domesday Survey, it is spoken of as Meretone and in the Saxon Chronicle, A.D. 871, it is also called Meretun.

Lambarde, in his "Perambulations of Kent, 1570," says this place was called "West Greenwiche," in ancient evidences and in Latine "Vadum profundum" (j). It

j Deep ford.

received the name of Depeford from its position on the Ravensbourne : the river here being of great depth, and as tenements were erected along the shore, it obtained the addition of Stronde, or Strand. We also find it sometimes termed Depeford-Stronde, alias West Greenwich, from its relative position to Greenwich ; in course of time, however, this latter appellation was disused, and it retained its present name of Deptford.

The word is variously spelt in many old books and manuscripts—viz. : "Depforde" in A.D. 1555 ; "Depeforde" in 1570 ; "Depford" in 1572 and 1649 ; "Detford" in 1648 ; "Dedford" in 1673 ; "Depthorde" in the Harlein MSS. ; "Debtford" in an old ballad of the 17th century entitled "The Debtford Plumb Cake ;" and on an ancient monument in St. Nicholas' Church "Deepford."

The Manors.

WEST GREENWICH OR DEPTFORD,

AFTERWARDS KNOWN AS

SAYES COURT.

" Here Cowley lived, dear to poetic fame,
And Evelyn, a classic lustre shed ;—
Resplendent stars, like meteors of flame,
That far and wide their radiance have spread,"
Holbert.

ON the death of Odo, the half-brother to the Conqueror, the Manor of West Greenwich was given to
Gilbert de Magminot, or Maminot, as more commonly
spelt, who was one of the eight barons associated with
John de Fienes, for the garrison and defence of Dover
Castle. For this service considerable lands were assigned
by the king to De Fienes, who divided them between
himself and the barons associated with him, binding
each of them, by the tenure of their lands, to furnish a
certain number of soldiers for the defence of the castle.
The estates granted to Gilbert de Maminot, Bishop of
Lisieux, consisted of twenty-four knight's fees, which
were held of this place, as the "caput baroniæ" or head
of the barony, and together with it, made the "Barony
of Maminot" as it was then called. Having fixed upon

Deptford as the site of the barony, (*a*) De Maminot proceeded to erect a castle here for his residence, every vestige of which has, long since, disappeared. Hasted, nevertheless, infers that "some stony foundations" existing in the last century, seemed "to point out the situation of it near Sayes Court, in Bromfield, on the brow of the Thames, near the mast dock." The date of his decease is unrecorded, but we find him living in A.D. 1085.

He was succeeded by his son, Hugh de Maminot, the father of Wakelin de Maminot, who after inheriting the estates, married the daughter of Robert de Ferrars. Wakelin gave the Manor of Deptford to the Monks of Bermondsey Abbey, Surrey, in the year 1145. "Wakelinus Mammynot dedit dimidiam partem totius Grenewich monarchis de Bermuneseye" (M. S. Harl: 231). Although this grant was, probably, never confirmed, on account of the very unsettled state of the country, yet it gave the Bermondsey Monastery a claim to interfere. He was Lord Warden of the Cinque Ports, and held Dover castle for the rightful heir to the crown (the Empress Maud, or Matilda, wife of Geoffrey of Anjou, and only surviving issue of Henry I). On being compelled by King Stephen to surrender his charge, he fled the country, leaving his possessions to his son, Wakelin, who married the Countess Juliana de Vere, daughter of Alberic de Vere, Great Chamberlain of England, and widow of Hugh Bigod, Earl of Norfolk. He was a good benefactor to the Monks of Bermondsey, to whom, in 1157, he gave ten shillings rent out of the "Mill of Deptford." In the twelfth year of the reign of Henry II., upon the assessment of the aid for marrying the king's daughter, he certified twenty-seven of his Knight's fees to be "de veteri feoffamento" and one "de novo." Dying without

a Philipot, in his "Villare Cantianum" says, "It may appear by the quire of Dover Castle, transmitted on record in the King's Exchequer, that it had the reputation of a barony."

Hac sunt feoda Baronia de Magminot. quæ tenentur de Willelme de Say. quæ ipse tenet de Rege per Baroniam : Et reddunt Wardam ad Castrum Dovoriæ Per 32 Septimanas.

issue in the third year of the reign of Richard I.,
A.D. 1191, his sister Alice became his coheir, and brought
Deptford, amongst many other vast estates, to her
husband, Geoffrey de Say (second son of William de
Say), who granted his manor of West Greenwich (as it
was then more generally termed) with the advowson of
the Church of St. Nicholas, and its appurtenances, to the
Knights Templars, in pure and perpetual alms *(Dugdale
Mon: Vol. II*, p. 555). "The enormous ransom
demanded by the Emperor of Germany, Henry VI., for
the release of Richard, Cœur de Lion, from captivity,
was taken by Geoffrey de Say, and other of the chief
barons and bishops. Freed from his confinement at
Trifels, Richard hurried with Geoffrey de Say, and his
other liberators to England, and landed at Sandwich,
March 13th, 1195" *(Dunkin)*. Geoffrey died in the six-
teenth year of the reign of King John, and was succeeded
by his son of the same name ; who A.D. 1214, had livery
of the inheritance of both of his parents, upon the payment of 400 marks to the king. He, shortly afterwards,
regained possession of the Manor of Deptford and the
advowson of the Church of St. Nicholas, from the
Knights Templars, in exchange for the Manor of
Saddlescombe, in the county of Sussex. He also ratified
to the Canons of Begham, or Bayham, the lands of
Brocile (Brockley) and the Church of St. Nicholas,
which had been alienated from his barony, and given to
the Knights Templars, by his father and mother. The
heavy fine exacted by the king, most probably induced
Geoffrey to join the barons, who had taken up arms
under the command of Robert Fitzwalter and William
Marshall, son of the Earl of Pembroke, driven thereto by
the tyranny and avariciousness of John, which resulted
in the signing of Magna Charta, at Runnymede,
A.D. 1215. Upon this provocation, John seized the
lands and fees of his rebellious vassal lying in Kent and
other counties, and bestowed them on Peter de Crohun.
Geoffrey, deprived of his castle at Deptford, joined Louis,
son of Philip, king of France, immediately he invaded
Britain ; the throne of which he claimed in right of his

wife. Louis, after besieging and taking the castle of
Rochester, was escorted by Geoffrey and many other
barons to St. Paul's Cathedral, London, where, after
prayers, they performed homage, and swore fealty to him,
with the "majores or nobiles" as the magnates of London
are called in the Year Books of the City. The unex-
pected death of King John at Newark, October 19th,
1216, entirely changed the policy of the barons: "The
evil will borne to King John seeming to die with him,
and to be buried in the same grave."

Pursuant to the terms settled at the conference between Pembroke and Louis, on an islet of the Thames,
near Kingston, the Manor of Deptford, together with his
former possessions, were restored to Geoffrey on the
11th of September, A.D. 1217. A.D. 1223, upon levying the
scutage of Montgomery, Geoffrey answered for twenty-
seven fees of the fees of Maminot. He died in Gascony,
upon the Monday preceding the Feast of St. Bartholomew, A.D. 1229, and was succeeded in the barony by his
son and heir, William de Say, who, after performing
homage, had livery of his father's lands ; King Henry
accepting one hundred pounds, by forty marks a year,
paid at Michaelmas and Easter for relief.

William de Say became Governor of Rochester Castle
in 1259 ; where we find him residing until the battle of
Lewes in 1264, when Simon de Montfort proved victorious and took the King prisoner. De Say together
with the Earl of Warenne, the King's half-brothers, and
other barons, fled from the field to Pevensey Castle,
whence they escaped to Damme, in Flanders, where the
Queen, in company with the exiled foreigners, Archbishop
Boniface, Bishop of Hereford, Peter of Savoy, and John
Mansell, had assembled an army of hired troops. William
de Say died in 1271, leaving a son and heir of the same
name, aged 19, who held this manor "in capite" by
barony, and the repair of a part of Rochester Bridge and
a certain part of Dover Castle, called from its possessors
"Sayes Tower." This William de Say accounted to the
Exchequer for the sum of £56 6s. 8d. for twenty-seven
fees of the Honour of Maminot ; viz., twenty-six of the

old feoffment, and one of the new. That he had free-warren and divers other privileges, is evident from an entry in the Hundred Roll.

On the 14th of June, 1293 (22 Edw. 1.) the King issued writs to the sheriffs, to summon all those who owed military service—amongst whom was William de Say—to attend the monarch on the first of September following at Portsmouth, sufficiently furnished with horse and arms, to proceed for the defence of Gascony, against the King of France, which the military tenants were not disposed to perform, and which they disputed the King's right to enforce.

He died in 1294, leaving Geoffrey his son and heir, aged 14. William de Leybourne paid a fine to the King, and obtained his wardship with the view of Geoffrey's marrying Idonea, Leybourne's daughter—an expectation fulfilled in due time.

Geoffrey obtained livery of his lands in 1305, after performing homage. He accompanied King Edward I. in the expedition which terminated in the conquest of Scotland ; and, probably, for his services obtained the ensuing year a charter from the King for a weekly market every Friday, and a fair yearly upon the eve and day of the Blessed Virgin, at his manor at Sawbrightesworth.

Geoffrey died in 1321, and his wife Idonea surviving, had an assignment of the Manor of Birling, and certain lands in Burgham, for her dowry. He was succeeded by his son and heir Geoffrey de Say, aged 17 ; Margaret de Badlesmere holding the wardship of Deptford during his minority.

Having made proof of his age in 1325 he had livery of his lands granted him, and was summoned to Parliament in the first year of the reign of King Edward III. He obtained, in 1334, the King's charter for free-warren for all his demesne lands in his lordship of Greenwich, Deptford, &c., with the view of frankpledge, infangtheft, outfangtheft, and divers other privileges.

He married Maud, daughter of Guy Beauchamp, second Earl of Warwick—" The Black Dog of Ardenne " who caused Piers Gaveston to be beheaded on Blacklow Hill—and by her had issue : William, son and heir, and three daughters, viz. : Idonea, who was married to Sir John de Clinton, of Maxtoke, Knight ; Elizabeth, who was married first to Thomas de Aldone and afterwards to Sir William Heron, Knight ; and Joane, who was likewise married twice, first to William de Fienes and afterwards to Stephen de Valoines.

Geoffrey de Say died on the 26th of June, 1360, and his wife Maud, surviving, had the manors of Birling and Burgham assigned to her in dower. She likewise, in consideration of her services to Queen Philippa and the Lady Isabel, the King's daughter, obtained, in the forty-second year of the reign of King Edward III., the grant of an annuity of 100 marks per annum, to be paid out of the Exchequer.

Geoffery was succeeded by his son and heir William de Say, who died in 1375, leaving an infant son and heir named John, who died in his minority and in ward to the King, A.D. 1382. His sister Elizabeth, then 16 years of age, being his heir, obtained Deptford, with other possessions. She was married first to Sir John de Falvesle, Lord of Falvesley in Northamptonshire. Soon after obtaining livery of the lands of her inheritance, her husband died ; she was afterwards married to Sir William Heron, Knight, " by reason whereof he had the title of Lord Say."

In 1395 Lord and Lady Say levied a fine on all their lands and manors in Kent, to the use of them and the heirs male of their bodies, with remainder to her own right heirs.

Lady Say died A.D. 1398, without issue, upon which this manor came to her lord, in her right ; and he died possessed of it in 1404. By the inquisition taken after her death it was found that Sir William de Clinton, Knight, son of Idonea, sister of William de Say last mentioned ; Mary, wife of Otho de Worthington and daughter of Thomas de Aldon, by Elizabeth, another sister of the said William de Say, with Maud, her sister ; and Roger de Fienes were her heirs and next of kin.

Sir William Heron, under the title of Lord Say, was, in the first year of King Henry IV., joined in commission with Walter, Bishop of Durham, and others, to treat with the Ambassadors of the King of France, upon that delicate question—the restitution of the goods and jewels of Queen Isabel, the late wife of King Richard II. His diplomatic abilities also led to his employment in other instances. His testament bears date the 30th of October, A.D. 1404.

This family of Say, mighty amongst the barons of their day and generation, fixed the name of " Say's Court " (or Sayes Court, as now generally spelt) on their Deptford abode ; a name preserved to the present day, despite of the vast changes and alterations Deptford has undergone in common with the other suburbs of London ; a name so firmly rooted in English literature that can never be forgotten whilst the English language exists.

The default of a male heir, now dissolved the barony of which Deptford, under the Maminots and Says, had been the " caput," whilst the divisions of the property amongst the co-heirs, caused a dissolution of the manorial ties Odo so arbitrarily combined.

Arms : Quarterly, Or and gules ; which bearing came to them from the Magminots, and again from the Says to the Peckhams, Parrocks and St. Nicholas's ; but these bore it only in chief.

According to another inquisition, made in 1414, it was found that Sir John Philipp, Knight, and Alice his wife, held the reversion of the superior manor of Sayes Court, and that Sir William Philipp, Knight, his brother, was his next heir.

The manor of Deptford-le-Stronde had previously passed into the hands of Edmund, Earl of March.

A.D., 1436. William de la Pole, Earl of Suffolk, having married Alice, daughter and heiress of Thomas Chaucer, widow of Sir John Philipp, Knight, after doing his fealty, had livery of the lands. Unboundedly ambitious, and with unusual attainments, William de la Pole, advanced himself to vast possessions and the highest dignities in the land ; availing himself of the fullest extent of the weakness of the monarch,—who, although he possessed some good qualities, yet they were of a kind more suitable to a cloistered monk, than to a king, whose destiny was either a camp or a court. Kings of such calibre invariably acquire a favorite—for which position the Duke of Gloucester contended with the Earl of Suffolk. Suffolk was the most successful—probably the best courtier—for, in the question of the marriage of the King, he carried his point, that "Henry should be united to a princess possessed of intelligence and spirit ; in order that the deficiencies of the consort might be counterbalanced."

Unhappily for the success of this notion, the bride selected, was Margaret, of Anjou, the French queen's cousin. She was the daughter of Renè, the titular King of Sicily and Jerusalem, who, although lord of many States, was very poor. The Earl of Suffolk, whilst negotiating this fatal marriage, became in as high favour with the French Sovereign as he was with his English royal master. Being great steward of the King's household, " he was sent to Sicilie, to perform the solemnity of marriage with Margaret, the daughter of the King of that province, as a proxie, on the behalf of King Henry ; and to conduct her into England (*Dudg, Baronage II*, 188) whereupon "in the month of November 23rd (Henry VI.) William de la Pole, with his wife and many honourable persons, both men and women richly apparelled, sayled into France, for the conveyance of the lady Margaret, nominated queene in the realme of England. This noble company came to the city of Towers (Tours) in Touraine, when they were honourably received and entertained, both of the French King, and of the Duke Reiner, when the Marquesse of Suffolke, as procurator to King Henry, espoused the said lady in the Church of St. Martin ;" escorting her afterwards to England, where she " was married to King Henry in the Abbey of Tichfield on the 22nd of Aprill." She was afterwards conducted, by easy stages, but with great ceremony, to William de la Pole's house at Deptford, whence, the following day, she was conveyed to Blackheath, " where shee was met by the

maior, aldermen, and sherrifes of the city in scarlet, and
the crafts of the same, all riding on horse-backe, in blue
gownes, with broydered sleeves, and red hoods, on the
28th of May, who conveyed her with her traine thorow
Southwarke, and so thorow the Citty of London, then
beautified with pageants of divers Histories, and other
shows of welcome, marvellous, costly, and sumptuous."
Stow, speaking of this marriage, says it " seemed to many
both unfortunate and unprofitable to the realme of England, and that for divers causes : first, the King had with
her no dowry, and for the fetching of her, and other
charges about her, the marques of Suffolk demanded
a whole fifteenth in open Parliament : and also there
was delivered for her the dutchie of Aniou (Anjou) the
city of Mans, and the county of Maine."

The same year, the marquis was one of the ambassadors sent, with the Archbishop of York, and Humphrey,
Duke of Buckingham, into France, to treat of peace
between the two realms. "And in consideration of his
long stay and great expenses there, upon that occasion,
and touching that marriage, obtained a grant to himself
and to the said Alice," his wife, (" in case he should
depart this life, leaving his heir in minority) ; that she,
the said Alice, with his executors should have the wardship and marriage of his heir " (*Dugdale*). Almost from
the day of the marriage, De la Pole and the queen monop-
olized and divided the whole authority of the government.
They were constantly together, and people said that
Suffolk appeared more like her husband and King of
England, than the unfortunate Henry. As greedy of
wealth as he was covetous of rank and power, he had,
previously to the royal marriage, besides other emoluments, " in consideration of his manifold services formerly
perform'd and the services of Alice, his wife, obtain'd a
grant to himself, and the said Alice, and to their issue
male, in case Humphrey, Duke of Gloucester, should die
without issue, of the name, title and honour of Earl of
Pembroke " and certain lordships, a castle and other
estates " to hold to himself, and the said Alice, and their
issue male, but for lack of such issue to revert to the

C

crown." He was made Lord Chamberlain; and in the following August, Lord High Admiral of England, besides obtaining several lucrative wardships.

Although the favorite was now most powerful, yet he was very unpopular amongst every class of society. A succession of defeats sustained by the English in France;—coupled with the loss of the Norman provinces—and the murder of Humphrey, "the good Duke" of Gloucester—were crimes attributed to the Marquis of Suffolk, whilst he, as if impelled to court his destruction by an exhibition of odious rapacity—seized the great estates of "the good duke," and after appropriating what best suited him, divided nearly all the remainder amongst his own family and most devoted adherents. As a climax—at this crisis—to show that he could rise in rank whilst his country sank in disgrace—he assumed the title of Duke of Suffolk. This impudence sealed his doom. It roused the spirit of the nobles and the people throughout the land, not only against Suffolk, but the queen, for they saw that the honour of the country was being sacrificed to the cupidity and fatuity of the one, and the treachery and tyranny of the other. The next two years, 1448-50, were most eventful ones—discontent brooded over the land, and turbulent meetings were held in many parts of England; one even in "the Broomfields, Deptford," near the very threshold of his mansion at Sayes Court, where his unpopularity was as great as in any part of the Kingdom. In East Kent, too, an insurrection was excited by one Thomas Thany, a fuller, who pretended to be a hermit, but more generally known by the soubriquet of "Blue Beard;" this rising was suppressed and its promoters, with others executed on the 9th February, 1450, at Canterbury.

The Duke of Suffolk had previously been impeached in Parliament (1446) for high treason in inducing the French to invade this country in order to depose Henry, and to place on the throne his own son, who was to marry the daughter of the Duke of Somerset, who was considered by the house of Lancaster as the next in succession to the Crown. He was also charged with the loss of the French provinces by his negotiations in that country, and with having betrayed the secrets of the State to the French leaders. By his consummate address and the favour of Queen Margaret, with whom in the last accusation he had been confounded, he averted this storm. But another Parliament assembled in Westminster in January, 1450, determined to overthrow him. On the 28th of that month the Speaker and members of the House of Commons appeared in the House of Lords, and after accusing the minister of treason, demanded his committal to the Tower. The Lords replied that a Peer of the Realm could not be committed without some specific charge against him. The Chancellor and Speaker gave to the King in Parliament, on the 7th of February, a formal accusation of the Duke, consisting of nine articles ; and on the 9th of March, the Commons, by their Speaker, exhibited a further accusation of high crimes and misdemeanours, containing sixteen articles. The King was now personally brought to interfere. To preserve the Duke from any further proceedings which might terminate unpleasantly, he directed the Chancellor to order Suffolk to quit the country, and remain in exile for five years. Upon learning the result the populace flew to arms, and in the metropolis upwards of two thousand persons collected to take away his life (b). The Duke, however, evaded the fury of the mob and escaped to Ipswich, where he embarked for the Continent, but was stopped between Dover and Calais by one of the largest vessels of war, the " Nicholas of the Tower" which carried one hundred and fifty men. The Commander of that ship compelled the Duke to come on board the " Nicholas," and, as he stepped over the gangway, greeted him with " Welcome, Traitor." Having been shriven by a Confessor, on the following day, he was ordered into a cock-bat which came alongside, where there were a block and an axe. He was then ordered by one of the clumsiest and meanest of the sailors " to put his head on the block, for he should

b March 14th, 1450. Libels against the Queen and Duke of Suffolk were affixed to the doors of St. Nicholas' Church, Deptford.

die by the sword !" Then, with a rusty sword, in half-a-dozen strokes, he severed the head from the body. The duke's remains were then thrown into the sea ; but were found on the sands next day, and taken to Wingfield, Suffolk, for interment. (*Dunkin*).

Agreeably to a grant already mentioned, the Duchess of Suffolk had the wardship of her son John, who was only seven years old at the time of his father's death. He afterwards married Elizabeth, the sister of King Edward IV., who, in consideration thereof, by letters patent, dated the 23rd of March, 1464, renewed to John the title of the Duke of Suffolk, it being doubtful whether his father's unparalleled attainder and illegal banishment had not rendered it void. In his place of Parliament, A.D. 1472, he acknowledged the title of Prince Edward, the "eldest son of that king, and made oath of fidelity to him." His mother Alice died in 1476 and was buried at Ewelme in Oxfordshire.

John, by his wife, had five sons :—John, Edmund (who on the death of his brother John, had the title of Earl of Suffolk), Humphrey, a clerk; Edward, arch-deacon of Richmond ; and Richard slain in battle at Pavia, 1525. He had also four daughters :—Catherine, wife of William Lord Sturton ; Anne, a nun at Sion ; Dorothy, and Elizabeth, who was married to Henry Lovel, Lord Morley. He died in 1491, and was buried near his father at Wingfield, in Suffolk.

During his lifetime the Manor of Deptford seems to have been held by his eldest son, John ; who, by a special charter dated March the 13th, 1466, because of his consanguinity to the king, was created Earl of Lincoln. Subsequently, he was made Lord Lieutenant of Ireland, and after the death of the king's son, he was proclaimed heir-apparent to the English crown. Upon the fall of King Richard III. on Bosworth field, August 22nd, 1485, Henry, Earl of Richmond, seized the crown, and John, with other men of note, became his prisoner, but he afterwards escaped to Flanders.

The Duchess of Burgundy had espoused the cause of Lambert Simnell, who pretended to be Edward (*c*), Earl of Warwick, son of George, Duke of Clarence, elder brother of Richard III. ; and to support his claim, she furnished two thousand mercenaries. These forces, with the Earl of Lincoln, went to Ireland, where, in conjunction with the Earl of Kildare, an army was raised to invade England. This Irish-Dutch army landed in Lancashire in May, 1487, and was joined by Sir Thomas Broughton, an opulent landholder of the north. By the 22nd of June, they had penetrated as far as Stoke, near Newark-upon-Trent, where they were met by the Earl of Oxford, and King Henry VII's troops. "Both armies joined and fought earnestly and sharply." (Hall.)

The invaders, about eight thousand in number, commenced the attack ; and more than half of them, including the Earl of Lincoln, were left dead on the field.

For this treasonable (?) attempt of its lord, the Manor of Deptford was forfeited to the Crown ; but Henry VII. did not long retain it, for, in the following year, he granted it to Oliver St. John, who died in 1499, leaving it by will dated 1496, to his son John St. John, who was possessed of it at his death in 1513.

Before the year 1538, this Manor seems to have again reverted to the crown, for, on the 3rd of September of that year, King Henry VIII. granted the Stewardship of the Manor of Sayes Court, alias West Greenwich, and others, near adjoining to it, to Richard Long, one

c This Prince was living at the time and was produced by Henry VII. in proof of the falsehood of the claim. He subsequently united his fortunes with those of Perkin Warbeck, who pretended to be Richard, Duke of York, younger brother of Edward V., and appeared to believe in him. On this account, having acknowledged Perkin as Richard IV., Warwick was put to death by Henry VII. He was called Earl of Warwick because through his mother he was grandson of the great Earl of Warwick, the "King Maker."

The claim of Perkin has since been disproved by the discovery of the skeleton of both princes in the Tower in 1674.

of the Esquires of his body, for the term of his life, with the yearly wages of £7 6s. 8d. and all profits and emoluments.

This Richard Long was an admirable courtier; he was one of the unscrupulous instruments used by Henry VIII. in breaking up his marriage with Anne of Cleves. He was also employed in other delicate affairs by his reckless and uxurious master—not however without profit and danger to himself.

By letters patent dated July 17th 1547, King Edward VI. granted to Sir Thomas Speke, Knight, for the term of his life, the Office of Stewardship of his lordships and Manors of Sayes Court and West Greenwich; and also the Office of Chief Steward of his Manor and Ville of Deptford-Strond; and also the Office of Bailiff of the said Manor of Sayes Court, in the King's hands and disposal, by the death of Sir Richard Long, Knight, with divers fees and emoluments therein mentioned.

On the death of Sir Thomas Speke the said Offices were granted, by the same Monarch by his letters patent, dated December 24th 1552, to Sir Thomas Darcy, Knight of the Garter, and Lord Darcy of Chiche; and again two years afterwards to William Sackville.

In 1568 we find the Manor in the possession of William Chaworth, of London, Cloth worker.

The Manor of Sayes Court, during the reigns of James I. and Charles I. was retained in the hands of the Crown; but the Mansion House of Sayes Court had already as it seems, according to Hasted, to have been granted for a term of years to Sir Richard Browne, Knight, soon after the tenth year of the reign of Queen Elizabeth. He died in May, 1604, aged 65, and was buried in St. Nicholas' Church, Deptford, near his wife Dame Joanna Vigorus, of Langham, Essex, who died November 18th, 1604, aged 74.

Sayes Court in the Survey bearing date the 25th of July, A.D. 1608, is described as follows:

"this Howse conteyneth Eightteene severall Roomes and twoo storis high and Nyne bayes and gardens and Orchards contayning by estimacon two Acres and a halfe also a Stable on the west end of the Stalles and a loft or gardener of foure bayes valued by the jury by the yeare, (in good repaire) iiij l."—

And again in the Survey, taken two years after the martyrdom of King Charles I.—viz., June 2nd, 1651 :—

"Manor house built with timber with the apptenances thereunto belongeinge commonly called Sayes Court, Deptford, * * * * consisteinge of one Hall, one plor, one Kitchen, one Buttery, one Larder, wth a Daryehouse, alsoe one Chamber and thre Celle^{rs.} In ye second Storie eight chambers with foure Clossetts, and three Garretts, two Stables, and one other litle Stable joyninge to the aforesaid Mano^r howse which aforesaid Mano^r howse together wth the said Garden Orchard and Court Yards conteine together two acres, two roodes, and sixteene pches. 2 a. 2 r. 16 p. xiiij li."—

The Honourable Roger North, describing a visit of his brother, The Lord Keeper Guilford, to Sayes Court, says :—

"His Lordship was once invited to a philosophical meal, at the house of Mr. Evelyn at Deptford. The house was low, but elegantly set off with ornaments, and quaint mottos at most turns ; but, above all, his garden was exquisite, being most boscaresque, and, as it were, an exemplar, of his book of forest trees. They appeared all so thriving and clean, that, in so much variety, no one could be satiated in viewing ; and to these were added plenty of ingenious discourses, which made the time short."

After the execution of King Charles I. the Commonwealth seized on the royal estates and on 16th July, 1649, passed an ordinance to vest the same in trustees in order to their being forthwith surveyed and sold to supply the necessities of State. In pursuance of which, a survey was soon afterwards taken of this Manor of Sayes Court and Deptford and le Strond, alias West Greenwich, by which it appears, that the quit rents, due to the Lord from the several freeholders in free socage tenure, amounted to 118s. 1½d. per annum.

The Court Baron and Court-leets, &c., were valued at 60 shillings yearly.

The relief from the freeholders was one half of the quit rent.

And further, that King James I., in consideration of the services done by Christopher Browne, Gent, (son of Sir Richard Browne) as well as of the charges he had been at in repairing the mansion house of Sayes Court and its appurtenances, by letters patent, dated January 17th, 1611, had granted to him, the said Manor House lying in Bromfield in Deptford with the Orchards, garden and two closes of four acres now in possession, and also sufficient hay and pasture for the keeping, feeding and pasturing twelve kine, one bull, and two horses in winter and summer, upon the grounds of Sayes Court for the term of forty years without any rent, and that King Charles had directed his Privy Seal to the trustees of his son Charles, Prince of Wales, who thereupon granted by indenture, dated October 1st, 1635, the above premises to the said Christopher Browne for twenty-four years, to commence from the 16th June, 1651 (being the expiration of the former lease) which was ratified by the king on the 24th of November following. All which premises were reported in 1649 to be in the possession of William Prettiman, Gent, executor of Christopher Browne, and guardian of Richard Browne, one of his grandchildren, to whom, by his will, he had given his interest in them.

That the yearly value of the Manor House and premises was in all £108 per annum, but that there were yearly reprisals out of the same to the Vicar of Deptford in consideration of tithes £12 and four loads of hay, valued at £6.

That there were 160 perches of Thames wall belonging to this Manor against Craine Meadow, to which there was one sluice belonging called the "King's or Craine's Sluice," for draining these lands and grounds.

That William Prettiman was likewise tenant to all the demesne lands from the then Commissioners of the public Revenue, amounting to about 164 acres at the yearly rent of £424 11s. 7¾d.

After this Survey, the Manor with its appurtenances and sundry premises in Greenwich and Deptford were sold by the said trustees to John Bachsted, Ralph Cobbet and others; and the Manor house to William Somerfield. In this state they remained until the restoration of King Charles II., A.D. 1660, when they returned to the royal revenue, of which, so long as any manorial rights were exercised, they continued to form a part.

Christopher Browne died in March, 1645, aged 70 years, and was buried with his wife Thomasin in St. Nicholas' Church ; leaving his possessions to his son Richard Browne, afterwards knighted. Sir Richard, being desirous of saving something from the wreck of his property by the Commonwealth confiscations, sent his son-in-law, John Evelyn, from Paris to endeavour " to compound with the soldiers " and to take possession of Sayes Court, with a view to his permanent residence there, " there being now so little appearance of any change for the better, all being in the rebels' hands." Mr. Evelyn repaired the Manor house, and planted the garden elms and groves about the seate (1665). "Sylva" Evelyn resided at Sayes Court for 40 years, leaving it in 1694 for Wotton, his birthplace; his brother George, having lost his sons, had settled the family estate upon him. And during this long residence he had the honour of being visited by many illustrious personages.

" 30th April, 1663. Came his Majesty " (King Charles II.) " to honour my poor villa with his presence, viewing the gardens, and even every room of the house, and was pleased to take a small refreshment. There were with him the Duke of Richmond, the Earl of St. Albans, Lord Lauderdale and several persons of quality." (*Diary*.)

" 1665, May 5th. After dinner, to Mr. Evelyn's; he being abroad, we walked in his garden, and a lovely noble ground he hath indeed. And among other varieties, a hive of bees, so as, being hived in glass, you may see the bees making their honey and combs mighty pleasantly." (*Pepy's Diary*.)

"May 1st, 1683. I planted all the out limits of the garden and long walks with holly, four hundred feet in length, nine feet high, aud five in diameter." *(Sylva, bk. II., chap. i.) (d)* Sayes Court gradually sank into decay after Evelyn's departure from Deptford, although two very distinguished tenants succeeded him. It was let, first to Admiral Benbow, then only a Captain ; of whom Evelyn writes, "I have let my house to Captain Benbow, and have the mortification of seeing, every day, much of my former labour and expense there impairing for want of a more polite tenant."

"30th January, 1698. The Czar of Muscovy, being come to England, and having a mind to see the building of ships, hired my house at Sayes Court, and made it his court and palace, new furnished for him by the King." During the Czar's residence in the house, Mr. Evelyn's servant writes to him—"There is a house full of people and right nasty. The Czar lies next your library, and dines in the parlour, next your study. He dines at ten o'clock and six at night ; is very seldom at home a whole day ; very often in the King's yard, or by water, dressed in several dresses. The King (William III.) is expected here this day ; the best parlour is pretty clean for him to be entertained in. The King pays for all he has."

"June 9th, 1699. To Deptford to see how miserably the Czar had left my house, after three months making it his court. I got Sir Christopher Wren, the King's surveyor, and Mr. London, his gardener, to go and estimate the repair, for which they allowed £150 in their

d The hithermost Grove I planted about 1656 ; the other beyond it 1660 ; the lower Grove, 1662 ; the holly hedge, even with the Mount hedge below, 1670. I planted every hedge and tree not onely in the Garden, Groves, &c., but about all the fields and house since 1653, except those large, old and hollow elms in the stable court and next the sewer ; for it was before, all one pasture field to the very garden, of the house, which was but small ; from which time also I repaired the ruined house, and built the whole end of the kitchen, the chapel, buttry, my study above and below, cellars and all the outhouses and walls, still-house, orangerie, and made the gardens, &c., to my great cost, and better I had don to have pulled all down at first, but it was don at several times. *(From the MSS. at Wotton.)*

report to the Lords of the Treasury." (*e*)   The gardens were perfectly ruined ; one of Peter's favourite recreations being to be wheeled by his attendants through the beautiful holly hedge, Evelyn had planted with so much pains, in one of Admiral Benbow's wheelbarrows.   Mr. Evelyn removed the remainder of his goods to Wotton on the 24th of May, 1700, and Sayes Court has never since been inhabited by any member of the family.   The mansion was let on the 18th of March to Lord Carmarthen, son of the Duke of Leeds.   Of the Duke of Leeds, Evelyn wrote to Dr. Bohun, A.D., 1692 : "Amongst other things, I had paid £300 for the renewing of my lease, with some augmentation of what I hold from the Crown, which the Duke of Leeds was supplanting me of."   In consequence of the Workhouse being out of repair, and not worth repairing, a vestry was held on the 24th of May, A.D. 1759, to consider the propriety "of renting Sayes Court."   On the 23rd of June, in the same year, a sixty-one years' lease of the premises (containing two roods, twenty-six perches) was granted to the parishioners of St. Nicholas, to be used as a Workhouse, from Michaelmas, 1759, at a rental of £2 per annum.   A renewal of lease, for a similar term at £50 per annum, was obtained in 1820 ; power being given by this lease to the parishioners of St. Nicholas to pull down or otherwise alter the said mansion house, so as to suit their purposes.   An Act of Parliament was passed in 1830 "for authorising the granting of building and other leases, late the property of Dame Mary Evelyn, deceased, in the Parishes of St. Paul and St. Nicholas, Deptford" (Private Act).

A workhouse for the Greenwich Union—of which the Deptford parishes form a part—having been erected in East Greenwich, Sayes Court was no longer required by the parishioners of St. Nicholas, and they surrendered the lease to W. J. Evelyn, Esq., on the 7th of September, 1848.

---

e Admiral Benbow was awarded £1 at the same time, for damage to wheelbarrows.

In 1852 the building was occupied by Mr. Richard
Cooper, as an Emigration Depôt, until the removal of
the Depôt to Southampton. The last emigrants embarked from the Deptford Depôt on the 23rd December,
1852. In 1853 it was tenanted by Mr. Cooper's sons,
and used by them for a manufactory for the clothing and
bedding of emigrants. This establishment was in connexion with the Colonial Emigration Commissioners.
Mr. Cooper materially altered the arrangements of the
building and perhaps destroyed " that fragment " of the
old structure which Mr. Alfred Davis, a gentleman well
acquainted with the antiquities of Deptford, writing in
1833, describes, as then remaining. Mr. Davis says
" The site of Sayes Court is no mean object of curiosity,
as there yet remains a fragment of the antient building,
undefaced,—certainly undestroyed. The mighty intellect
of Sir Walter Scott has thrown around the place a most
fascinating spell ; and Sayes Court has, therefore, additional claims upon the attention of readers of romance.
A few passages in which the localities are peculiarly
striking, may well be substituted for any infirm description of my own."

"An hour's riding brought them to the present
habitation of Lord Sussex, an antient house called Say's
Court near Deptford, which had long pertained to a
family of that name, but had for upwards of one hundred
years been possessed by the ancient family of Evelyn *(f)*.
The present representative of that antient house took a
deep interest in the Earl of Sussex and had willingly
accommodated both him and his numerous retinue in his
hospitable mansion. Say's Court was afterwards the
residence of the celebrated Mr. Evelyn, whose " Sylva "
is still the manual of British planters." *(Vide Sir W.
Scott's " Kenilworth.")*

"A forlornly looking, ragged mulberry tree, standing
at the bottom of Czar Street, was the last survivor of the
thousands of arborets planted by " Sylva " Evelyn in the
gardens and grounds surrounding his residence at

f A chronological error, as in the reign of Queen Elizabeth, Sayes
Court was not in possession of the Evelyn family.

Ebelyn Family.

Possessors of Sayes Court marked red.

GEORGE EVELYN, of Kingston and Wotton, Surrey, died, 1603
(Great Grandson of William Avelin or Evelin,
of Harrow, Middlesex, who died, 1476.)

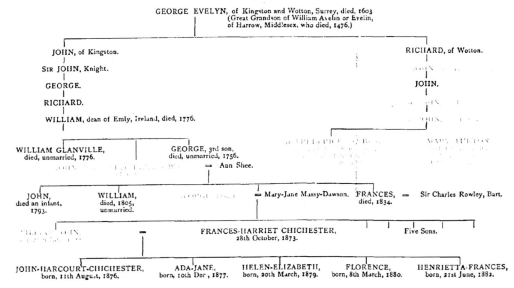

JOHN, of Kingston.

SIR JOHN, Knight.

GEORGE.

RICHARD.

WILLIAM, dean of Emly, Ireland, died, 1776.

RICHARD, of Wotton.

JOHN.

JOHN.

WILLIAM GLANVILLE,
died, unmarried, 1776.

GEORGE, 3rd son,
died, unmarried, 1756.
= Ann Shee.

MARY HUTTON

JOHN,
died an infant,
1793.

WILLIAM,
died, 1805,
unmarried.

= Mary-Jane Massy-Dawson.

FRANCES,
died, 1834.

= Sir Charles Rowley, Bart.

FRANCES-HARRIET CHICHESTER,
28th October, 1873.

Five Sons.

JOHN-HARCOURT-CHICHESTER,
born, 11th August, 1876.

ADA-JANE,
born, 10th Dec., 1877.

HELEN-ELIZABETH,
born, 20th March, 1879.

FLORENCE,
born, 8th March, 1880.

HENRIETTA-FRANCES,
born, 21st June, 1882.

Deptford. It may be interesting to know that a piece of this tree is built in the New Coal Exchange, London.

For some years past the old building was occupied, as a residence, by the head gardener of the Sayes Court Estate.

In the spring of 1881, the house was fitted up to accommodate old residents and tenants on the Evelyn Estates, in receipt of parochial relief, and is now known as the

EVELYN ALMSHOUSES,

SAYES COURT.

There are at the present time some twenty-one inmates in these almshouses and it is most gratifying to know that Mrs. Evelyn takes a great interest in these old people—most of whom are sexagenarians—coming over from Wotton, periodically, expressly to visit them ; and providing them regularly with a gratuitous supply of illustrated and religious papers. Mr. Evelyn has recently handed over—under agreement—the entire management of Sayes Court Museum and Grounds, to a Committee of ten of his Deptford tenantry, to be used as a recreation ground for the inhabitants of the surrounding district.

THE EVELYN FAMILY—PEDIGREE.

THE Evelyn Family is supposed to be a branch of the Norman Family of Ivelin. John Evelyn, author of " Sylva," states that there were some of this name both in France and Italy, written Ivelin and Avelin ; that in old deeds he found the name written Avelyn, alias Evelyn, and that a member of the family was taken prisoner at the battle of Agincourt, 25th October, 1415.

In the reign of Queen Elizabeth the representative of the English branch of the family was George Evelyn, of Long Ditton, Kingston, and Wotton, Surrey, Esq., who died the 30th of May, A.D. 1603, aged 77 years, leaving, besides other issue, four sons. His first wife, Rose, daughter and heiress of Thomas Williams, brother and heir of Sir John Williams, Knt., was buried at Long Ditton, 21st July, 1577. His second wife, Joan Stint, died in 1613, and was buried at Wotton. From the second son, John Evelyn, of Kingston, Surrey, the present head of the family, William John Evelyn, Esq., is directly descended ; the youngest son, Richard Evelyn, succeeded to the Wotton Estate. Richard married Ellen, daughter and heiress of John Stansfield, of Lewes, in Sussex, Esq., by whom he had issue : George, of Wotton ; John, of Sayes Court, Deptford ; Richard ; Elizabeth, married to Thomas Darcie, of Dartford ; and Jane, married to William Glanville, of Devon.

Richard Evelyn, Esq., died 20th December, 1640, and was succeeded by his eldest son, George, who died without issue male in 1699, having devised the Wotton Estate to his brother John, who had become possessed of Sayes Court (or more properly Say's Court), by marrying Mary, only daughter and heiress of Sir Richard Browne, son of Christopher Browne, by Thomazine, daughter of Benjamin Gonson, widow of Captain Edward Fenton, and sister of the Lady Katherine, first wife of Admiral Sir John Hawkins. John (Sylva) Evelyn, Esq., had five sons, four of whom died in infancy at Sayes Court, and three daughters, Mary, Elizabeth, and Susannah.

Mary died unmarried, March 17th, 1685, æt 19. Elizabeth was married to Sir John Tippet, and Susanna to William Draper, of Adscomb, near Croydon, in Surrey.

(*For biographical sketch of " Sylva Evelyn," see chapter on Parish Worthies*).

John, eldest and only surviving son of " Sylva " Evelyn was the ingenious author of several books and poems (see " Parish Worthies ") ; having married Martha, daughter and co-heiress of Richard Spencer, Esq., died in his father's lifetime, March 24th, 1699, leaving one son, John, and one daughter, Elizabeth, who was married to the Hon. Simon Harcourt.

The last-mentioned John Evelyn was by his grandfather's will, dated February, 25th, 1706, made his executor and residuary legatee, and, as such, became possessed of both the terms in Sayes Court, and the other premises in Deptford, granted by Charles II. In July, 1713, he was created a baronet by Queen Anne, and was a Fellow of the Royal Society, of which his grandfather had been a promoter and benefactor.

In 1724 King George I., granted the freehold of these premises (an Act of Parliament having been passed to enable him so to do) to Francis, Earl of Godolphin, and Hugh, Viscount Falmouth, in trust for Sir John Evelyn and his heirs for ever ; paying the yearly rent of £1 2s. 6d. as a quit rent, and a valuable consideration besides to His Majesty for the same.

Sir John married at Lambeth Chapel, September 18th, 1705, Anne, daughter of Edward Boscawen, Esq., of Cornwall, and sister of Hugh, Viscount Falmouth, by whom he had issue :—

Sir John Evelyn, the 2nd Baronet.

Charles, who married Susanna, daughter of Peter Prideaux, Esq.

William, a General in the Army, and Colonel of the 29th Regiment of Foot, who died a bachelor in 1783.

Sydney, who also died unmarried, and two daughters Anne and Mary, who both died unmarried, the first-named in 1771, and the other in 1779.

Sir John, the 1st Baronet, died in 1763, and was succeeded by his eldest son, Sir John, who married Mary, daughter of Hugh Boscawen, 1st Viscount Falmouth. He was Clerk of the Green Cloth to Frederick, Prince of Wales, and to King George III., and served in Parliament as member for Helston. He had issue :—

Lucy, who died in 1754, unmarried.

Augusta, who was married to the Rev. Dr. Henry Jenkin, Rector of Wotton, and died childless in 1812, five years before her husband ; and

Sir Frederick, the 3rd Bart.

Sir John, the 2nd Bart., died June 11th, 1767, aged 61, and was succeeded by his only son.

Sir Frederick, who married Mary, daughter of William Turton, of Staffordshire, Esq., by whom he had no issue. Sir Frederick was an officer in Elliott's Light Horse, at the famous battle of Minden, in 1759, when that regiment, but newly raised, had a large share in the glory of the day.

Sir Frederick Evelyn, who was a member of the Jockey Club, died on the 1st of April, 1812, having devised his estates to his relict, Lady Mary. The baronetcy descended to his cousin, Sir John Evelyn, 4th Baronet, who died in 1833, aged 75, and was succeeded by his brother, Sir Hugh Evelyn, 5th Baronet, who was born at Totnes, Devonshire, 31st January, 1769, and died at Sydenham, 28th August, 1848, without issue, and was buried at Wotton. At the death of Sir Hugh, the Baronetcy became extinct. Sir Hugh married Mrs. Henrietta Harris (relict of an officer) about the year 1831, who died July 16th, 1836, aged 58 years, and was buried at South Repps, Norfolk. On the 12th November, in the same year, he married Mary, daughter of John Kennedy (relict of James Thomas Hathaway, of London, merchant), at the Church of St. Martin-in-the-Fields, Middlesex. Lady Evelyn died on the 12th of November, 1817, and the estates reverted to the family in the person of her devisee, John Evelyn, Esq., who was fifth in direct descent from George Evelyn, of Long Ditton and Wotton, the common ancestor.

This John Evelyn was the second son of William Evelyn, Dean of Emley, Ireland, who married Margaret, daughter of Christopher Chamberlain, Esq., in 1739, and died at Dublin on the 25th of March, 1776, aged 58 years. The Dean's eldest son, William, born at Arklow, Co. Wicklow, survived his father little more than seven months. He was Captain in the 4th or King's Own Regiment, and, having served in the American War of Independence, was mortally wounded in action, and died at New York on the 6th of November, 1776. John, who then succeeded as heir to his brother, was born at Arklow 1st June, 1743. He served in the Honourable East India Company's Civil Service from 1770 to 1790, and married at Dacca, Bengal, 14th April, 1787, Ann, the seventh and youngest daughter of Anthony Shee, Esq., of Castlebar, Co. Mayo (by Marjory, daughter of Edmund Burke, of County Mayo), and sister to Sir George Shee, Bart., of Dunmore, County Galway, and had issue :—

John, born at Calcutta 25th January, 1788, and dying at the age of five years, was buried at Bath.

William, born at Calcutta 16th December, 1788. He was Ensign in the 41st Regiment, and was drowned in the wreck of the "Two Friends" Transport, in the Gulf of St. Lawrence, on the 22nd of October, 1805, and buried at Louisburg in the Island of Cape Breton. He died unmarried.

George, born at Galway, 16th September, 1791, of whom presently,

Francis, only daughter, born at Bath in 1797, was married at Wotton Church, in August, 1822, to Captain Rowley, (afterwards Sir Charles Rowley, Bart.,) of Hill House, Herts. She died and was buried at Florence, in 1834.

John Evelyn, Esq., was a Deputy Lieutenant and Justice of the Peace for the county of Surrey, and dying at Wotton 27th November, 1827, was succeeded in the family estates by his third but only surviving son George.

George Evelyn, Esqre., was just entering on his 37th year at the time of his father's death. He was educated at Warminster and Harrow, and, afterwards having entered the Army, served under the Duke of Wellington in the Peninsular War, as Lieutenant and Captain in the 3rd Regiment of Foot Guards. Subsequently he was severely wounded in the left arm, in the defence of the Château of Hougoumont, at the memorable battle of Waterloo, 18th of June, 1815. He was a Fellow of the Society of Antiquaries, and a Justice of the Peace for the county of Kent, and a member of the Athenæum Club.

He took a very great interest in all that related to the welfare of Deptford, and was one of the Vice-Presidents of the Royal Kent Dispensary. He married at Mary-le-

D

bone Church 12th July, 1821, Mary Jane, eldest daughter of James Hewitt Massy Dawson, Esqre. (of Ballinacourte, Co. Tipperary, M.P. for Clonmel, and Grandson of Hugh, first Lord Massy) and had issue :—

I. WILLIAM JOHN (of Wotton and Deptford), born in Mary-le-bone, on the 27th of July, 1822.

II. GEORGE PALMER, of Hartley Manor, Dartford, J.P. for the county of Kent, Colonel Commandant of the 1st Regt. Royal Surrey Militia ; late Captain in the 1st Battalion of the Rifle Brigade. He served in the Rifle Brigade in North America and at the Cape of Good Hope. He was on special service during the Crimean War, and was present at the battles of Alma and Balaclava, at the siege of Sebastopol and at the defence of Eupatoria. He was decorated with a medal and four clasps for the Crimea, 4th Class for the Mejidie and Turkish Medal. He married in 1855, Esther Emiline, second daughter of Lewin Philips, Esq., and grand-daughter of the Rev. Philip Philips, of Frankfort, and by her had issue :—

(1). GEORGE ROWLEY JOHN, late 2nd Lieutenant in the 3rd Regiment (Buffs). He was born 12th August, 1857, and died during the late Zulu War at Fort Ekowe, Zululand, 30th March, 1879.

(2). Charles William Glanville, born 21st March, 1860.

(3). Edward Shee, born 30th December, 1866.

(4). Mary Emiline.

III. CHARLES FRANCIS, of Horns Lodge, Tunbridge, Lieutenant Colonel of the 3rd Royal Surrey Militia, married on the 31st of July, 1880, at St. Mary Abbot's, Kensington, Emma Brook, daughter of the late Rev. Charles Paul, Vicar of Wellow in Somerset ; issue— Francis Alvin, born 4th January and baptized 9th February, 1882, at Sunning Hill, Ascot, Berkshire.

IV. FREDERICK MASSY, married Miss Oretta Cocks, of Ipswich, 21st May, 1848. He was Vicar of Oakwood, Surrey. He died at Margate, 12th August, 1877, and was buried at Oakwood, leaving issue :—

(1). William Frederick, born 7th September, 1857.

(2). John Dawson, born 29th March, 1862.

(3). Mary Adelaide, married 3rd February, 1882, to the Rev. S. E. Andrew, of Leeds, Kent.

V. JAMES, Lieut. and Captain in the Grenadier Guards, died at Paris 6th November, 1874, and was buried at Wotton. He married Anne Antoinetta, daughter of John Davis, Esq., of Richmond, Surrey, at Boulogne-sur-Mer, and by her left issue :—

(1). James Boscawen, born 12th July, 1868, who died on the 19th March, 1869, and was buried at Wotton.

(2). Alberta Silva.

VI. EDMUND BOSCAWEN, of Yaldham, Sevenoaks, sixth and youngest son, late Rector of Wotton, Surrey, was born 29th December, 1828, and married 20th August, 1857, Lucy Emma, daughter of the Rev. C. F. Johnson, Vicar of White Lackington, in Somersetshire, where the marriage ceremony was solemnized.

George Evelyn, Esq., died on the 15th of February, 1829, and was buried at Wotton, being succeeded by his eldest son, William John Evelyn, Esq. (of Wotton, Surrey ; St. Clere and Deptford, Kent), M.A., Oxon ; Fellow of the Royal Geographical Society ; F.S.A.; late M.P. for West Surrey, 1849-57 ; Deputy Lieutenant ; Justice of the Peace ; and in 1860 High Sheriff for the county of Surrey. On the 28th of October, 1873, he married at Randalstown, Co. Antrim, Ireland, Frances Harriet, eldest daughter of the Rev. G. V. Chichester, Rector of Wotton, Surrey, and brother of Baron O'Neil, of Shanes Castle, Co. Antrim—issue :—

(1). John Harcourt Chichester, born at Wotton, 11th August, 1876, and baptised in Wotton Church, 9th September, 1876.

(2). Ada Janet, born at Wotton, Surrey, 10th of December, 1877, and baptised 6th January, 1878.

(3). Helen Elizabeth, born in the parish of St. George's, Hanover Square, 20th March, 1879, and baptised at Mary-le-bone Parish Church, 17th April, 1879.

(4). Florence, born in the parish of Mary-le-bone, 8th March, 1880, and baptised at Mary-le-bone Parish Church, on the 5th April, 1880.

D2

(5). Henrietta Frances, born at Wotton, 21st June, 1882, and baptised 20th of July, 1882, in Wotton Church.
ARMS—Azure, a griffin passant, Or, a chief of the last.
CREST—A griffin passant, Or, ducally gorged.
MOTTO—Durate.

HATCHAM.

IN the Domesday Book, compiled by order of William the Conqueror, 1087, the manor of Hatcham is noticed in the following terms :—"In Brixton Hundred the Bishop of Lisieux holds of the Bishop of Baieux Hachesham, which Brixi held of King Edward. It was then assessed at three hides, as it now is; the arable land amounts to three caracutes. There are nine villanes and three bordars, with three caracutes; and there are six acres of meadow; the wood yields three swine : from the time of King Edward (the Confessor) it has been valued at forty shillings."

In the reign of Henry II. Hatcham was the seat of a family of the same name ; for we find by a certificate returned into the Exchequer at that time that Gilbert de Hatcham (or Haachesham, as then spelt) accounted for four Knights' fees of the Barony of Wakelin de Maminot. In the next reign as stated in the "Testa de Nevill," two Knights' fees in Hatcham and Camberwell were held of Humphrey de Bohun, Earl of Hereford, by William de Say, and the heirs of Richard de Vabadun. Sarah, the daughter and heiress of de Vabadun, married Roger de Bavant, who in the 46th year of the reign of Henry III. accounted to the Exchequer for two Knights' fees, pertaining to the above-mentioned barony. A composition was made in 1274 between the Prior of Bermondsey and the Abbot of Begham, of Hatcham, in the Parish of West Greenwich, which was let to the Abbot for the sum of 13s. 4d. per annum. In the 13th year of the reign of Edward I., 1285, Adam de Bavant, son of Roger, had a grant of free warren, but it appears that he alienated a portion of the estate directly afterwards to Gregory de Rokesley, an eminent citizen of London. who had filled the office of Lord Mayor from A.D. 1275 to 1281 ; was keeper of the Royal Exchequer, and essay-master-in-chief of all the English Mints. De Rokesley obtained a faculty from the Abbot and Convent of Begham, that same year, for his oratory, which he had built for the use of himself and family here ; saving to themselves all oblations and other rights. He died in 1292, and Roger Busslep, who may have been his heir, sold or mortgaged the estate to Robert Burnell, Bishop of Bath and Wells ; and on his death in October, 1292, an extent was taken both of this and the Manor of Hatcham—Barnes, from which it appears that here was a capital messuage, garden and fish-pond, with lands, and rents of assize, valued together at £6 0s. 2½d. The Bishop's claim on the estate descended to his nephew Philip Burnell, who died in the 22nd year of King Edward I.'s reign. His son Edward dying without issue in 1316, the inheritance devolved on his daughter Maud, who married first, William Lord Lovell, and afterwards John de Handlo. The descendants of the latter succeeded to the possession of the Burnell Estates under the sanction of a settlement ; but on the failure of male heirs of that family the estates reverted to William, Lord Lovell, who, however, in 1442, transferred Hatcham to Walter, Lord Hungerford of Heytesbury, and his son, Sir Edmund Hungerford, who had married a co-heiress of the Burnell family.

The subsequent descent of this estate is uncertain, but it may possibly have passed by the marriage of an heiress, from the Hungerford to the family of Hastings, as there was a building between Camberwell and Stock-well, called Loughborough-house, which may have been founded by Edward Hastings, created Baron Lough-borough by Queen Elizabeth in 1558. or by Henry Hastings, who obtained the same title from Charles I, in 1643, but neither of whom left heirs to continue the title. In 1749 Cowper and his wife levied a fine to Gordon of one-third of the Manor of Little Hatcham in Peckham and Camberwell, which possibly may have reference to this part of the Burnell estate now under notice.

Aymer de Valence, Earl of Pembroke, was found, at his death, to have been possessor of the Manor of Hatcham in Deptford-castle (as it is expressed). This earl was murdered in France, when in attendance on Queen Isabella, wife of Edward II, the "She-wolf of France."

That portion of the estate retained by Adam de Bavent, was distinguished by the name of Hatcham-Bavant, or Hatcham-Barnes, and was, together with other properties in different parts of England and Wales, conveyed by Roger de Bavent, Knt., to King Edward III, his wife, Hawise, resigning at the same time all her rights in it. Edward III by letters patent dated July 20th, 1371, confirmed the grant made in 1370, to the Prioress and Convent at Dartford—newly founded by him—of this Manor, with its appurtenances lying in the counties of Kent and Surrey, for the use of the religious there, in pure and perpetual alms; to hold of the same lords as it did before it came to his hand. It continued here until the dissolution of Monasteries by Henry VIII, in the 22nd year of his reign, when it became vested in the Crown, where it remained until the time of Philip and Mary, who assigned it, with other estates, for her life, to Ann, widow of George Seymour, Duke of Somerset. James the First in 1610 granted the Manor of Hatcham-Barnes and the lands, etc., in West Greenwich and Lewisham, in the counties of Kent and Surrey, with the perquisites of Courts, formerly belonging to the Monastery at Dartford, to George Salter and John Williams. They transferred the estate by sale to Peter Vanlore; and he to a person named Brookes, by whom it was conveyed to Sir John Gerrard and Sir Thomas Lowe, Aldermen of London; Robert Offley and Martin Bond, citizens and haberdashers, in trust for the foundation and support of an almshouse and Free Grammar School at Monmouth. It is still in the possession of the Haberdasher's Company, who amongst other improvements have erected Middle Class Schools for boys and girls on the top of Plow-Garlic-hill, an account of which will be found in the chapter dealing with the Educational establishments in the parish.

Lysons, writing about 1790, informs us that the Manor of Hatcham was reduced to a single house; but this is incorrect, as evinced by several long leases, granted under the authority of the Court of Chancery, in 1763, 1767, and 1778.

Hatcham House, surrounded by a brick-moat, well stocked with fish; situated near the old New Cross Turnpike Gate, was advertised to be let in February, 1775. The old house with its moat and park, has now disappeared, the site being covered with new streets of cottages, nothing being left but the name—"Hatcham Park," by which the locality is at present known.

DEPTFORD-LE-STROND.

THE position of the Manor of Deptford-le-Strond is at once perceptible from its name. Like Hatcham, it was held of the Barony of Maminot, and of the superior Manor of Sayes Court or West Greenwich, with which it has sometimes been confounded. The earliest account of this as a distinct Manor is in the 22nd year of Richard II. (A.D. 1399), when Roger Mortimer, Earl of March, was found to have died possessed of a certain site styled Le-Stronde, in Greenwich, and seventy-three acres of land in Deptford Strond (*Cal. Inquis. post. mort. sub. an.*)

His son Edmund, the last Earl of March, died in 1425, possessed of this site, called his Manor of West Greenwich, alias the Strond.

Leaving no issue, this Manor descended to his nephew, Richard, Duke of York (the son of his sister Ann). Richard was slain at the battle of Wakefield, his head being struck off and placed on the gates of York—when this, with other estates, devolved on his son, Edward, afterwards King Edward IV., who gave it, with other property, to his mother, on 1st June immediately after his accession to the throne.

That Richard, Duke of York, possessed a messuage in Deptford Strond, is evident from the escheats of 7th Edward IV., "Esceat' de anno Septimo Edwardi Quarto:"—"Ric'us dux Ebor' Deptford Strond mess'."

Upon the death of the Duchess, the Manor reverted to the Crown, where it remained till granted to Lord Darcy. Thomas, Lord Darcy having been attainted, his honours became forfeited, and on the 8th June, 28th Henry VIII. (A.D. 1536) he was beheaded.

Henry VIII. settled it, as part of her jointure, upon his queen, Jane Seymour. After her decease a lease of the property for twenty-one years was granted to Thomas Hatcliffe, Esq.

On the 30th May, 1554, the manor was granted by Queen Mary, subject to this lease, by the description of the manor of Deptford Stronde, Camberwell, and Redderith (Rotherhithe) in the Counties of Kent and Surrey, to Sir Thomas Pope; being parcel of the lands of Jane, late Queen of England, to hold to Sir Thomas and Elizabeth his wife; and of the heirs male of Sir Thomas, with remainder to John Basford, gent., son of the said Elizabeth, and the heirs of his body; remainder to John Orpwood, junr., and the heirs of his body; remainder to Elizabeth Pope, daughter of John Pope, Esq., brother of Sir Thomas, and the heirs of her body; remainder to the right heirs of Sir Thomas. It subsequently became the property of the late Benjamin Way, Esq., of Denham Place, near Uxbridge, Buckinghamshire, who died in 1808. He was Sheriff in 1777 and M.P. for Bridport in 1765. He however, did not long retain the Manor, because of its remoteness from his residence and other estates.

BROCKLEY.

BROCKLEY is situated in the southern extremity of the parish, a portion being in the Parish of Lewisham. It was once accounted a Manor and granted with its appurtenances by Wakelin de Maminot in the latter end of the reign of King Henry II., to Michael de Turnham, to hold free and quietly to him and his heirs by the yearly rent of 12 pence, in lieu of all services, for which grant the said Michael became his feudatory tenant and paid him 40 shillings.

Michael de Turnham afterwards sold his land of Brocele, as his free gravilikinde and stockikinde to the Countess Juliana, wife of Wakelin de Maminot, that she might found a religious house here, Stephen de Turnham, his nephew, consenting to it.

The religious of the Premonstratensian Order (g), who were first settled at Ottham, in the County of Sussex, by Ralph de Dene, finding that place very inconvenient to them, resolved to quit it for one more suitable ; and in all likelihood it was these to whom the Countess Juliana

g The Premonstratensian Order was founded by Saint Norbert, Confessor and Archbishop of Magdebourg. He was born at Santen, in the Duchy of Cleves, in the year 1080, died in 1134, and canonized by Pope Gregory, XII., in 1582.

St. Norbert built a monastery in the lonesome valley of Premontre in the forest of Coucy, in 1121.

The order of Premonstratensians, or Norbertins, according to Helyot, is divided into thirty provinces and contains 1300 monasteries of men, and 400 of women. In its primitive institution it was very austere. The religious never wore linen and observed a perpetual abstinence from flesh. and a yearly rigorous fast of many months. For Hubert de Romanis. the disciple of St. Dominic and general of his Order, writes that this holy foundation borrowed these observances from the Premonstratensian rule. But several mitigations were introduced into it ; which gave occasion to various reformations approved by Gregory IX., and Eugenius, IV., and one in Spain of all others the most rigorous. confirmed by Gregory, XII. The Premonstratensians were called by our ancestors White Canons, and had in England 35 houses according to BishopTanner. (Butler). (There are now but two houses of the Order in England, one near Spalding and the other near Doncaster, both in Lincolnshire).

and Michael de Turnham gave this place, in pure and perpetual alms, for an habitation, which gift was confirmed by Geoffrey de Say, the land being part of his barony.

But they did not remain here long; for Robert de Turnham *(h)*, nephew of Michael, gave them an estate at Begham in Sussex, to which they quickly removed themselves, with the consent of Ela de Sackville, daughter of Ralph de Dene; and he gave or rather confirmed to them his land here at Brockley, in pure and perpetual alms to hold of Geoffrey de Say and his heirs, freely and quietly, paying him the accustomed rent of 12 pence in lieu of all service and secular exactions; which gift was confirmed by his brother Stephen de Turnham.

King John in the ninth year of his reign confirmed the land at Brokele to the Abbot and Convent of Regham.

Edward III. in 1329 granted them free-warren in their lands at Brokele.

This remained with them till the dissolution of their Abbey in 1526, when, being one of those smaller monasteries which Wolsey had obtained from the King for the endowment of his College at Oxford, it was settled by him on Cardinal College. Wolsey, being cast in a præmunire in 1529, all the estates of this foundation both real and personal were forfeited to the King and continued in the hands of the Crown till 1532, excepting

---

h This chivalrous and zealous knight accompanied King Richard Cœur de Lion in his crusade to the Holy Land, and concerning him the chronicler Gloucester sings:—

" King Richard with gud intent
　　To yat cité of Jafes went
　　On morn he sent after Sir Robert Sakvill,
　　Sir William Waterville,
　　Sir Hubert, and Sir Robert of Turnham,
　　Sir Bertram Brandes and John de St. John."

From this disastrous enterprise Robert de Turnham never returned.

" Robert de Turnham with his fauchion
　　Gan to crack many a crun."

but as it was observed by Weever, amidst this scene of blood and carnage, he could not save his own head from the frenzy of an army of enraged and offended Saracens.

such as were begged from time to time by the hungry courtiers, which were not a few.

That part of this estate, situated in the Parish of Deptford, was granted by Queen Elizabeth by letters patent in the 10th year of her reign—May 4th—by the description of the site and capital messuage of the Manor of Brockill to Philip Conway.

Hasted writing in 1778, says : " This is now called Hither or Upper Brockley Farm, and is situated near New Cross, in part of St. Paul's parish ; it is, and has been for some generations, in the family of Wickham, of Garsington, Oxfordshire ; Mary and Anne, daughters and co-heiresses of the Rev. William Wickham, carried this and another considerable estate in the parish of St. Nicholas, Deptford, into the family of Drake, of Shardeloes, Amersham, Bucks.   Mary, the eldest daughter married the Rev. John Drake, rector of Agmondesham, whilst her sister Anne espoused on August 8th, 1870, his eldest brother Thomas, who had assumed in 1776, the name of Tyrwhitt, in accordance with the testamentary injunction of Sir John de la Fountain-Tyrwhitt, Bart., the surname and arms of Tyrwhitt ; but, upon inheriting the estates of his own family at the death of his father, 8th August, 1796, he resumed, in addition, his paternal name, and became Tyrwhitt-Drake.

The first ancestor of the Drake family, according to Burke, from whom lineal descent can be traced is John Drake, of Exmouth, Devonshire, " a man of great estate, and a name of no less antiquity " who lived in the time of Henry V.

ARMS—Quarterly, 1st and 4th, a wivern with wings displayed and tail nowed ; gules for Drake. 2nd and 3rd gules, three tirwhitts, or lapwings, or, for Tyrwhitt.

CRESTS—For Drake, 1st a naked dexter, hand and arm erect, holding a battle axe, sa headed arg. For Tyrwhitt, a savage man ppr cinctured and wreathed vert, holding in both hands a club.

ANCIENT BUILDINGS.

———

THE HERMITAGE.

IN the 3rd year of the reign of King Edward VI. there was a decree in the Court of Augmentation concerning the Hermitage, which was extant in Deptford, in the 4th year of the reign of King Henry IV., A.D. 1403. (*Rym. Fœd. Vol. III. p.* 163, *1st ed.*)

THE MOATED PLACE, OR STONE HOUSE,
OR KING JOHN'S HOUSE.

HASTED asserts that tradition has assigned the latter appellation to an old house, formerly existing at the north-western extremity of the parish, which had, at "several times been the residence of the Kings of England" from King John having been supposed to have been the builder of it ; but with what truth is not certainly known.

Edward III. frequently resided here (*Rym. Fœd., Vol. V. pp.* 68, 638.)

And Henry IV. is said to have made it his residence whilst his leprosy was being cured. A.D., 1405. "Rex Henricus lepra percussus" (*Leland, Antiq. Col. ij.* 314). In the month of July A.D. 1412, we find two charters of Henry IV. dated from this place.

In Hardyng's Chronicle (*cap. ccx., p.* 370), Henry IV. on his death-bed is made to allude to this fearful affliction in the following affecting strain :—

> "Lorde, I thanke the with all my herte,
> With all my soule and my spirytes clere,
> This worme's mete, this caryon full unquerte,
> That some tyme thought in worlde it had no pere,
> This face so foule that leprous doth apere,
> That here afore I have had such a pryde,
> To purtraye ofte in many place full wyde ;

Of which ryght nowe ye porest of this lande,
Except only of theyr benignyte,
Wolde loth to looke vpon I vnderstande,
Of which. good Lorde, that thou so visyte me,
A thousand tymes, the Lord of Trinyte.
With all my herte, I thanke the, and comend
Into thyne handes my soul withouten ende."

"And so," says Hardyng, "he died." This shews that if cured of the leprosy itself, it had left *its mark* upon him.

This Royal Residence remained in the hands of the Crown under the martyrdom of King Charles I. in 1648 ; after which it came under the management of the trustees appointed by ordinance of Parliament, July 16th, 1649, for the sale of that King's lands, and was, by their surveyor, certified to be within the County of Surrey.

GUILD OF OUR LADY OF ROUNCEVAL.

"KING EDWARD VI., on November 16th, in the sixth year of his reign, granted to Edward, Lord Clinton, and Lord Saye, sundry lands in this parish, parcel of the Gild of Our Lady of Rounceval."

DEPTFORD MILL.

IN the 16th year of the reign of Edward II., John Abell held a mill at Deptford, which then escheated to the Crown.

SKINNER'S PLACE.

"IN 1547 Thomas Basingburne held a messuage and tenement, and one dovecote called Skinner's Place, and all houses, lands, &c., belonging to it in Deptford-Strond, alias West Greenwich, being parcel of the possessions of

Thomas-a-Beckett's Hospital (St. Thomas' Hospital),
within the borough of Southwark ; and Edward Draper
then held certain pieces of land belonging to the same
hospital in this parish. All which were then held by them
of the king in capite, by the service of the hundreth part
of one Knight's fee.   Richard Stonely afterwards held
Skinner's Place.   John Leach held the tenement and the
heirs of Robert Tyerborne and Henry Abraham held
others of the premises ; but in 1568 we find the Lady
Anne Parry in possession of them " (*Hasted*).

ROYAL DOG KENNELS.

ON the east side of Mill Lane, erst Dog Kennel Row, is
an ancient wall, now incorporated in a building connected
with the Deptford Brewery, which, according to local
tradition, belonged to the Royal Dog Kennels erected
here by King John and used by Charles I. during his
residence in the neighbourhood.

DEPTFORD BRIDGE

AND ITS HISTORICAL ASSOCIATIONS.

On Keston Heath wells up the Ravensbourne, (a)
A crystal rillet, scarce a palm in width,
Till creeping to a bed, outspread by art,
It sheets itself across, reposing there ;
Thence, through a thicket, sinuous it flows,
And crossing meads and footpaths, gath'ring tribute,
Due to its elder birth from younger branches,
Wanders in Hayes and Bromley, Beckenham Vale,
And straggling Lewisham, to where Deptford Bridge
Uprises in obeisance to its flood,
Whence, with large increase it rolls on to swell
The master current of the " mighty heart"
Of England.

(Hone's Table Book, p. 642).

(a) An old legend is told to account for the name of this stream, which was formerly sometimes called Brome, from Bromley. "It is said that Julius Cæsar, on his invasion of Britain, was encamped with all his force a few miles distant from its source. The army was suffering a good deal from want of water, and detachments had been sent out in all directions to find a supply but without success. Cæsar, however, fortunately observed a raven frequently alighted near the camp, and conjecturing that it came to drink, he ordered its arrival to be carefully noted. This demand was obeyed and the visits of the raven were found to be a small clear spring on Keston Heath. The wants of the army were supplied, and the spring and rivulet have ever since been called the Raven's Well, and Ravensbourne."

Hasted, in his History of Kent (folio vol. 1, 129) gives a view of the Roman intrenchments on Holwood Hill, and figures the ancient road to the spring of the Ravensbourne. as running down to it from where Holwood gates now stand ; he also figures the spring with twelve trees planted round it.

Such was the character of the stream—which forms the
eastern boundary of the parish—in bygone days :—

> " But, oh ! how changed with changing years,
> 'Tis now the vilest stream on earth,
> Polluted from its place of birth !
> The Kent and Surrey hills, no more
> Can shew their limpid rills of yore."
>
> (JOHNSON).

From the time of Henry VIII., "the banks of this
river were under the direction of a Commission of
Sewers, the jurisdiction of which extends from the head
of it down to Lombard's Wall, near Greenwich." In
1849 it became the boundary of the first Metropolitan
Commissioners of Sewers. The present Commissioners
have powers over the drainage and watercourses into it,
but not over the embankments. Obstructions on the
stream, as affecting drainage, are subject to their inter-
ference.

The river at its debouchure into the Thames is called
Deptford Creek, and is navigable for lighters and vessels
of 500 tons at the mouth. - Deptford Creek was a
favourite resort, during the fifth century, of the warlike
Teutonic tribes, who eventually became possessed of the
greatest portion of the kingdom ; as it was again during
the ninth, tenth, and eleventh centuries of the hardy
Norsemen. And it was here that the daring Sir Francis
Drake landed after his memorable voyage round the
world.

As "it would not be in accordance with the dignity
and greatness of the Roman nation to have recourse to
ferries," it is scarcely feasible that a deep narrow gully
like the Ravensbourne, at this spot, would have been
permitted to remain only as a dangerous and unsound
ford, daily affected by tidal influences, in a military way
of such a substantial character as the Watling Street. It
is not unreasonable, therefore, to suppose that a Roman
bridge existed here, which in all probability was
destroyed, for strategical purposes, by the Danes, whose
fleet lay moored for a considerable time in the Creek
below.

A wooden bridge was in existence in the fourteenth century, for, by an inquisition taken in 1395, it appears that it was the duty of the whole hundred to repair it— "totum hundredum de Blakeheth, videlicit, West-grenewych, Estgrenewych, Wolewych, Leuesham, Eltham, Burg de Modyngham, Kelebrok, Lee et Cherltone debent reparare pontem, quæ vocatur Depevord Brege." But this finding was not satisfactory to the men of the hundred; for in the next year we find the following :— "Quod reparatio pontis de Depeford, pertinet ad homines Hundredi de Blackheath, et non at homines villarum de Eltham, Modingham et Woolwich (*Record in the Tower, Esc. Anno 20 Edw. III, n.* 66).

A.D. 1570 Lambarde says "there was lately re-edified a fayre wooden bridge also, over the Brooke called Ravensbourne, which riseth not far off, and setting on woorke some Corne Milles, and one for the glasing of Armour, slippeth by this Towne into the Thamyse."

A.D. 1628, an inscription bearing this date formerly existed on the bridge : "This bridge was re.edified at the only charge of King Charles, in the fourth year of his reign.

This statement is erroneous ; the bridge being much decayed, was probably enlarged and materially altered by King Charles, but not erected by him. During the next year it was "partially swept away by a sudden flood, caused by a succession of heavy rains, but was immediately repaired.

In 1652 we again find the bridge seriously injured by very heavy storms which flooded the Ravensbourne. This tempest is mentioned by Evelyn. "May 25th, after a drowth of neare 4 monethes, there fell so violent a tempest of haile, raine, wind, thunder, and lightning, as no man had seene the like in this age ; the haile being in some places four or five inches about, brake all glasse about London, especially at Deptford, and more at Greenwich."

According to the Parish Minute-book October 6th, 1706, we find the "parish indicted,—bridge not in good repair ;" and on October 18th, 1724, the churchwardens

E

and overseers of the parish were represented at Maidstone Quarter Sessions by William Pemmell, for the non-payment of the bridge money collected by Pemmell, Thomas, Hutchinson, and Foster. These parties, "having a considerable sum now remaining in their hands which they have given no account of," the vestry ordered them to be prosecuted.

On January 29th, 1809, a sudden and rapid thaw set in after an unusually heavy snow storm, which caused the waters of the Ravensbourne to rise above the archway of the bridge, carrying away the parapet and some four yards of the bridge itself. From the Waterworks on the top of Mill Lane, the stream rushed in torrents ; chairs, tables and furniture of various descriptions being washed away and carried through the Creek into the Thames. The body of a man was also observed carried forward with the torrent. Another flood in 1824 carried away the houses and warehouses on each side of the bridge, together with the tide mill below, and its embankments. It is said that the value of the property lost by this flood would have rebuilt the bridge twice over.

The architecture of the old stone bridge showed three several periods :—

I.—The centre piece which was probably of the time of King Edward III.

II.—Two semi-circular arches, apparently of the period of the Stuarts, and supposed to have been those erected at the charge of Charles I. in 1628.

III.—The modern cast iron girders, which were laid down at the expense of the county, to widen the roadway on account of the increase of traffic.

Three insurgent armies have crossed here on their march to London, viz. : That under Wat Tyler (b) in 1381 ; Jack Cade in 1450 ; and Sir Thomas Wyatt in

b In Haydn's Dictionary of Dates, 14th ed., under the article "Rebellions," he is called Walter the Tyler, of Deptford ; although historians speak of him as belonging to Dartford.

the reign of Queen Mary. Sir Thomas Wyatt (c) encamped with his army in Deptford from Friday afternoon till Monday morning. But the most memorable event connected with Deptford Bridge was the sanguinary conflict between the Royal troops and the Cornish rebels in 1496, which is graphically described in "Grafton's Chronicle" as follows:—

"On the Saterday night he (King Henry VII.) sent the Lorde Dawbeney wyth a great companie (John, Earl of Oxford; Henry Burchier, Earl of Essex; Edmond de la Pole, Earl of Suffolk, Sir Ryves ap Thomas and Sir Humphrey Stanley, being the royal commanders under Daubeny) to set on them (the Cornish rebels under Lord Audley) earlye in the morning, which first gat the bridge at Detford-Strande, which was manfully defended by certeyne Archers of the rebeles, whose arowes, as is reported, were in length a full yard. While the Erles set on them on every syde, the Lord Dawbeney came into the field with his companie, and without long fighting the Cornishe men were overcome, but first they tooke the Lord Dawbeney prisoner, and whether it were for feare or for hope of favour, they let him go at libertie, without any hurt or detriment. There were slain of the rebels which fought and resisted, two thousand men and mo, and taken prisoners an infinite number, and amongest them the blacke smith and chief capitaynes which shortly after were put to death.

This Mighell Joseph, surnamed the blacke smith, one of the capitaynes of this donghill, and draffe sacked ruffians, was of such stowte stomacke and haute courage, that at the same time that he was drawen on the Hardle towards his death, he sayd (as men do report) for that mischievous and ungracious act, he should have a name perpetuall, and a fame permanent and immortall. So

c "On the 3rd February, 1554, Wyatt and his host (who are indifferently estimated at 2,000 and at 8,000 men) marched from Deptford (where they had been for three days) along the riverside towards Southwark." (Craik and Macfarlane). Queen Mary offered as a reward to the man that should take or kill Wyatt, lands worth £100 a year to him and his heirs.

(you may perceyve) that desyre of vaine glory and fame enflameth and encourageth aswel poore and meane persons, as the heartes of great Lordes and puyssaunt Princes to travayle and aspire to the same. Some affirme that the King appoynted to fight with the rebelles on the Monday, and preventyng the time by pollicie, set on them upon the Saterday before being improvided and in no array of battaile, and so by that pollicy obteyned the field and victory." The royalists sustained a loss of three hundred slain. James Twichet, Lord Audley, was drawn from Newgate to Tower Hill in a coat of his own arms painted upon paper, reversed and torn, and then beheaded. Thomas Flammock, a lawyer, and Michael Joseph, a blacksmith of Bodmin, were drawn, hanged and quartered on the 28th of June, 1496 ; the latter part of their sentence, which ordered that their quarters were to be pitched on stakes and set up in divers places of Cornwall, was not carried out. being set up in London and other places instead.

The cause of this revolt was the imposition of what the Cornish men deemed an unjust tax, and they had reckoned on the co-operation of the Kentish men—in which they were deceived—which accounts for their marching into this county previous to their contemplated attack on London.

Lambarde, referring to Audley's revolt in his Perambulations of Kent, 1570, says the tax " was unseasonable, for that it was exacted when the heads of the common people were full of Parkin Warbeck."

The Canterbury Pilgrims must have passed here on their way from the " Tabard " in Southwark to the Shrine of St. Thomas á Becket at Canterbury ; as must also the gorgeous processions of the civic dignitaries and citizens of London, to Blackheath, on many occasions—notably in 1415 to welcome Henry V., on his return from the victory of Agincourt, and again in the year following to meet and conduct in state to Lambeth the Emperor Sigismund, who had come to negotiate terms of peace between England and France. That which welcomed Henry VI. in 1431 on his return from Paris whither he had gone to be crowned in Notre Dame ; and some years later his queen, Margaret of Anjou. And the memorable procession of May 29th, 1660, of King Charles II. at the Restoration.

An agitation commenced some fifteen years ago for widening the bridge and its approaches—in which Messrs. Joseph Liddiard and William Gurley Smith took a very active part—which resulted in the Metropolitan Board of Works adopting the plans of these gentlemen. The old stone bridge was removed last year, being replaced by an iron one of much greater dimensions, and the roadway was widened on the north side in Deptford and south side in Greenwich to an uniform width of 60 feet. The roadway previously in its narrowest part was only 21 feet 10 inches, with 4 feet 9 inches and 4 feet 8 inches respectively of footway. Between the hours of 8 a.m. and 8 p.m. from the 19th to the 24th of January, 1874, during very foggy weather, 18,541 foot passengers and 2,960 vehicles passed over the bridge, a sufficient proof that the recent improvements were much needed.

TRINITY HOUSE CORPORATION

𝔘𝔫𝔦𝔱𝔞𝔰 𝔦𝔫 𝔗𝔯𝔦𝔫𝔦𝔱𝔞𝔱𝔢.

Motto of the Guild.

This Society or Guild,—founded by Sir Thomas Spert (commander of the great ship "Harry Grace-a-Dieu") for the increase and encouragement of the study of navigation, the good government of the seamen, and the better security of merchant shipping on our coasts,— was incorporated by Henry VIII., March 20th, 1512, who confirmed to them, not only the ancient rights and privileges of the Company of Mariners of England, but their several possessions at Deptford-Strond, which, together with grants made by Queen Elizabeth and King Charles II., were confirmed by letters patent in 1685 by their first name of "The Master, Wardens and Assistants of the Guild or Fraternity of the Most Glorious and Undivided Trinity, and of St. Clement, in the Parish Church of Deptford-Strond, in the County of Kent."

The Corporation is governed by a Master, four Wardens and eighteen Elder Brethren ; the inferior members of the fraternity, called younger Brethren, being of an unlimited number, for every Master or Mate of a ship expert in Navigation may be admitted as such ; and these serve as a continual nursery to supply vacancies among the Elder Brethren, occasioned by death or otherwise. The Master and two of the Wardens are chosen annually, on Trinity Monday ; formerly at their ancient house at Deptford-Strond ; the other being for life.

The Master, Wardens, Assistants, and Elder Brethren are by Charter invested with the following powers :—

1.—The Examination of the Mathematical children of Christ's Hospital.

2.—The examination of Masters of H.M. ships; appointing pilots to take charge of ships belonging to the Royal Navy, as well as merchant ships; and the amercing of such as shall presume to act as Master of a ship of war, or as a pilot, without their licence, in a pecuniary mulct. An Act of Parliament was passed in the 5th year of George II., for the better regulation of these pilots.

3.—The settling of the several rates of pilotage, and the erecting and maintaining of light-houses, buoys, beacons, and other sea-marks, upon the several coasts of the Kingdom, and in the mouth of the River Thames, with license to alter and shift the same as occasion may require, from time to time, for the good of navigation and the better security of ships, according to an Act of the 8th of Queen Elizabeth. To which end the Brethren frequently survey the North and South Channels leading to the Thames, as well to observe the alteration and increase of all lands and shoals, as to place buoys and other sea-marks, for the direction of mariners, who pass the same, for which service all ships pay a rate of $\frac{1}{2}$d. per ton.

4.—The granting of licenses to poor seamen, not free of the City, to row on the Thames for their support in the intervals of sea service, or when past going to sea.

5.—The preventing aliens from serving on board English ships without their license, upon the penalty of £5 for each offence.

6.—The hearing and determining the complaints of officers and seamen in the Merchant Service; but subject to an appeal to the Lords of the Admiralty, or the Judge of the Court of Admiralty.

To this Corporation belongs the Ballast Office for clearing and deepening the River Thames, by taking from thence a sufficient quantity of ballast for the supply of all ships sailing out of it. In this service are a number of barges (60 in the year 1870) with two men in each. The ballast is delivered at the ship's side at a charge of 1s. per ton. (Act of Geo. II.)

After the maintenance of light-houses and other necessary expenses of the Corporation, the remainder of the revenue is applied wholly to the relief of poor decayed seamen, their widows and orphans and none other ; by yearly, monthly or other temporary charities, more or less, according to their necessities.

The benefits and revenues to support these Charities are derived from light-money, buoys, beaconage, ballastage, and the benefactions of the Brethren. In their hall in London are tables of the names of these benefactors, and the several gifts made.

In consideration of these weighty and necessary services to the public, and that their ships and servants are to be at Her Majesty's call, they have several privileges, immunities and exemptions granted to them from time to time, such as the not serving upon juries and inquests and other like burdens, which others are subject to. This favour extends to all the Brethren both elder and younger, their officers and servants.

The Corporation had two hospitals at Deptford, erected at different times,—one in the Stowage abutting on St. Nicholas' Churchyard which contained 21 houses, and the other in Church-street, overlooking St. Paul's Churchyard, containing 38 houses. The latter was much the finer edifice and had large gardens attached to it. Sir Richard Browne, of Sayes Court,—elder Brother, and Master in 1672—gave the inheritance of the land on which these alms houses were erected ; and they were partly built by a benefaction of £1,300 left to the Trinity House by Capt. Richard Maples, who died commander of a ship in the East Indies in 1680. The Hospital in Church-street has recently been demolished, and some new streets of artizans' dwellings erected on its site. The old hall still remains, but it is a disgrace to the Corporation. The other house in Stowage is let out in tenements and called Rose Cottages. On Trinity Monday, 1837, the Duke of Wellington was elected Master for the first time ; and he held the office for 16 years, never failing to be present at each anniversary, and on these occasions the

town was always *en fête*. The procession, consisting of
the Duke and Elder Brethren, came from the Tower in the
Trinity barges and landed at Deptford Green, where they
were met by the vicar and parish officers, and proceeded
at once to the Hall, where the Oath of Allegiance was
taken by the Master and Deputy Master. The "Loving
Cup" was then passed round, the Master himself first
partaking of it ; and then followed a distribution of
finger biscuits. It is said the Duke never failed to bring
a bouquet with him, which he held in his hand whilst
he looked around him and selected the youngest and
fairest lady, to whom he presented it. On these grand
occasions the Hall was strewn with rushes, and on the
ledges round the room was laid that "Herb of Grace,"
rue—thus keeping up the old custom of decorating apart-
ments on special festivals.

At the conclusion of the ceremonies at the Trinity
Hall, the procession made its way to the Parish Church
of St. Nicholas, being preceded by two girls, dressed in
white, strewing flowers. After service and sermon the
Master and Brethren returned to London. There is
always a dinner given by the Master and Brethren of the
Trinity House, which takes place in London, and
always concludes with the following old Grace, A.D.
1310.

> " Alla Trinita beata
> Da noi sempre adorata
> Trinita gloriosa ;
> Unita meravigliosa
> Tu sei manna superna
> E tutta desiderata."   Amen.   Amen.

By some remains of glass that constituted part of the
window in the ancient Hall at Deptford, containing
the arms and names, with dates, there appears an
authentic record, although none other exists, of several
Masters and Wardens holding office under the charter
of Henry VIII.

1570		WM. LAWSON.
		JOHN DOYIER.
		JAMES RUDDAM.
		HY. CHURCHE.
1572		C. G.
		NICHOLAS FISHBORNE, Warden.
		JOHN BROLLING.
		JOHN DYER.
1573		WM. THOMAS, Warden.
1581		WM. B., Warden, Master in 1585.
1587		D. B. R. C., Master.
		WM. HARRIS, Warden.
1588		ROBALL SIMON, Master.
1615		ROBERT CHESTER, ,,
1617		ROBERT SALMON, ,,
1624		— CHRISTOPHER, Warden.
1629		WALTER COOK, Master.
1635		JOHN TOTTER, ,,
1637		ANTHONY FULCHER, Master.
1638		WM. GOODLAD, ,,
		MICHAEL EDMONDS, ,,
1660		DUKE OF ALBEMARLE.
1662		SIR RICHARD BROWNE, Bart.
		EARL OF CRAVEN.
1671		SIR THOMAS ALLEN, Bart.
1675		LORD OSSORY.
1676		SAMUEL PEPYS, Esq.
1683—	84	LORD DARTMOUTH.
1685		SAMUEL PEP S, Esq.
1686		CAPT. THO ˆ BROWN.
1687		SIR RICHARD HADDOCK.
1688		CAPT. JOHN NICHOLS.
1689		EARL OF TORR NC_ON.
1690—	92	ADMIRAL RUSSELL.
1692—	94	EARL OF PEMBROKE.
1694		CAPT. JOHN H LL.
1695—	96	SIR MATHEW ANDREWS.
1697—	98	LORD LUCAS.
1699		CAPT. RALPH SANDERSON.
1699		CAPT. ROBERT FISHER.

1700		CAPT. THOMAS WILLSHAW.
1701		CAPT. SAMUEL ATKINSON.
1702—	4	CAPT. HENRY RISBE.
1704		SIR GEORGE ROOKE.
1705—	7	ADMIRAL GEORGE CHURCHILL.
1707—	9	SIR HENRY JOHNSON.
1709—	11	SIR JOHN LEAKE.
1711—	13	SIR GEORGE BYNG.
1713—	15	EARL OF STRAFFORD.
1715—	19	EARL OF BERKELEY.
1719—	21	SIR WILLIAM SANDERSON.
1721—	23	SIR CHARLES WAGER.
1723—	25	SIR JOHN JENNINGS.
1725—	27	SIR JOHN NORRIS.
1727—	28	SIR THOMAS COLLY.
1729—	31	SIR THOMAS HARDY.
1731—	33	CAPT. SAMUEL JONES.
1733—	37	SIR CHARLES WAGER.
1737—	41	SIR JOHN NORRIS.
1741—	45	DUKE OF RICHMOND.
1745—	48	DUKE OF BEDFORD.
1749—	51	EARL OF SANDWICH.
1751—	56	LORD ANSON.
1756—	59	DUKE OF BEDFORD.
1759—	64	EARL OF SANDWICH.
1764—	68	DUKE OF BEDFORD.
1768—	70	DUKE OF MARLBOROUGH.
1770—	73	VISCOUNT WEYMOUTH.
1773—	75	LORD NORTH.
1775—	77	EARL OF ROCHFORD.
1777—	82	EARL OF SANDWICH.
1782—	86	VISCOUNT KEPPEL.
1786—	90	SIR GEORGE POCOCK.
1790—1806		RIGHT HON. WILLIAM PITT.
1806—	7	EARL SPENCER.
1807—	9	DUKE OF PORTLAND.
1809—	16	MARQUIS CAMDEN.
1816—	37	EARL OF LIVERPOOL.
1837—	52	DUKE OF WELLINGTON.

The Trinity Monday Visit to Deptford has been discontinued since the "Iron Duke's" death.

The Royal Dockyard.

"Such place hath Deptford, navy-building town."

POPE.

DEPTFORD, having been long a rendezvous for ships, was fixed upon by King Henry VIII., in 1513, as a site for a Royal Dockyard. The first building erected was, probably, the Store House mentioned by Lombarde, "for the better preservation of the Royall Fleete." "There is a floating tradition that a monastery once existed on the site of the Dockyard, which appears to be unfounded, in fact, as neither Dugdale nor Strype allude to any monastic establishment here. Most probably the building referred to by Lysons in his Environs of London, was the "Stonehouse," and the tradition may have originated through the residence at Deptford of Henry IV., whilst that monarch was afflicted with leprosy" (*Dunkin*). The Government works appear to have rapidly extended and improved until Deptford became the most considerable of all the Royal Dockyards, for according to a list of the Navy taken on the 5th of January, 1548, we find six war vessels here. Unlike the other Royal Yards, Deptford had no particular commissioner, but was under the immediate inspection of the Board of Admiralty, which had under it a resident clerk of the Checque and Survey, a Storekeeper and Master Shipwright.

The first recorded visit of royalty occurred on the 19th of June, 1549; an account of which, written by King Edward VI., is still preserved in the Cottonian MSS. in the British Museum. He says, " I went to Deptford, being bidden to supper by the Lord Clinton, where before supper i saw certaine (men) stand upon a bote without hold of anything, and rane one at another til one was cast into the water. At supper Mons. Vieedam and Henadey supped with me. After supper was ober a fort (was) made upon a great lighter on the Temps (Thames), which had three walles and a watch tower, in the meddes of wich Mr. Winter was captain, with forty or fifty other soldiours in yelow and blake. To the fort also apperteined a galery of yelow color with men and municion in it for defence of the castel; wherfor ther cam four pinesses with other men in wight ansomely dressed, wich entending to give assault to the castil, first drove away the yelow piness and after with clods, sciubs, canes of fire, darts made for the nonce, and bombardes assaunted the castill, beating them of the castil into the second ward, who after issued out and drone away the pinesses, sinking one of them, out of wich al the men in it being more than twenty leaped out and swamme in the Temps. Then came th' Admiral of the Navy with three other pinesses, and wanne the castil by assault, and burst the top of it doune, and toke the captain and under captain. Then the Admiral went forth to take the yelow ship, and at length clasped with her, toke her, and assaulted also her toppe and wane it by compulcion, and so returned home."

There was no increase in the establishment during the reign of Queen Mary, but Deptford Yard became noted for its ship-building and scientific master shipwrights. The names of Pett, Shish, Addey, Gasker, &c., occupy a place of pre-eminence in the annals of naval architecture during the 16th and 17th centuries, of which Deptford may be justly proud, and most of these men were born and lived in the riverside portion of the parish, which at the present day is so much despised.

Some of the earliest expeditions despatched by the

government of this country on voyages of discovery were fitted out here.

A.D. 1576.   Sir Martin Frobisher sailed from Deptford on the 8th of June of this year, to try and find a north-east passage to China.   Queen Elizabeth, who took a great interest in the expedition, watched the two small vessels, the Gabriel and Michael, from a window of the palace, as they sailed past Greenwich.

Frobisher was accompanied in these Arctic voyages by Fenton, who afterwards distinguished himself.   He is buried in St. Nicholas Church.

A.D. 1577.   Sir Francis Drake sailed from England on 13th December, 1577, in command of the " Pelican," on his memorable voyage round the world.   He returned home November 3rd, 1580, with treasure amounting to some £800,000 ; and his vessel by express command of the Queen, was placed in the Dock at Deptford, to be preserved as a memorial of his daring adventure.   Four months afterwards (4th April, 1581) Queen Elizabeth condescended to partake of a banquet given by Drake in the cabin of the " Pelican," and before her departure conferred on him the honour of knighthood.   On the occasion of this Royal visit to Deptford Dockyard, Camden (who calls the vessel the "Golden Hind") *(a)* says " there was such a concourse of people, that the wooden bridge over which they passed broke, and upwards of a hundred persons fell into the river, by which accident, however, there was nobody hurt, as if, says he, that ship had been built under some lucky constellation." Upon this occasion, the following verses made by the scholars of Winchester College, were nailed to the mainmast.

Plus Ultra, Herculeis inscribas, Drace, Columnis
Et magno, dicas, Hercule major ero.

In English, thus—

His pillars pass'd, thou Drake may'st boldly claim
Than Hercules the great, a greater name.

a " Drake's old ship the ' Pelican,' named after the famous voyage the ' Golden Hind,' was long an object of veneration to the Seamen of Deptford."   *Payne's voyages of the Elizabethan Seamen, p.* 144.

Drace, pererrati quem novit terminus orbis,
  Quemque simul mundi vidit uterque Polus ;
Si taceant homires, facient te sidera notum.
  Sol nescit comitis non memor esse sui.

Which may be rendered—

Expos'd to thee have earth's last limits been,
  Thou at like distance both the Poles hast seen ;
Were mankind mute, the stars thy fame would blaze,
  And Phœbus sing his old companions praise.

Digna Ratis quæ stet radiantibus inclyta stellis ;
  Supremo cœli vertice digna Ratis

Thus translated—

Amidst the stars, thy ship were fitly plac'd,
  And stars in gracing it, be doubly grac'd.

Drake's ship soon became one f the lions of the metropolis, and its cabin appears to have been fitted up as a refreshment saloon, for the accommodation of the numerous visitors who daily crowded the Dockyard to see the first English ship that had accomplished the circumnavigation of the globe. In course of time the old ship fell into decay, and was broken up ; but the Master Shipwright of the Dockyard—Mr. John Davis—anxious to preserve some memorial of it, caused a chair to be constructed from its timbers, which he afterwards presented to the University of Oxford ; where it is still to be seen in the Bodleian Library. Abraham Cowley, the poet, who was frequently at Deptford with his dear friend "Sylva" Evelyn, wrote a Pindaric Ode upon his sitting drinking in this chair :—

" To this great ship, which round the world has run
And match'd, in race, the chariot of the sun ;
This Pythagorian ship (for it may claim),
Without presumption. so deserved a name,
By knowledge once, and transformation now)
In her new shape this sacred port allow.
Drake and his ship, could not have wish'd from fate,
A more blest station or more blest estate,
For, lo ! a seat of endless rest is given,
To her in Oxford and to Him in Heaven."

Cowley again speaks of " Drake's Brave Oak " in his *Sixth Book of Plants, p.* 145, *Ed.* 1693. Trans. by Mrs. A. Behn, as follows :—

> "And Drake's brave Oak that past to Worlds unknown.
> Whose toils O Phœbus, were so like thy own ;
> Who round the earth's vast globe triumphant rode,
> Deserves the celebration of a God.
> O let the Pegasean ship no more
> Be worshipt on the too unworthy shore,
> After her watery life, let her become
> A fixt star shining equal with the Ram.
> Long since the Duty of a Star she's done
> And round the earth with guiding light has shone"

And again—

> "Great Relic ! thou, too, in this port of ease,
> Hast still one way of making voyages ;
> The breath of fame, like an auspicious gale,
> (The greater trade-wind, which does never fail)
> Shall drive thee round the world, and thou shalt run
> As long around it as the sun.
> The straits of time too narrow are for thee—
> Launch forth into an undiscover'd sea.
> And steer the endless course of vast eternity ;
> Take for thy sail, this verse, and for thy pilot, me."

To Cowley's let us add another, first published in the *Biographia Britannica* A.D., 1750.

> "Thy glory Drake, extensive as thy mind,
> No time shall tarnish, and no limits bind ;
> What greater praise ! than thus to match the sun
> Running that Race ; which cannot be outrun,
> Wide as the World thou compass'd spreads thy Fame,
> And with that World, an equal date shall claim."

Charles Kingsley gives an interesting account of Drake, and his ship the "Pelican" in "Westward Ho!"

In allusion to Sir Francis Drake, it not may be amiss to note the following quaint lines written over the sign of the "Queen's Head and Admiral Drake" at a house kept by an old sailor, viz. ;—

> "Oh, Nature ! to old England still
> Continue these mistakes,
> Still give us for our Kings such Queens,
> And for our DUX such Drakes."

A.D., 1589. "It was here that Sir Walter Raleigh equipped a fleet chiefly with volunteers, who were attracted by his reputation. But after leaving Deptford, he was so long detained by contrary winds, that he only took one vessel and destroyed another. Thomas White, a Londoner, who fitted out a few ships at his own cost, had better fortune. He took two Spanish ships freighted with 1,400 chests of quicksilver, and with goods of another and a curious kind,—2,072,000 indulgences, purchased by his Catholic majesty at 300,000 florins, with the charitable purpose of re-selling them to his Mexican subjects at five millions in gold." A.D., 1596, a fleet of 17 men-of-war of the 1st class, with 153 smaller vessels were equipped partly at Deptford, and partly at other ports, afterwards they were collected at Plymouth, whence they sailed. The loss of the Spaniards by this expedition, which operated off Cadiz was estimated at twenty million ducats." (*Dunkin*).

A.D. 1597 another armament, still stronger than the former, was fitted out, partly also at Deptford, which consisted of 17 first rates and 43 smaller vessels of war.

Three small vessels captured by some of Elizabeth's ships were brought to Deptford in 1560. James I. took a great delight in visiting his ships, and particularly Deptford Dockyard.

On October 3rd, 1625, a fleet of 80 ships, large and small, which had partly been fitted out at Deptford, sailed, under the command of Viscount Wimbledon, to attack the Spaniards.

A.D. 1776. On the 10th of February, 1776, the celebrated circumnavigator, Captain James Cook, hoisted the pendant on board H.M. sloop "Resolution," having received his commission to command her on the preceding day; Captain Clerke, who had been his second lieutenant on board the "Resolution," during his second voyage round the world, being appointed to the command of the "Discovery," which had been commissioned to accompany him in his third and fatal voyage of discovery to the then imperfectly known Pacific Ocean. Both ships were equipped for sea at Deptford Dockyard, from which they sailed on the 29th of May following.

F

A.D. 1784. A society of gentlemen fitted out a large ship here, for the purpose of making discoveries in the Arctic regions. This vessel was Dutch built and equipped with every kind of accommodation.

A.D. 1791. Captain George Vancouver, who had served under Cook in the Pacific, fitted out an expedition, in Deptford Yard, to prosecute the survey of the North-West Coast of the American Continent, which had been commenced by Cook, shortly before his death. Captain Vancouver sailed from here on the 7th of January, 1791, in the "Discovery," being accompanied by the "Chatham" armed tender in command of Lieut. William Robert Broughton.

This expedition, besides adding greatly to the geographical knowledge of the time, resulted in the annexation to the British Crown of a rich and extensive territory known at the present day as the Colonies of Vancouver Island and British Columbia. The names of these vessels, together with those of the officers on board, will be found to occupy prominent positions on the charts of the survey of this coast concluded some twenty years ago by the late Hydrographer to the Admiralty, Admiral Sir George Henry Richards, C.B., R.N., &c., who for some time past has been residing in the immediate neighbourhood of Deptford.

During the Commonwealth the Dockyards at Deptford were vastly increased and filled with workmen. Ship after ship was built with great rapidity and men to man them were drafted out of the Army.

The new wet dock near the Red House was finished in November, 1704.

In 1780 a long range of store houses were built under the direction of Sir Charles Middleton.

A fire broke out in the sail rooms on the 8th of July, 1793, and did much damage.

In March, 1863, by direction of the Admiralty, the ancient State barge and shallop, built at Deptford in the reign of James I., was removed from the store house here and, after being renovated and decorated, was forwarded to Virginia Water. The barge, which is clinker built, is an interesting specimen of naval architecture ; it contains a large dining saloon, and, notwithstanding its great age, the timbers are perfectly sound.

The last official document printed by order of the House of Commons was the report of the Hydrographer (Captain Richards), April 28th, 1864, shewing the amount of Dock, Basin, and Quay accommodation in her Majesty's Naval Yard at Deptford, which is as follows :—

"The area of the yard in Deptford consists of 27 acres, 1 rood, and 23 perches.

There are two fourth-class docks.

There is one basin, which contains 1 acre, 1 rood, and 8 perches.

The available length of quay accommodation in basins consists of 500 feet.

The length of quay accommodation outside is 2000 feet.

Ships cannot lie alongside the Dockyard at most stages of the tide.

The front of the wharf wall at Deptford Dockyard is about 1700 feet in length and mean breadth of the yard 650 feet. There are three building slips for ships of the line on the face next the river and two for smaller vessels which launch in a basin or wet dock, 260 feet by 220 feet. There are two dry docks which open into each other for using when required, and one large dock of 2 acres communicating with the Thames."

The poplar trees in the Dockyard were cut down on the 13th of March, 1834.

Many famous ships have been built here ; and the following list, however imperfect, will, nevertheless, convey an idea of the important part Deptford has played in the naval annals of the country.

It disputes with Woolwich and Erith the building of the great ship that carried Henry VIII. across the Channel, to meet Francis I., King of France, at the Field of the Cloth of Gold—the "Harry-Grace-a-Dieu," commanded by Sir Thomas Spert or Sprat, who was a native of the town, and resided here.

F 2

The " Regent of England " which was built at Woolwich,—according to an article in Hone's Year Book,
p. 1227—in 1512, the year previous to the establishment
of the dockyard here, has been attributed by some to
have been the first war vessel built at Deptford.

A.D.	NAME OF SHIP, TONNAGE AND ARMAMENT.
1595	" Repulse," (a) 700 tons.
1595	(b)
1609	" Red Lion." (c)
1610	(d)
1619	" Constant Reformation," (e) 750 tons, 40 guns.
,,	" Happy Entrance," (e) 850 tons.
1631	" St. Denis."
1633	" Henrietta Maria." (f)

a A.D., 1595. Repulse was built by Mr. Baker, and was commissioned to carry the Admiral's flag in Lord Essex's squadron against
Cadiz.

b The Earl of Cumberland built at Deptford in 1595 a ship of his
own of 900 tons, which Queen Elizabeth at the launching named " The
Scourge of Malice."—*Entick's Naval Hist., p.* 369.

c " On the 7th of June (1609) the ' Red Lion,' which was newly
built by Mr. Baker, of Deptford, was launched, where were present
the King's Majesty and the Prince ; I attending then near the place
at the great store-house end, where his Majesty had his standing, he
was pleased very graciously to confer with me, and to use me with
extraordinary expressions of his princely favour."—*Phineas Pett's
Diary.*

d " In the beginning of January, 1610, there were two new ships
built at Deptford for the East India merchants to be launched, whereat
his Majesty (James I.) with the Prince and divers lords were present,
and feasted with a banquet of sweetmeats on board the great ship in
the dock, which was called ' The Trades Increase ;' the other was
called ' The Pepper Corn,' the names being given by his Majesty."—
Pett's Diary.

e On 8th November, 1619, the King, accompanied by the Prince
and the Lord Admiral, came to his Majesty's timber-yard at Deptford,
where he gave names to the two new ships, which were built in the dry
dock, which ships were the first that were undertaken by the Commissioners of the Navy.—*Pepy's Miscellanies, vol.* 3, *p.* 592.

f 31st of January, 1633, was launched here " The Henrietta
Maria," the King and Queen being present ; and again in February,
1634, his Majesty was present at the launching of the " James," which
had been built by his nephew, Peter Pett.—*Phineas Pett.*

1634 " James." (*a*)
1650 " Assistance."
1652 " Diamond." ⎫
   ,,   " Ruby." ⎬ (*b*).
1652 " Naseby." (*c*)
1655 (*d*)
1658 " Reserve," (*e*) 573 tons.
1661 (*f*)
1666 " Loyal London."
1667 (*g*)

a " 1634, in the month of February, the 'James,' built by my nephew Peter Pett, was launched at Deptford, his Majesty being present, where I attended all the while."—*Phineas Petts's Diary*.

b " 1652, March 15th. I saw the Diamond and Ruby launch'd in the Dock at Deptford, carrying 48 brasse cannon each. Cromwell and his Grandees present with greate acclamations."—*Evelyn's Diary*.

c This vessel, which bore the flag of Admiral Blake in the ocean-battles of the Commonwealth, was re-christened the " Royal Charles " at the Restoration, and despatched to Scheveling, in the Netherlands, to convey his majesty (Charles II.) to Dover.

> " The Naseby now no longer England's shame,
> But better to be lost in Charles' name."

As flagship of James, Duke of York, in 1665, she was engaged in the action with the Dutch ; who afterwards captured her along with the " London," " Royal Oak," " James " and some other vessels when they sailed up the Medway ; and so, forsooth, she *was* " lost in Charles' name." Dryden celebrates her in his Annus Mirabilis.

d 1655, April 9th. I went to see the greate ship newly built by the usurper Oliver, carrying 96 brasse guns and 1000 tons burthen. In the prow was Oliver on horseback, trampling 6 Nations under foote, a Scott, Irishman, Dutchman, Frenchman, Spaniard, and English. as was easily made out by their several habits. A Fame held a laurel over his insulting head ; the word, *God with us.*—*Evelyn's Diary*.

e Built by Peter Pett.

f 1661. January 19th. The King hath been this afternoon at Deptford, to see the yacht that Commissioner Pette is building, which will be very pretty.—*Pepy's*—*Bohn's edit. I.*, 143.

g April 28th, 1667.—To Deptford, and there I walked down the Yard, Shish and Cox with me, and discoursed about cleaning of the wet docks. and heard. which I had before, how, when the docke was made, a ship of near 500 tons was there found ; a ship supposed of Queene Elizabeth's time, and well wrought, with a great deal of stone shot in her, of eighteen inches diameter. which was shot then in use ; and afterwards meeting with Captain Perriman and Mr. Castle at

1668	" Charles." (a)
,,	" Cambridge," (b) 70 guns.
1678	" Hampton Court," 70 guns, 1072 tons.
,,	" Hope," 70 guns, 1082 tons.
,,	" Lenox," 70 guns, 1072 tons.
1679	" Duchess," 90 guns, 1418 tons.
,,	" Sterling Castle," (c) 70 guns, 1087 tons.
,,	" Elizabeth," 70 guns, 1114 tons.
1683	" Neptune," 90 guns, 1448 tons.
1703	" Nottingham," 4th rate.
1704—5	(d)
1710	" Princess Augusta," 184 tons, 40 men.

Half-way Tree; they tell me of stone-shot of 36 inches diameter, which they shot out of mortar-pieces.—*Pepy's Diary, vol. IV., p.* 28.

a 1668. March 3rd. Was launch'd at Deptford that goodly vessell " The Charles." I was neere his Majesty (Charles II.) She is longer than the " Soveraine," and carries 110 brasse canon ; she was built by old Shish, a plaine honest carpenter, master builder of this dock, but one who can give very little account of his art by discourse, and is hardly capable of reading, yet of greate abilitie in his calling. The family have been ship carpenters in this yard above 100 years.— *Evelyn's Diary.*

Pepy's was also present at the launching of this ship, he says " Down by water to Deptford," where the King. Queene and Court, are to see launched the new ship built by Mr. Shish, called " The Charles." And then he piously wishes " God send her better luck than the former !" for, she had been captured by the Dutch in the Medway. —*Pepy's Diary.*

b Built by Mr. Shish.

c Lost on the Goodwin Sands during the great storm in November, 1703, when only 70 out of a crew of 276 men were saved.—*Captain Johnson.*

d There was great activity at this Dockyard during these years, consequent upon the frightful loss sustained by the navy in the great storm of November, 1703. The devastation which occurred in Deptford Yard was very serious. In the town the ravages of the storm were frightful. Nearly all the roofs of the houses of the inhabitants were injured and nearly all the chimneys blown down. Every vessel in the river between London Bridge and Deptford (excepting four) broke from her moorings and was either driven on shore or sunk. The storm began in the middle of November and reached its greatest height on the morning of the 27th. when the Eddystone Lighthouse was destroyed in which Mr. Winstanley, its builder, and others perished. The destruction caused throughout the country by this storm was so great that a general fast was appointed to be kept.

1716 " Barfleur " (a hulk), 1565 tons.
1720 " Catherine " (a large yacht), 166 tons, 40 men.
1723 " Berwick " (a hulk), 1147 tons.
1724 " Fubbs " (yacht), 157 tons, 40 men.
  ,, " May " (yacht), 164 tons, 40 men.
1729 " Torrington," (a) 5th rate, 40 guns, 200 men.
  ,, " Namur," (b) 2nd rate, launched in September.
  ,, " Windsor," 4th rate, 60 guns.
1732 " Deptford." (c)
1724 " Prince of Orange " (hulk), 1128 tons.
1739 (d)
1742 " Monmouth," 10 guns, (rebuilt).
1742 (e)
  ,, " Revenge," 1258 tons, 480 men. (f)
1744 Spanish Launches " (g)
  ,, " Winchester."
  ,, Two vessels of 70 guns each, names not given.
1745 " Yarmouth," 1359 tons.
1749 " Royal Charlotte," 10 guns, 232 tons, 70 men.

a This vessel was launched in July and commissioned to carry the Earl of Kinnoul to Turkey, his Lordship having been appointed agent for the Turkey Company at Constantinople.

b The Namur was launched in September, Admiral Sir Charles Wager, Sir Thomas Littleton, with several other great officers and persons of distinction, being present, and a vast crowd of spectators.

She was engaged at the blockade of Brest in 1759; and in Earl St. Vincent's squadron off Cadiz.

c " Tuesday, Aug. 22nd. Several Lords of the Admiralty went to Deptford yard, and viewed the Deptford, a 4th rate of 60 guns, rebuilt after a model designed by Sir Jacob Acworth. She is quite flush fore and aft on both decks, with several curious contrivances in her powder room, and two half decks that will keep the watch dry in the worst of weather."—Gent's. Mag.

d The fearful storm on September 10th of this year did serious damage to the yard; and war breaking out with Spain in October caused great activity.

e In August of this year thirty sail of transports were lying here to embark troops for Flanders; and press gangs were actively at work.

f Engaged at the blockade of Brest in 1759.

g Built to cope with a similar class of vessels constructed by the Spaniards.

1751   " Buckingham," (rebuilt).
1753   " Dorset " (yacht), 14 guns, 164 tons, 50 men.
1754   " Seaford," 434 tons.
1755   " Cambridge," 1615 tons, 200 men.
  ,,   " Medway," 1285 tons.
1756   " Deal Castle," 400 tons.
1757   " Shannon," 28 guns, launched August 13th.
  ,,   " Preston," 1044 tons, 350 men.
1758   " Dublin," 1561 tons, 600 men.
1759   " Hercules," 1608 tons.
1760   " Superb," 1612 tons.
  ,,   " Dragon," 1614 tons.
1762   " Kent," 74 guns, 1617 tons, 600 men.
1763   " Albion," 1662 tons.
1765   " Monarch," 74 guns, 1612 tons, launched July
           20th.
1766   " Magnificent," 1612 tons, 600 men.
1767   " Marlborongh," 1642 tons. (a)
1768   " Egmont," 1643 tons. (b)
1770   " Resolution," (c) 70 guns.
1771   " Grafton," (d) 1652 tons.
1774   " Enterprise," 594 tons.
1776   " Culloden," 1659 tons, 600 men. (a) (e)
  ,,   " Galatea," 429 tons
1777   " America," 1370 tons.

a   The " Marlborough," " Culloden," " Pegasus" and " Impregnable" took part in the action on " the glorious First of June," 1794, when as Dibdin sings :—

> " Howe made the Frenchmen dance a tune,—
>   An admiral great and glorious ;
> Witness for that the First of June.—
>   Lord ! how he was victorious."

b   In Earl St. Vincent's squadron off Cadiz.

c   The " Resolution" was built in room of one of the same name, lost in pursuing the enemy in that memorable engagement on the French coast, under the command of Sir Edward Hawke.

d   The Earl of Sandwich was present at the launching.

e   The " Culloden" and " Alexander" were engaged at the Battle of the Nile.

1778	" Alexander," 1621 tons. (*e*)
"	" Amphitrite," 24 guns, 514 tons, 164 men.
1779	" Alcide," 1625 tons.
"	" Pegasus," 594 tons, 28 guns. (*a*)
1780	Vessel launched, (*a*) March 22nd, name unknown.
"	" Magnanime," launched 14th Oct., 1370 tons.
"	" Myrmidon," 481 tons.
"	" Goliath," 74 guns, 1604 tons.
1782	" Resistance," (*b*) a frigate, 44 guns, launched in July.
1783	New yacht, (*c*) in room of " Katherine," launched.
1786	" Impregnable," 2nd rate. (*a*)
"	" Vanguard," 3rd rate. (*d*)
"	" Standard," 64 guns, 1370 tons, 64 guns.
1787	" New Union," 90 guns, three-decker.
1793	" Hawke," 16 guns.
1797	" Neptune," 98 guns. (*e*)

According to Lysons, the following ships were built between the years 1800 and 1810, viz. : "Fame," "Blake," "Bombay," "Colossus," 74 guns, (*e*) "Courageux," 74 guns, four frigates and three sloops, names not given, and "Queen Charlotte," 120 guns, launched 17th July, 1810.

| 1803 | (*f*) |
| 1803 | " Repulse," 74 guns, launched July 22nd. |

(Showell's Collection.)

Vide note *e*, p. 80.

Vide note *a*, p. 80.

a The Earl of Sandwich attended Prince William Henry at the launch of this vessel, previous to which his Royal Highness had carried the Spanish and French colours to the Tower as military trophies.

b This vessel was commissioned by Captain King, the circumnavigator with Captain Cook.

c This yacht was fitted out to fetch H.R.H. Prince Frederick (Bishop of Osnaburgh) from Williamstadt.

d Flagship of Lord Nelson in the Mediterranean, in 1797.

e At the Battle of Trafalgar in which these vessels were engaged, the "Colossus" suffered more severely in her aggregate of killed and wounded than any other British ship.

f The "Marlborough," 74 guns, was launched from Barnet's dock.

No date.   " Blenheim," 74 guns.
  "   " Orpheus," 36 guns.
1819   " La Blonde," 46 guns (a frigate), launched 12th
            January.
1822   " Comet."
1833—34. (a)
1843   " Worcester," (b) 50 guns.
1844   " Porcupine," 3 guns, 582 tons.
1845   " Spitfire," 3 guns, 432 tons.
  "   " Terrible," (c) 21 guns, 1850 tons, 800 H.P.
           " Emerald."
           " Termagant." (d)
           " Leopard."
           " Imperieuse."
1854   " Hornet," 17 guns, 950 tons.
  "   " Curlew."
  "   " Hannibal," 91 guns, 3136 tons.
1857   " Racer."
1858   " Forte," 51 guns, 2364 tons.
  "   " Icarus," 11 guns, 950 tons.
1859   " Ranger," 5 guns, 427 tons.
  "   " Mutine," 17 guns, 950 tons.
1859   " Rattler," 17 guns, 950 tons.
  "   " Rosario," 11 guns, 669 tons.
  "   " Rapid," 11 guns, 669 tons.
  "   " Speedwell," 5 guns, 425 tons.
  "   " Zebra," 17 guns, 950 tons.
  "   " Newcastle," 51 guns, 3027 tons.

   a In 1833 the yard was closed, and in the following year utilized
in breaking up old Men-of-War.

   b The " Worcester " was laid down in 1816 and completed ready
for launching in 1831. She was not, however, launched until the 10th
of October, 1843 ; when the slip was required for the building of the
paddle-wheel steamer " Terrible " of 800 horse power.

   c The " Terrible " was afterwards nick-named the " Black Sea
Cat " in consequence of the active part played by her during the
Crimean War.

   d The compiler of this work served on board the " Termagant "
at the bombardment of Bomarsund in August, 1854, and afterwards for
three years on the West India and North American Station, bearing
the broad pendant of Commodores, Henderson and Kellett.

1860 " Landrail," 5 guns, 425 tons.
  „   " Endymion," 36 guns.
  „   " Favorite," 22 guns.
      " Dido," 22 guns.
      " Sappho," 17 guns.
      " Columbine," 11 guns.
      " Ariadne," 26 guns, 3214 tons,
      " Cameleon," 17 guns, 950 tons.
1864 " Enterprise," (a) 1000 tons.
  „   " Favourite," 8 guns, 2000 tons (iron-cased cor
      vette).
1869 " Druid," (b) launched 13th March.

Deptford Yard, being unsuited for the construction of the class of war vessels that have supplanted the " wooden walls of Old England," was finally closed on the 31st of March, 1869 ; and afterwards sold to Mr. T. P. Austin for the sum of £70,000 ; who subsequently disposed of about twenty-two acres of the ground, to the Corporation of London, for £94,640, for the site of a Foreign Cattle Market. The Market was opened for use on the 28th of December, 1871.

a " The armour-plated sloop 'Enterprise' built according to the plans of the Navy Constructor, Mr. Reed, was launched on Tuesday, the 9th of February, from the Royal Yard, Deptford. The young Prince Arthur, accompanied by Major Elphinstone, witnessed the interesting sight ; and the Admiralty was represented by the Comptroller, Admiral Robinson."—*Kentish Mercury.*

b The Druid was the last vessel launched from this yard ; H.R.H. the Princess Louise being present at the launching.

ROYAL VICTORIA VICTUALLING YARD.

THE Royal Victoria Yard occupies the site of the Old Red House, "so called as being a collection of warehouses and storehouses built of red bricks," which was burnt down in July, 1639. On being re-built, it was included in the grant, to Sir John Evelyn, of Sayes Court, A.D., 1726, and was then described as 870 feet in length, 35 feet wide, and containing 100 warehouses. The whole of the land comprised in the present yard has been purchased by the Government from time to time from the Evelyns, the latest addition being a portion of the once famous gardens of " Sylva Evelyn" which was purchased from the owner of the estate in 1869. The East India Company rented the premises for some time; but on being re-purchased by the Crown from the Evelyns, a new victualling house was built in 1745, to replace the old victualling office on Tower Hill, the lease being then almost expired. This new building was accidentally burnt down in 1749, with great quantities of stores and provisions. It was subsequently rebuilt, and now comprises extensive ranges of stores, workshops, &c., with river-side wharf, and all the necessary appliances for carrying on the work of the yard. It received its present name of " Royal Victoria Yard " in July, 1858, by command of Her Majesty the Queen, after her visit to it ; Grove-lane, at the same time being changed into Victoria-road. This yard is the largest of the three Home Victualling Establishments ; of which the other two are situated at Gosport (the Royal Clarence) and Devonport. It is under civilian management, and gives employment to upwards of 400 persons ; the amount paid in wages and salaries being upwards of £36,000 per annum.

It is here that a large proportion of the biscuit used in the navy is manufactured, together with chocolate, mustard, pepper, and other comestibles ; and it is hence that the Naval Depôts abroad draw their supplies of every description of clothing, food, tobacco, rum and medical stores—an office for which the yard by reason of its proximity to the docks is admirably fitted. The value of stores of this description, received under contract, annually amounts to upwards of £500,000. The buildings, being devoted strictly to business purposes, are not of a very interesting character, though the scale on which the supplies are maintained is calculated to impress the mind of the visitor,—one of the rum vats alone being capable of containing upwards of 32,000 gallons.

The figure head of the "San Josef," captured at the battle of Navarino on the 14th of February, 1797 adorns the loft devoted to sailmaking; while the safety of the yard from invasion is insured by 10 brass carronades of brilliant appearance, though somewhat antique date, one of them bearing the legend "Cast in the presence of His Majesty, October the 5th, 1639—Mountjoy, Earle of Newport, Major Generall of the Ordnance," while the identity, both of this *formidable* weapon as well as that of one of its companions is insured by the further inscription, "John Browne made this peece." These guns were probably those placed in the yard, June, 1667, for defensive purposes, when the Dutch sailed up the river as far as Sheerness, which they burnt. It was to this yard that the Board of Admiralty retired to hold their sittings when driven from London by the ravages of the Great Plague.

There is a Museum in the yard, but the majority of articles of interest which it contained at one time, have been withdrawn : there are still, however, some minor Arctic relics, models of ships, and a large fragment of the keel of the ill-fated "Royal George," besides a tea cup and saucer, inscribed to the effect that they once were the property of Napoleon Buonaparte.

The present Superintendent of the yard is T. G. Grant, Esq., who was appointed in 1870, and Assistant Superintendent, C. F. Miller, Esq.

PARISH WORTHIES.

___

"Lives of great men all remind us
We can make our lives sublime,
And departing, leave behind us
Footprints on the sands of time."

Longfellow.

THE roll of persons connected with the parish of Deptford, either by birth or residence,—who have elevated themselves to distinction by their eminent attainments in literature, science, art, invention or heroism,—is, by no means, a short one; and it will be impossible for us to give more than very abbreviated sketches of their history. From the most approved authorities, we shall, however, present all those particulars which it may be most important to know.

___

PETER THE GREAT.

PETER THE GREAT, in 1698, having established a regency, to direct the government during his absence, departed from his dominions as a private gentleman, in the train of the ambassadors that he had sent to the principal courts of Europe. Amsterdam, at that time, one of the most flourishing commercial cities in Europe, was the first place that arrested his attention ; he entered himself as a common carpenter, in one of the principal dockyards, labouring and living exactly like the other workmen. Thence he came to England, and for some time worked as a ship carpenter in the Royal Dockyard at Deptford ; residing, with his retinue, at Sayes Court, which he had hired from John Evelyn, Esq., who, at that time, had retired to the seclusion of his country residence at Wotton, in Surrey.

A wooden tablet in one of the old ship-building sheds with the following inscription :—" Here worked, as a ship carpenter, Peter, Czar of all the Russias, afterwards Peter the Great, 1698 ;" a small street near the Dockyard Gates, called Czar-street—now in process of demolition,—and the sign of a public house in the Cattle Market, are all that is left to mark the residence in Deptford, of one of the greatest of Russian Emperors, and founder of the modern capital of the Empire, St. Petersburgh.

Incidents connected with the Czar's life at Deptford will be found recorded in notices of Sayes Court and the Quaker's Meeting House.

THE EARL OF NOTTINGHAM.

CHARLES HOWARD, Lord Howard, of Effingham, was born in 1536. As Lord High Admiral of England, he was entrusted, by Queen Elizabeth, with the command of the fleet which destroyed the Spanish " Invincible Armada," in 1588. In 1596, he, with the Earl of Essex, burnt a second Spanish fleet in Cadiz harbour, for which service he was created Earl of Nottingham. After Queen Elizabeth's death, he still continued to enjoy the most distinguished posts under her successor, James I., discharging every duty with a singular ability and honourable zeal.

Lord Nottingham resided at a house on Deptford Green, where the Admiralty for a long time held their board, and governed the destinies of the English navy.

This house was subsequently converted into the " Gun
Tavern." In the Board-room, which had a window with
a balcony fronting the Thames, was a splendid mantle-
piece, bearing the arms of Sir Thomas Howard, K.G.,
Earl of Surrey, and afterwards Duke of Norfolk ; who in
April, 1514, succeeded his brother, Sir Edward, the first
Lord High Admiral, who was appointed by indenture,
8th April, 1512, with an allowance of ten shillings a day
for his own maintenance, wages and rewards.   He was
killed at Conquest, on the 24th of April, 1514.

This chimney piece, which was for many years an
object of interest to curious visitors, was removed some
50 or 60 years ago, by the late Benjamin Tucker, Esq.
to his residence in Cornwall, Tremarten Castle, probably,
as a fixture or heir-loom to the property, granted him,
for three lives by King George, IV.   It is of oak ; six
feet, one inch wide, and four feet, three inches high.
The carved figures (male and female) are gilded, and alos
the lion's head, with the flowers or pateras in the
triangular compartments and mouldings, immediately
surrounding the four panels.   The top ones contain
drawings or plates of the celebrated " Harry Grace a
Dieu " built by Henry VIII., at Woolwich.   One panel
shows that ship afloat ; and in the other are projected
the various shipwright's lines and sheer planes of the
same vessel.

In the compartment to the left, is the following
inscription written in gold :—

" Soon after his accession to the throne, Henry VIII.,
settled the present constitution of the Royal Navy
Offices."

In the opposite panel, is the inscription as under,
written in gold :

" In the spring of 1514, the Lord High Admiral
entered the port of Brest, with forty-two ships of war,
and some small vessels, where he found the French fleet
protected within the batteries, and a range of twenty-
four hulks linked together ; whilst there, Monsieur
Pregent, arrived in the Bay of Conquest, with six gallies
and four foists, which he secured between two rocks, well

furnished with ordnance. Nevertheless, the Lord High Admiral resolved to attack them, and having prepared two gallies and four boats, he embarked in one of the galleys, which he laid alongside of Monsieur Pregent, and himself headed the boarders; but his galley, by accident, swinging off before she could be lashed, and when only seventeen of his men had been able to follow him, he was killed the 24th of April, 1514."

The moulding surrounding the coat of arms and the shield are properly blazoned.

There is a finely executed drawing of this mantle-piece in the British Museum.

SIR RICHARD BROWNE, Knight.

Sir Richard Browne, the elder, owner and occupier of Sayes Court, was a personage whose career and character are well worthy our highest regard. A zealous and faithful servant of the Crown, he discovered, nevertheless, an uncompromising attachment to the cause of the people.

Beginning life as a student in the Temple, we find him very early taken into the service of the Crown by Robert Dudley, the great Earl of Leicester, when sent by Queen Elizabeth as Governor of the United Netherlands. In that mission Sir Richard Browne filled the post of Chief Secretary, and continued in it for several years, exhibiting evidences of no ordinary capacity and judgment. On his return home he was at once appointed Clerk of the Green Cloth to Queen Elizabeth,—an office at that time of grave responsibility, attended in its discharge with innumerable difficulties—its duties not being confined, as they are at present, to the arrangement of the ceremonial and appointments at the palace on state occasions, but more resembling those which appertain to the Chancellor of the Exchequer. In this office he continued in the succeeding reign, holding in connection with it, that of Master of the Household and

G

Cofferer to King James I.   His duty of Clerk of the
Green Cloth, was to superintend the conduct and
accounts of the purveyors to the Crown, who were invested
with powers, which they too often used to their own
purposes, and to the severe oppression of the people ;
and by checking and reducing these powers, and punish-
ing their abuse, to the relief of the taxpayer, Sir
Richard Browne rendered the most signal service.

"He died" says the records of the time "by the
rupture of a vein, in a vehement speech he made about
the compositions 'of the purveyors' in a Parliament of
King James."   Sayes Court was his home, and St.
Nicholas' Church, Deptford, his resting place.   He died
in May, 1604, aged 65 years.

SIR RICHARD BROWNE, Baronet.

SIR RICHARD BROWNE, Knight and Baronet, was the
only son of Christopher Browne and Grandson of Sir
Richard Browne.   He was Gentleman of the Privy
Chamber to King Charles I, and Clerk of the Council to
Kings Charles I and Charles II.   He was Ambassador to
the Court of France from these monarchs, from 1641
until the Restoration of King Charles II. in 1660.   His
death and funeral is described in *Evelyn's Diary* :—
"February 12th, 1683.   This morning I rec'd news of
the death of my father-in-law, Sir Richard Browne, who
died at my house at Sayes Court, in the 78th year of his
age.   The funeral was solemnized the 19th at Deptford,
with as much decency as the dignity of the person and
our relation to him required.   There were invited, the
Bishop of Rochester, several noblemen, knights, and all
the fraternity of the Trinity Corporation (of which he
had been Master), and others of the country.   The Vicar
(Rev. Richard Holden) preached a short but proper discourse on (Psalm xxxix. 10.) the frailty of our mortal
condition, concluding with an ample and well-deserved
eulogy on the defunct, relating to his honourable birth

and ancestors, education, learning in Greek and Latin, modern languages, travel, public employments, signal loyalty, character abroad ; and particularly the honor of upholding the Church of England in its public worship, during the persecution by the late rebels, by the suffrages of divers bishops, doctors of the Church and others, who found such an asylum in his house and family at Paris, that, in their disputes with the Papists (then triumphing over it as utterly lost,) they used to argue for its visibility and existence from Sir Richard Browne's chapel and assembly there. Then he spake of his great and loyal sufferings during the thirteen years' exile with his present Majesty, his return with him in 1660, his honourable employment at home, his timely recess to recollect him self, his great age, infirmities and death. He gave to the Trinity Corporation, that land in Deptford on which are built those almshouses for twenty-four widows of emerited seamen. He was born in the famous year of the Gun-powder treason, in 1605, and being last male of his family, left my wife, his only daughter, heir. Thus ended this honourable person, after so many changings and tossings to and fro, in the same house, Sayes Court, where he was born."

"By a special clause in his will, he ordered that his body should be buried in the Churchyard under the south-east window of the Chancel, adjoining the burial place of his ancestors ; he being much offended at the novel custom of burying everyone within the body of the Church and Chancel, that being a favour heretofore granted only to martyrs and great persons."

JOHN EVELYN, LL.D., D.C.L., F.R.S., &c.

JOHN EVELYN (familiarly known as " Sylva " Evelyn, from the title of his great work on Forest Trees,) " is one of the greatest and most estimable characters which any age has produced, and of whom " the town of Deptford " may be proud." Born to rank and fortune, he used both unselfishly, employing them to befriend the people and benefit his generation. With incomparable talents, and the most comprehensive acquirements, his chief delight was to patronize, in the place of envying, genius in others. Howard was not a greater or more persevering philanthropist. In extensive erudition and accurate observation few have been his equals. In the many public duties with which he was charged, through a long series of years, none have been more assiduous and upright. Strongly and from honest conviction attached to the doctrine and practice of the Church of England, he entertained, nevertheless, and advocated the most liberal sentiments for all who differed from him in opinion, respecting in every one the rights of conscience, and rejoicing to see its responsibility felt. For monarchy he had a strong predilection, strengthened, no doubt, by his personal attachment to Kings Charles II. and James II., formed during their residence in Paris; but he was at the same time utterly averse to the arbitrary measures of those monarchs. He lived in intimacy with men of all persuasions, never breaking connections with any one on account of differences of political or religious faith; " God will make all things manifest," he used to say, " in His own time; only let us possess ourselves in patience and charity; this will cover a multitude of imperfections." He must have conducted himself with no ordinary prudence, for he had personal friends in the following of Cromwell, while he was known openly to be the faithful servant of the exiled royal family, and to be in correspondence with his father-in-law, Sir Richard Browne, the King's representative at Paris. He was master of several modern languages, German, French, Italian and Spanish, &c. He had travelled through Europe " not to count steeples," but to study people, their customs and antiquities, and to expand his mind by intercourse with his fellow men. He took a very active and prominent part in the formation and establishment of the Royal Society, to whose transactions he contributed papers of high merit. In his public employments, he sat as City Commissioner in

1662, to inquire into the conduct of the Lord Mayor concerning the Gresham Charities; and, later, as a Commissioner of Public Works, of Trade, and Plantations; filling at the same time places at other boards, without emolument, and attended with much labour and expense. Horace Walpole passes this just panegyric upon him :— "I must observe" he says "that his life, which was extended to eighty-six years, was a course of inquiry, study, curiosity, instruction and benevolence. He really was the "neighbour" of the Gospel, for there was no man that might not have been the better for him. He was one of the first promoters of the Royal Society, a patron of the ingenious and indigent, and particularly serviceable to the lettered world; for, besides his writings and discourses, he obtained the Arundel Marbles for the University of Oxford, and the Arundel Library for the Royal Society. Nor is it the lowest part of his praise that he who proposed to Mr. Boyle the erection of a Philosophical College, for retired and speculative persons, had the honesty to write in defence of active life against Sir George Mackenzie's Essay on Solitude. He knew that retirement, in his own hands, was industry and benefit to mankind, but in those of others laziness and inutility."

Bishop Burnet styles him, "that most ingenious and virtuous gentleman, Mr. Evelyn, who is not satisfied to have advanced the knowledge of this age by his most useful and successful labours, about planting and divers other ways, but is ready to contribute everything in his power to perfect other men's endeavours."

He was born at Wotton, Surrey, October 31st, 1620 and received the earliest rudiments of education from "One Frier, at the Church porch of Wotton." At the age of eight years he began to learn Latin at Lewes, and was afterwards removed to the free school at Southorn, near that town. In 1637 he was placed as a gentleman Commoner at Baliol College, Oxford, where he remained for three years, and afterwards entered himself of the Middle Temple. Whilst there his father died. "The ominous appearance of the political horizon determined him to visit the continent when about twenty-one years old. As the French and Dutch were besieging Genappe, thither Evelyn journeyed, and voluntered his services to one of the belligerents. "For a week" he "trailed a pike,"—and then abandoned a military career. After his return to England, he studied a little, but, to use his own words, "danced and fooled more."

On the breaking out of the Civil War in 1642, Evelyn went with his horse and arms to Brentford to join the King; but "was not permitted to stay there." Having obtained the King's licence to travel again, we find him in Paris at the close of the year, where he remained for the winter. On leaving Paris he made a tour of Europe and spent some time at Rome, returning to the French metropolis in July 1646 ; where being recommended to Sir Richard Browne, Bart, the King's minister there, he made his addresses to his only daughter, Mary, whom he married in 1647, and in her right became possessor of Sayes Court. In proof of the happiness of this union, we need but to quote the lines of his friend Abraham Cowley, the poet, who says,—

> "Happy art thou whom God does bless,
>   With the full choice of thine own happiness ;
>   And happier yet, because thou'rt blest,
>   With prudence how to chuse the best.
>   In books and gardens thou hast plac'd aright,
>   (Things which thou well dost understand,
>   —And both dost make with thy laborious hand,)
>   Thy noble innocent delight.
>   And in thy virtuous wife, where thou again dost meet,
>   Both pleasures more refin'd and sweet ;
>   The fairest garden in her looks,
>   And in her mind the wisest books.
>   Oh, who would change these soft, yet solid joys !
>   For empty shews, and senseless noise ;
>   And all which rank ambition breeds,
> Which seem such beauteous flowers, and
>   are such poisonous weeds, &c."

A few Extracts from Mr. Evelyn's invaluable "Diary" will best shew his life at Sayes Court.

"1647, Oct 14. To Sayes Court at Deptford in Kent, (since my house), where I found Mr. Pretyman, my wife's uncle, who had charge of it and the estate about it during my father-in-law's residence in France." The men of Kent, ever loyal, endeavour to preserve their monarch Evelyn says " May 30th 1648. There was a rising now in Kent, my Lord of Norwich being at the head of them. Their first rendezvous was in Broome field next to my house at Sayes-Court, whence they went to Maidstone, and so to Colchester, where was that memorable siege."

Ev-lyn commenced the year 1649 by taking up his abode at Sayes Court, where, says he, " I had a lodging and some bookes." " Jany 22, 1649 I went thro' a course of Chymistrie at Sayes Court. Now was the Thames frozen over, and horrid tempests of wind."

" 25th Feb. came to visite me Dr. Joyliffe, discoverer of the lymphatic vessells, and an excellent anatomist. June 17 " got a passe from the rebell Bradshaw, then in greate power " and paid a visit to his wife in Paris having been absent from her ' above a yeare and a halfe.' In the beginning of 1652 Evelyn arrived in England with the intention of settling down at Sayes Court.

" Feb. 9, 1652. I went to Deptford, where I made preparation for my settlement, no more intending to go out of England, but endeavour a settled life, either in this or some other place, there being now so little appearance of any change for the better, all being entirely in the Rebells hands, and this particular habitation and the estate contiguous to it (belonging to my father-in-law actually in his Majesty's service), very much suffering for want of some friend to rescue it out of the power of the usurpers ; so as to preserve our interest, and take some care of my other concerns, by the advice and endeavour of my friends I was advis'd to reside in it, and compound with the souldiers. This I was besides authoriz'd by his Majesty to do, and encourag'd with a promise that what was in lease from the Crowne, if ever it pleas'd God to restore him, he would secure to us in fee-ferme. I had also addresses and cyfers to correspond with his Majesty and Ministers abroad : upon all which inducements I was persuaded to settle henceforth in England, having run about the world, most part out of my owne country, neere 10 years. I therefore now likewise meditated sending over for my wife, whom as yet I had left at Paris.

"Jany 17th 1653. I began to set out the ovall garden at Sayes Court, which was before a rude orchard and all the rest one entire field of 100 acres, without any hedge, except the hither holly hedge joyning to the bank of the mount walk. This was the beginning of all the succeeding gardens, walks, groves, enclosures, and plantations there.

"January 21. I went to London and there seal'd some of the writings of my purchase of Sayes Court.

"February 19th. I planted the orchard at Sayes Court.

"February 22nd. Was perfected the sealing, livery and seizin of my purchase of Sayes Court. My brother Geo. Glanvill, Mr. Scudamor, Mr. Offley, Co. William Glanvill (son to Serjeant Glanvill, sometime Speaker of the House of Commons), Co. Stephens, and severall of my friends dining with me. I had bargain'd for £3,200, but I paid £3,500.

"11th October. My sonn John Stansfield was borne, being my second child, and christened by the name of my mother's father, that name now quite extinct, being of Cheshire. Christened by Mr. Owen in my Library at Sayes Court, where he afterwards churched my wife, I always making use of him on these occasions, because the Parish Minister durst not have officiated according to the forme and usage of the Church of England, to which I always adhered.

"25th October. Mr. Owen preach'd in my Library at Sayes Court . . . . He afterwards administered to us all the Holy Sacrament.

"2 April, 1655. This was the first weeke that my V. Pret. (Uncle Pretyman) having parted with his family from me, I began housekeeping, till now sojourning with him in my owne house.

"5 Jany., 1656. Came to visit me my Lord Lisle, sonn to the Earle of Leicester, with Sir Charles Ouseley, two of the usurper's Council; Mr. John Hervey, and John Denham, the poet.

"28 May. Came to visit me the old Marquess of Argyle (since executed), Lord Lothian, and some other Scotch noblemen, all strangers to me. *Note.*—The Marquess tooke the turtle-doves in the aviary for owles.

"The Earl of Southampton (since Treasurer) and Mr. Spencer, brother to the Earle of Sunderland, came to see my garden.

"Jany. 1662. Having notice of the Duke of York's intention to visit my poore habitation and garden this day, I return'd, when he was pleas'd to do me that honor of his owne accord, and to stay some time viewing such things as I had to entertaine his curiosity. Afterwards he caus'd me to dine with him at the Treasurer of the Navy's house, and to sit with him cover'd at the same table. There were with his Highness the Duke of Ormond and several lords. Then they viewed some of my grounds about a project for a receptacle for ships to be moor'd in, which was laied aside as a fancy of Sir Nicholas Crisp.

"14 August, 1662. This afternoon the Queene Mother with the Earle of St. Alban's and many greate ladies and persons, was pleased to honor my poor villa with her presence, and to accept of a collation, She was exceedingly pleased and stay'd till very late in the evening." And next day "Came my Lord Chancellor (the Earle of Clarendon) and his lady, his purse and mace borne before him, to visit me.

1664. "This spring I planted the Home-field and West-field about Sayes Court with elmes, being the same yeare that the elmes were planted by his Majesty in Greenwich Park.

"1668, August 14. His Majesty was pleased to grant me a lease of a slip of ground out of Brick Close to enlarge my fore court, for which I now gave him thanks ; then entering into other discourse he talked to me of a new varnish for ships instead of pitch, and of the gilding with which his new yacht was beautified. I shew'd his Majesty the perpetual motion sent to me by Dr. Stokes from Collen (Cologne) ; and then came in Mons. Cobbert, the French Ambassador.

"1672. 12 Jany. His Majesty renewed us our lease of Sayes Court pastures for 99 years, but ought, according to his solemn promise (as I hope he will still perform), have passed them to us in fee forme." This written promise—which still exists at Wotton—like almost all those of Charles when in adversity, was forgotten "when fortune dawned upon him."

"1674. 27 June. Mr. Dryden, the famous Poet and now Laureat, came to give me a visite. It was the anniversarie of my marriage, and the first day I went into my new little cell and cabinet, which I built below towards the South court, at the east end of the parlor.

"9th July. Paid £360 for purchase of Dr. Jacomb's son share in the mill and land at Deptford, which I bought of the Beechers.

"1694. May 4th. I went this day with my wife and four servants from Sayes Court, removing much furniture of all sorts, books, pictures, hangings, bedding, &c., to furnish the apartment my brother assigned me, and now, after more than 40 years, to spend the rest of my days with him at Wotton, where I was born; leaving my house at Deptford full furnished, and 3 servants to my son-in-law Draper, to pass the summer in, and such longer time as he should think fit to make use of it."

Of Evelyn's children, his three daughters Mary, Elizabeth, and Susanna were very talented. Mary died of small-pox in the 19th year of her age, and was buried in St. Nicholas Church. Many noble persons honoured her funeral, some in person, others sending their coaches, of which there were six or seven with six horses, viz.: the Countess of Sunderland, Earl of Clarendon. Lord Godolphin, Sir Stephen Fox, Sir William Godolphin, Viscount Falkland, and others. Her father says, "Thus lived, died, and was buried the joy of my life and ornament of her sex and of my poor family."

Elizabeth died also of small-pox soon after her marriage with a nephew of Sir John Tippet, surveyor of the Navy and one of the Commissioners. She was likewise buried in St. Nicholas Church.

Susanna was married to William Draper, Esq., in the chapel of Ely House, by Archbishop Tenison (then Bishop of Lincoln). "She was a good child, religious, discreet, ingenious, and qualified with all the ornaments of her sex;" a good linguist, and specially skilful in needlework, and painting in oil and miniature; using her talents with great modesty; and in addition to these qualifications was a great beauty.

John Evelyn died at his house in Dover Street, London, 27th February, 1706, aged 85. He was interred at Wotton, above ground, in a stone coffin, on the marble slab of which is the following inscription: "Here lies the Body of JOHN EVELYN, ESQ., of this place, second son of Richard Evelyn, Esq., who, having served the Publick in several employments, of which that of Commissioner of the Privy Seal in the Reign of King James the 2d., was most honourable, and perpetuated his fame by far more lasting monuments than those of Stone or Brass, his learned and useful works, fell asleep on the 27th day of February, 1705—6, being the 86 year of his age, in full hope of a glorious Resurrection, thro' faith in Jesus Christ. Living in an age of extraordinary Events and Revolutions, he learnt (as himself asserted) this Truth, which, pursuant to his intention, is here declared—

"That all is vanity which is not honest,
And that there is no solid wisdom but in real Piety.

Of five sons and three daughters born to him from his most virtuous and excellent wife Mary, sole daughter and heiress of Sir Richard Browne, of Sayes Court, near Deptford in Kent, onely one daughter, Susanna, married to William Draper, Esq., of Adscomb in this County, survived him; the two others dying in the flower of their age, and all the sons very young, except one named John, who deceased 24th March, 1698—9, in the 45 year of his age, leaving one son, John, and one daughter Elizabeth."

"SYLVA" EVELYN'S WORKS.

I.—Of Liberty and Servitude. 1649. 12mo.

II.—A Character of England, as it was lately presented in a letter to a Nobleman of France ; with Reflections upon Gallus Castratus. 1651.

III.—The State of France. London, 1652.

IV.—An Essay on the First Book of Lucretius de Rerum Natura, interpreted and made into easy English Verse. 1656.

V.—Dedicatory Epistles, &c., to The French Gardener. London, 1658.

VI.—The Golden Book of St. Chrysostom, concerning the Education of Children. London, 1659.

VII.—An Apology for the Royal Party. London, 1659.

VIII.—The late News from Brussels Unmasked. London, 1660.

IX.—The Manner of the Encounter between the French and Spanish Ambassadors at the landing of the Swedish Ambassador.

X.—A Panegyrick at His Majesty King Charles' Coronation. London, 1661.

XI.—Instructions concerning the erection of a Library written by Gabriel Nande, published in English with some improvements by J. Evelyn, London, 1661.

XII.—Fumifugium ; or the Inconvenience of the Air and Smoke of London, dissipated. London, 1661. Reprinted in 1772.

XIII.—Tyrannus ; 1661, 8vo.

XIV.—Sculptura ; or the History and Art of Chalcography and engraving in Copper and Mezzotinto. London, 1662. 8vo.

XV.—Sylva ; or a Discourse on Forest Trees. London 1664 fol. Five editions printed to 1729. Several times republished since by Dr. A. Hunter, with additions.

XVI.—Dedicatory Epistles, &c., to Parallel of Ancient and Modern Architecture. London, 1664.

XVII.—Another part of the History of Jesuitism. London, 1664.

XVIII.—Kalendarium Hortense. London, 1664.

XIX.—Public Employment and Active Life preferred to Solitude, in Reply to Sir George Mackenzie. London, 1667.

XX.—History of the Three Late Impostors. London, 1669.

XXI.—An Idea of the Perfection of Printing, translated from the French of Roland Freart, 1668.

XXII.—Navigation and Commerce; their Origin and Progress. London, 1674.

XXIII.—Terra; a Philosophical Discourse of the Earth. London, 1675.

XXIV.—Mons. de la Quinlynye's Treatise of Orange Trees and Complete Gardener; translated from the French. London, 1693.

XXV.—Advertisement to the Translation of the Complete Gardener, by M. de la Quinlynye, 1693.

XXVI.—Ditto to M. de la Quinlynye's Directions concerning Melons.

XXVII.—Ditto, ditto, ditto, Orange Trees.

XXVIII.—Numismata; a Discourse on Medals. London, 1699.

XXIX.—Acelaria; a Discourse of Salads. London, 1699.

XXX.—An Account of Architects and Architecture— a tract.

XXXI.—Letter to Viscount Brouncker, concerning a New Engine for Ploughing, 1669—70.

XXXII.—Dedication to Renatus Rapinus. Of Gardens, 1673.

XXXIII.—Letter to Mr. Aubrey, concerning Surrey Antiquities, 1670.

XXXIV.—An abstract of a Letter to the Royal Society concerning the damage done to his Gardens in the preceding Winter, 1684.

XXXV.—The Diary and Letters. Published in 1818.

XXXVI.—Miscellaneous Writings, collected and edited
      by Mr. Upcott.
XXXVII.—Life of Mrs. Godolphin, 1847. The manu-
      script of this work passed into the hands of Mr.
      Evelyn's great-great-grandson, His Grace the
      Hon. Edward Venables-Vernon Harcourt, late
      Lord Archbishop of York, by whom it was
      entrusted for publication to Dr. Wilberforce, late
      Bishop of Oxford.
XXXVIII.—History of Religion, 1850, from the original
      manuscript at Wotton.

*MUNDUS MULIEBRIS, an anonymous work pub-
lished at London in 1690, has been recently and erroneously
attributed to John Evelyn.*

JOHN EVELYN, Esq.

JOHN EVELYN, Esq., third son of " Sylva," born 14th Jan.,
1654-5, and early in life shewed signs of possessing the
literary tastes of his father, who sent him to Oxford in
1666 ; where he remained in the house of the ingenious and
learned Dr. Ralph Bathurst, then President of Trinity
College, before he was admitted a gentleman Commoner,
which was in the Easter term of 1668. It is not clear at
what time he left Oxford ; but Mr. Anthony á Wood seems
to be positive that he took no degree there, but returned to
his father's house, where he prosecuted his studies under
the directions of that great man. There is, however, good
reason to believe that it was during his residence in
Trinity College, and when he was not above fifteen years
of age, that he wrote that elegant Greek poem which is
prefixed to the 2nd edition of his father's celebrated
work, entitled " Sylva ; " and is a noble proof of the
strength of his genius and wonderful progress in learning
in the early part of his life.

In November, 1675, he set out for Paris with Lord
Berkley, Ambassador to the French Court. but returned
to England in the following May.

In 1673, he published his first work, a treatise " Of Gardens," four books first written in Latin verse by Renatus Rapinus, and now made English by John Evelyn, Esq. His father annexed the second book of this translation to his "Sylva," and it must be allowed that the sense is very faithfully rendered and the poetry is more easy and harmonious than could have been expected from a youth of his age. His second work was " The life of Alexander the Great," translated from the Greek of Plutarch, printed in the 4th volume of Plutarch's Lives by several hands ; which was followed in 1677 by " The history of the Grand Visiers Mahomet and Achmet Coprogli ; of the three last Grand Signiors, their Sultanas and chief favourites ; with the most secret intrigues of the Seraglio." This was a translation from the French, and has been esteemed an interesting and instructive history. He also wrote some original poems : two of which are printed in Dryden's Miscellanies, and more in Nichol's Collection of Poems. One " On Virtue," is esteemed excellent by the best judges, and another styled " The Remedy of Love," is also much admired.

Mr. Evelyn, who had been introduced to the Prince of Orange in 1688, was two years later made one of the Chief Clerks of the Treasury, and on quitting that situation in 1691, became one of the Commissioners of the Revenue of Ireland, which country he visited in 1692. In all probability he would have been advanced to higher appointments, had he not been cut off in the prime of life ; dying at his house in Berkley Street, London, March 24th, 1698, in his 45th year. He had two sons and three daughters, of whom Richard his eldest son and Martha Mary, his eldest daughter died young at Sayes Court. His second daughter Elizabeth, married Simon Harcourt, Esq., eldest son and heir of Simon, Lord Viscount Harcourt, Lord High Chancellor of Great Britain, by whom she became the mother of the first Earl Harcourt.

SIR THOMAS SMITH.

SIR THOMAS SMITH, who had been farmer of the Customs to Queen Elizabeth, and was sent by King James I. as his Ambassador to the Court of Russia in 1604, had a magnificient house at Deptford, which was burnt down on the 30th January, 1618. His travels in Russia are in print; but they are supposed not to have been written by himself.

VICE ADMIRAL BENBOW.

JOHN BENBOW was born in 1650 and early entered the merchant service. In 1680 he commanded a merchant ship in the Mediterranean, with which he beat off a Sallee rover. Charles II. of Spain invited him to court, and induced James II. to give him an appointment in the British navy. William III. dispatched him to the West Indies to protect the British colonies. On his return to England, the King rewarded him for his services, by advancing him to the rank of Vice-admiral, and, after a short period, during which he was sent to blockade Dunkirk, he was again, in 1701, dispatched to the West Indies. Shortly after his arrival there, he fell in with the French squadron under Admiral Du Casse, near Santa Martha, on the Spanish Main, when a skirmishing action commenced, which continued three or four days; in the last day, the Admiral was singly engaged with the French, his other ships having fallen astern. Though a chain shot had shattered his leg, he would not be removed from the quarter deck, but continued the fight till morning, when the French bore away for Carthagena. The Admiral made signal for his ships to follow; but his orders were disobeyed. He then returned to Jamaica, and on his arrival ordered those officers who had behaved so cowardly to be confined, and, on their return to England, were tried by court-martial, when the most culpable of them suffered according to their deserts.

The Admiral's leg was amputated, but before the wound was healed, he was attacked with a fever which soon carried him off. He died November 4th, 1703. The following anecdote, though probably well known, claims a place here. When one of his Lieutenants expressed his sorrow for the loss of the Admiral's leg, "I am sorry for it too" replied the gallant Benbow, "but I had rather have lost them both, than have seen this dishonour brought upon the English nation. But, do you hear? If another shot should take me off, behave like brave men, and fight it out."

Admiral Benbow, if not a native, was a resident of Deptford during his intervals of sea-service, and had a son born at his own house in Hughes' Fields, which was still standing in 1843; the heraldic bearings being then nearly obliterated. He also lived for some short time at Sayes Court which he rented from Mr. Evelyn.

"Admiral Benbow, as to whose character, his bitterest enemy cannot deny him the honest reputation of a brave, active, and able Commander; while on the other, his warmest friends and admirers must allow, he wanted those conciliatory manners which is necessary to secure the personal attachment and regard of the officers he commanded. Honesty, integrity and blunt sincerity were the prominent features of his private character; and we can only lament the depravity of human nature, when we find ourselves obliged to confess these truly valuable qualities are not sufficient to acquire the love of our contemporaries, though they can scarcely fail of engaging the warmest esteem of every succeeding generation.

"It has been positively asserted by many, that the Admiral's body was buried at Jamaica, but in a note inserted by Campbell from the 'Mercure Historique et Politique,' it is said, it was sent for home, in order to be solemnly interred at the public expense. This appears to be confirmed by the testimony of several very ancient people still living at Deptford, who, although they don't

H

remember the funeral itself, have a perfect recollection of hearing it spoken of as a recent event. According to this information he was buried in the Churchyard of St. Nicholas, Deptford, in the North-west angle formed by the projection of the steeple beyond the body of the Church. A plain flat stone was lain over his remains; but through the miserable inattention of his posterity, and the disgrace of national gratitude, has been long since destroyed. The only evidence, at the present day, of the place of his interment, is the tradition just given." —Charnock's " *Biographia Navalis*," 1794. *Vol. II., pp.* 241-2.

CAPTAIN EDWARD FENTON.

CAPTAIN EDWARD FENTON accompanied Sir Martin Frobisher in search of a north-east passage, and after the failure of Frobisher's attempt he sailed in the spring of 1582, on a similar expedition, with four vessels. He did not, however, accomplish the object of his voyage, but meeting with a Spanish squadron, he gave them battle, and, after a severe conflict sunk their Vice-Admiral's ship. He returned home in 1583, and had a command in the fleet opposed to the Spanish Armada in 1588, distinguishing himself by bravery and skill in sundry encounters with the enemy. He died at Deptford in 1603, and was buried in the chancel of St. Nicholas' Church. A monument to his memory was afterwards erected in the Church, by his nephew, the Earl of Cork.

CAPTAIN GEORGE SHELVOCKE.

CAPTAIN GEORGE SHELVOCKE, was descended from an ancient family in Shropshire, but was long an inhabitant of this town. He was bred to the sea-service, under Admiral Benbow, and served in the Royal Navy during the wars of King William III. and Queen Anne. In 1726 he published a work entitled : " A Voyage round the World by the Way of the Great South Sea." Performed in the years 1719-22 in the Speedwell, of London, of 24 guns and 100 men (under Her Majesty's Commission to Cruise on the Spaniards, in the late war with the Spanish Crown) till he was cast away on the Island of Juan Fernandez, in May, 1720, and afterwards continued in the " Recovery," the " Jesus Maria " and " Sacra Familia," &c.

His sojourn on the Island of Juan Fernandez from May 25th till October 6th, reads something like Robinson Crusoe, except that he had a mutinous crew to contend with, who gave him much trouble ; and when he left the island in a leaky yawl of 20 tons burthen some 11 or 12 of the crew refused to sail with him. He died in London November 30, 1742, and was buried near his wife (Susanna, daughter of Captain Richard Strutton) in St. Nicholas' Churchyard.

CAPTAIN YOUNG.

CAPTAIN YOUNG, of Deptford,—" a sober man and an excellent seaman,"—died in 1693, and was buried on the 17th of November. Evelyn says " he was the first who in the first war with Cromwell against Spain took the Governor of the Havanna ; and another rich prize, and struck the first stroke against the Dutch fleet in the first war with Holland, in the time of the Rebellion."

JOHN BENBOW.

MR. JOHN BENBOW, son of Admiral Benbow, was born at Deptford about the year 1650. He was shipwrecked in the year 1702 (being then a mate on board the " Degrave " East Indiaman) on the coast of Madagascar ; where, after many dismal and dangerous adventures, he was obliged to live with and after the manner of the Malagees, his biographer says many years, but as he is likewise said to have lived several years after his return, his sojourn on the island could not have been so long. He was liberated by a Dutch captain, who brought him to England, after his friends had given him over as dead. Mr. Benbow wrote a work entitled "A complete Account of the South Part of the Island of Madagascar; treating of the climate, soil, natural productions, inhabitants &c." This was a large and very comprehensive book, containing a multitude of very curious circumstances which occasioned its being often borrowed by some one or other of his acquaintances. The MSS. was destroyed by a fire at his brother's lodgings in 1714. Mr. Benbow spent the remainder of his days in strict retirement at Deptford. He died here in 1708 and was buried in St. Nicholas' Church. His tombstone in the pavement of the North aisle bears the following inscription :—"Here lyeth the body of Mr. John Benbow, eldest son of Admiral John Benbow, viz., Admiral of the White, by Martha his wife. He died November the 17th, 1708, in the 27th year of his age."

PHINEAS PETT.

PHINEAS PETT, son of Peter Pett, was born at his father's house at Deptford-Strond, November 1st, 1570. He remained at home till he was nine years old, when he was sent to a private school at Greenwich, kept by one Mr. Adams. At this establishment he tells us in his diary "he so well profited, that in three years he was fit for Cambridge." While at Emmanuel College, his father died, and he was compelled to leave Cambridge without taking his degree, so that for want of better employment, he was apprenticed to Mr. Richard Chapman, one of His Majesty's Master Shipwrights at Deptford Dockyard. He adds " my allowance from him to find myself tools and apparel was barely £46 8s. od. per annum ; and my master dying when I had served almost two years, I was left to the wide world." He then went to sea for two years, and on his return obtained employment in the Dockyard here, where we find him in 1595, making ready for the voyage of the celebrated Drake, who was then fitting out his expedition against the Spaniards in the West Indies and Central America, where he died. Mr. Pett framed a model of a vessel on a peculiar scale, while residing in lodgings on Deptford Green. His merits became known to the Earl of Effingham, who took him by the hand. On June 30th, 1600, he was sent for to Court, then at Greenwich, which resulted in his being appointed as Keeper of the Plank Yard, &c., at Chatham. He afterwards removed to Woolwich as master builder, where he designed and built in 1637, the "Sovereign of the Seas," named by the Dutch the "Golden Devil," from the gilded work on her stern, and the havoc she caused to the Dutch fleet in the war between England and Holland.

In the *Naval Chronicle* of 1807, is the following account of this vessel :—

"Before the breaking out of the Civil War, King Charles I. built a ship called the " Sovereign of the Seas ;" the following description of which is taken from a publication of that time by Thomas Heywood, the old historian, addressed to the King :—

" This famous vessel was built at Woolwich in 1637. She was in length by the keel 128 feet, or thereabout, within some few inches ; her main breadth, 48 feet ; in length from the fore-end of the beakhead to the after end of the stern, 232 feet ; in height from the bottom of her keel to the top of her lanthorn, 76 feet ; bore five lanthorns, the biggest of which would hold ten persons upright ; had three flush decks, a forecastle, half-deck, quarter-deck and round house. Her lower tier had thirty ports for cannon and demi-cannon ; middle tier, thirty for culverines and demi-ditto ; third tier, twenty-six for other ordnance ; forecastle, twelve ; and two half-decks having thirteen or fourteen ports more within board for *murdering pieces*, besides ten pieces of chase ordnance forward and ten right aft and many loopholes in the cabines for musket shot. She had eleven anchors, one of 4,400 lbs. weight. She was of the burthen of 1,637 tons. She was built by Peter Pett, Esq., under the direction of his father, Captain Phineas Pett, one of the principal officers of the Navy. She hath two gallies, besides, and all of most curious carved work, and all the sides of the ship carved with trophies of Artillery, and types of honour, as well belonging to sea and land, with symbols appertaining to navigation ; also their two sacred Majesties' badges of honour ; arms with several angels holding their letters in compartments, all which works are gilded over, and no other colour but gold and black. One tree, of oak, made four of the principal beams, which was 44 feet, of strong serviceable timber, in length, three feet in diameter at the top, and ten feet at the stub or bottom.

Upon the stern-head a Cupid or child bridling a lion ; upon the bulk-head right-forward stand six statues, in sundry postures ; these

figures represent Concilium. Cura, Conamen, Vis, Virtus, and Victoria.
Upon the hamers of the water are four figures, Jupiter. Mars, Neptune
and Eolus ; on the stern Victory, in the midst of a frontispiece ; upon
the beak-head sitteth King Edgar, on horseback, trampling on seven
Kings.

The " Sovereign of the Seas " was the largest ship that had ever
been built in England, and is said to have been designed only for
splendour aud magnificence ; but being taken down a deck lower, she
became, according to report, one of the best men-of-war in the world.
She was in almost all the great engagements that were fought between
England and Holland.   She was rebuilt in the year 1684 and called
the " Royal Sovereign," and on the 27th January, 1696, being laid up
at Chatham in order to be rebuilt a second time, she accidentally took
fire and was totally consumed.   Evelyn recording this event says that
this ship " having given occasion to the levy of Ship-money was
perhaps the cause of all the after troubles to this day."

A fine model of this vessel was worked from Pett's
draughts some years ago, by order of the Lords of the
Admiralty, and afterwards placed in the model-room at
Somerset House.   It is now in the Museum at Greenwich
Hospital.

Phineas Pett was the first scientific naval architect,
whose principles of ship-building have never been
disputed.

On the formation of the Shipwrights' Company, he
was elected the first Master.

He married (May 15th, 1598) Ann, daughter of
Richard Nichols, of Highwood Hill, Hendon, Middlesex,
by whom he had several children (a).

a His son Phineas, afterwards Knighted, who was born January
24th, 1618, became resident Commissioner of the Navy at Chatham in
the reign of Charles II.   Of him Evelyn says " Passing by Chatham
we saw his Majesty's Royal Navy, and din'd at Commissioner Pett's,
master-builder there. who shewed me his study and models, with other
curiosities belonging to his art.   He is esteem'd for the most skilfull
ship-builder in the world.   He hath a pretty garden and banquetting-
house, pots, statues. cypresses, resembling some villas about Rome
(Diary Aug. 10th. 1663).   Sir Phineas held the office of Commissioner
in 1667, the year in which the Dutch fleet sailed up the Medway and
destroyed several ships ; for which in the ensuing year he was
impeached in the House of Commons on a charge of inattention to
the security of the harbour.   The parliamentary prosecution, however,
soon dropped, it being well known that the culpable neglect was not in
him, but in the king, who had idly squandered the large sums of
money granted for the national defences.

The following curious extract appears in Mr. Pett's diary, which was published in the "*Archæologia*," *Vol. XII.*

His father died, December 6th, 1589, "whose loss' says he "proved afterwards my utter undoing almost, had not God been more merciful to me, for, leaving all things to my mother's directions, her fatal matching with a most wicked husband, one Mr. Thomas Num, a minister, brought a general ruin to herself and family." In 1599 Mr. Pette relates the ill-treatment of his sisters by his father-in-law, who for a very slight offence, "furiously fell upon Abigail, the eldest, beating her so cruelly with a pair of tongs and a fire-brand, that she died within three days after the beating." He mentions "that, upon a complaint being made to a justice, the body, which had been privately buried, was taken up, and so, by the Coroner's inquest which passed upon her, and miraculous tokens of the dead corpse, as fresh bleeding, sensibly opening one of her eyes, and other things, the father-in-law was found guilty of her death, and so committed and bound over to answer the matter at the next general Assizes to be held at Bury." Num was committed of manslaughter and died soon afterwards.

Mr. Pett was author of a poetical tract entitled :— "Time's journey to seeke his daughter Truth, and Truth's letter to Fame of England's Excellence :" Imprinted by F. K. for Humfrey Lownes, 1590. It was dedicated to the Earl of Effingham at Deptford and is of the utmost rarity.

In it the following mention of Spenser occurs :—

" And he that in this kynd can temper well
    Profit with sweet delight ; unto his prayse
Well may we yeald, and say he doth excell
    And for his skill, his fame to heaven up rayse,
So may we speake of Spencer's golden layes
Whom never any man could equall yet,
That in our tougue hath as a poet writ."

PETER PETT.

PETER PETT, son of Richard Pett, one of Queen Elizabeth's master shipwrights was born at Deptford in 1593, and like his uncle Phineas Pett became an eminent shipbuilder. Although his claim to the invention of that class of war vessels called frigates, has been disputed, he, at least, introduced them into the British Navy, and built the first, named the "Constant Warwick," which took as "much money from privateers" during the Dutch war "as would have laden her." "The Constant Warwick" says Pepys "was the first frigate built in England. She was built in 1649 by Mr. Peter Pett, for a privateer for the Earl of Warwick, and was sold by him to the States. Mr. Pett took his model of a frigate from a French frigate, which he had seen in the Thames, as his son Sir Phinehas Pett acknowledged to me."

He died in 1652 and was buried in St. Nicholas' Church. The Latin inscription and epitaph on his monument will be found in the account of St. Nicholas' Church.

Sir Peter Pett, son of the above-mentioned Peter Pett, was born at Deptford and baptized in St. Nicholas' Church, October 31st, 1630. He became Judge Advocate of Ireland and M.P., and received the honour of Knighthood from the Duke of Ormond, Lord Lieutenant of Ireland. He was the author of many learned works, amongst which are; "A Discourse of the growth of England and populousness since the Reformation"; "On the Clerical Revenue, the same asserted to be reasonable and necessary"; Of the number of People of England, from Authentic Sources"; "On the necessity of future Publick Taxes for the support of Government and our Religion, &c.

―――――

JONAS SHISH.

The Petts were not the only eminent ship-builders of which Deptford may be justly proud. On the 13th of May, 1680, Evelyn says " I was at the funeral of old Mr. Shish, master shipwright of his Majesty's yard here, an honest and remarkable man, and his death a public losse, for his excellent success in building ships (tho' altogether illiterate), and for breeding up so many of his children to be able artists. I held up the pall with three knights, who did him that honour, and he was worthy of it. It was the costome of this good man to rise in the night, and to pray kneeling in his owne coffin, which he had lying by him many years. He was borne in that famous yeare of the gunpowder plot, 1605." So that at his death he was 75 years old. Also see foot-note *a*, p. 78.

He was succeeded as master shipwright here by his son, Evelyn's " kind neighbour," who built the " goodliest vessel of the whole navy," the "Neptune," which was launched on the 17th of April, 1683. This was the last of the 30 ships ordered to be built by Act of Parliament.

———

MUNGO MURRAY.

MR. MURRAY lived and died a working shipwright in Deptford Dockyard, although he published in 1754 the only English Treatise on ship-building that can lay any claim to a scientific character ; and was a man " whose conduct was irreproachable."

———

THE VERY REV. GEORGE STANHOPE, D.D.

DEAN STANHOPE was born March 5th, 1660, at Hartshorn or Hertishorn, a village in Derbyshire, of which his father, the Rev. Thomas Stanhope, was rector. He was sent to school, first at Uppingham and then at Leicester, and afterwards removed to Eton, from whence he entered King's College, Cambridge, of which he was Scholar and Fellow. His first preferment was the rectory of Tewing, in Hertfordshire. He was for 38 years Vicar of St. Mary's, Lewisham ; and 26 years Vicar of St. Nicholas,

Deptford. In 1703, he was made Dean of Canterbury; and was thrice chosen Prolocutor of the Lower House of Convocation.

He founded the Charity School in High Street, Deptford, known as Dean Stanhope's School, an account of which will be found elsewhere. "Sylva" Evelyn, after hearing him preach at Whitehall says, " he is one of the most accomplished preachers I ever heard, for matter, eloquence, action, voice, and I am told, of excellent conversation." His personal qualifications, prudence and public spirit, bore a considerable resemblance to those of that eminent divine Bishop Andrews.

His life is best known by his literary labours; his principal works being :—

I.—A Paraphrase and Comment upon the Epistles and Gospels, in 4 vols.

II.—A Translation of Bishop Andrews' Greek Devotions.

III.—Pious Breathings; being the Meditations of St. Augustine, to which are added select Contemplations from St. Anselm and St. Bernard.

IV.—Epicletus's Morals with Simplicius's Comment, done into English.

V.—Parsons his Christian Directory; being a Treatise of Holy Resolution, in two parts.

VI.—The Christian Pattern, or a Treatise of the Imitation of JESUS CHRIST; in four books, written originally in Latin by Thomas à Kempis. to which are added Meditations and Prayers for Sick Persons.

VII.—The Truth and Excellence of the Christian Religion asserted against Jews, Infidels and Hereticks: 16 Boyle Lectures preached at St. Paul's Cathedral in 1701-2.

VIII.—Of Wisdom; written originally in French by the Sieur de Charron, with an account of the Author; three Vols.

IX.—Several sermons upon special occasions.

After his death a plain marble monument was erected for him by his widow in the chancel of St. Mary's Church, Lewisham, where he lies buried. This monument, after laying for some time in the vault of the Church is now affixed to the north wall of the nave, a little to the westward of the north door, and bears the following inscription :—

IN MEMORY

of the very Revd. GEORGE STANHOPE, D.D.,
38 years Vicar of this Place, and 26 of
the Neighbouring Church at DEPTFORD ;
Constituted Dean of CANTERBURY, A.D. 1700,
And thrice PROLOCUTOR of the Lower House
of Convocation,
Whose Piety was real and rational,
His Charity great and universal,
Fruitful in Acts of Mercy, and in all good Works ;
His Learning was Elegant and Comprehensive,
His Conversation Polite and Delicate,
Grave without Preciseness, Facetious without Levity :
The good Christian, the solid Divine
and the fine Gentleman,
in him were happily united ;
Who, tho' amply qualified for the Highest
Honours of his Sacred Function,
Yet was content with only deserving them.
In his Pastoral office a Pattern to his People,
And to all who shall succeed him in the Care of them.
His Discourses from the PULPIT
Were equally pleasing and profitable,
A beautiful Intermixture of the clearest Reasoning
with the purest Diction,
Attended with all the Graces of a just ELOCUTION ;
As his Works from the PRESS have spoke the Praises
Of his happy Genius ; his Love of God and Men ;
for which Generations to come
will bless his Memory.
He was born March the 5th, 1660. He died March the 18th, 1727.
Aged 68 years.

Rev. CHARLES BURNEY, D.D., LL.D., F.R.S., F.S.A., and A.S.

——"Fashioned to much honour ; from his cradle
He was a scholar, and a ripe, and good one ;
Exceeding wise, fair spoken. and persuading,
Unto all those who sought him, sweet as summer.

     *   *   *   *   *   *

And to add greater honours to his age,
Than man could give him, he died fearing GOD !"

DR. CHARLES BURNEY was born at Lynn, in Norfolk, December 10th, 1757, and educated at the Charter House, in London, Caius College, Cambridge, and at King's College, Aberdeen, where he formed an intimate friendship with Dr. Dunbar, a Scottish professor of some distinction. He spent some time as a schoolmaster, and in that employment—unlike most of the race—won considerable wealth as well as honour. This fortune enabled him to collect a Classical Library, almost unrivalled in beauty and value. It was the gathering of a deeply read critic, as well as an open-handed purchaser.

The bias of Dr. Burney's learning and taste in literature led him to a preference of the Greek classics far above Latin, and naturally, his library bore this character (in counterpart). He aimed at collecting Greek authors— and especially the dramatists—in such a way that the collection of his copies gave a sort of chronological view of the literary history of the books and of their successive recensions.

For the tragedians, more particularly, his researches were brilliantly successful. Of Æschylus, he had amassed forty-seven editions ; of Sophocles, one hundred and two ; of Euripides, one hundred and sixty-six.

His first publication was a sharp criticism (in the *Monthly Review*) on Mr. (afterwards Bishop) Huntingford's Collections of Greek poems, entitled " Monostrophica." This was followed in 1789, by the issue of an Appendix to Scapula's Lexicon ; and in 1807 by a collection of the correspondence of Dr. Bentley, Regius Professor of Divinity at Cambridge, and other Scholars. Two years later, he gave to students of Greek, his "Tentamen de Metris ab Æschylo in choricis cantibus adhibitis," and to the youthful theologians his meritorious abridgment of Bishop Pearson's "Exposition of the Creed." In 1812, he published the Lexicon of Philemon. His only theological publication, other than the abridgment of Pearson's Exposition, was a sermon which he had preached in St. Paul's Cathedral in 1812.

Like his father and others of his family, he was a very sociable man. He lived much with Parr and with Porson, and like those eminent scholars he had the good and Catholic taste, which embraced in its appreciation, and with like geniality, old wine, as well as old books. He was less wise in nourishing a great dislike to cool breezes. "Shut the door," was usually his first greeting to any visitor, who had to introduce himself to the Doctor's notice; and it was a joke against him in his latter days that the same words were his parting salutation to a couple of highwaymen, who had taken his purse as he was journeying homewards in his carriage, and who were adding cruelty to robbery by exposing him to the fresh air, when they made off.

Some of Dr. Burney's choicest books were obtained when the Pinelli Library was brought to England from Italy. The prime ornament of his manuscript collection, a 13th Century copy of the Iliad of great beauty and rich in scholia, was bought at the sale of the fine Library of Charles Towneley, Collector of the Marbles. Although classical literature was the strength of the Burney Collection, it was also rich in some other departments. Of English newspapers, for example, he had brought together nearly seven hundred volumes of the 17th and 18th centuries, reaching from James I. to George III.; and some three hundred and eighty-five classical manuscripts.

Dr. Burney was Rector of St. Paul's, Deptford, and of Cliffe, in Kent; Prebendary of Lincoln; Chaplain in Ordinary to the King; Professor of Ancient Literature in the Royal Academy, and Honorary Librarian to the Royal Institution. He died December 28th, 1817, having just entered on his 61st year ; and was buried at Deptford, amidst the lamentations of his parishioners at his loss. After his death, the parishioners agreed to erect a monument to his memory. "As a record of their affection for their revered pastor, monitor and friend ; of their gratitude for his services, and of their unspeakable regret for his loss." There is a fine medallion bust of him on his monument in the Church. A meeting of his old pupils was called which met under the chairmanship of the excellent Dr. Kaye, then Regius Professor of Divinity at Cambridge, and afterwards Bishop of Lincoln, and they subscribed for the placing of a monument to their old Master in Westminster Abbey.

On the 23rd of February 1818, the Trustees of the British Museum presented to the House of Commons a petition praying, that Dr. Burney's library should be acquired for the public. The petition was granted and the library was purchased for the sum of £13,560 ; the total number of printed books amounted to nearly 13,500 and 520 manuscripts.

It was estimated that the collection had cost Dr. Burney a much larger sum, and that, possibly, if sold by public auction, it might have produced to his representatives more than £20,000.

DR. COLIN MILNE, LL.D., D.D., F.L.S.

The REV. COLIN MILNE was born at Aberdeen, in the University of which city he received his education, under the superintendence of his uncle Dr. Campbell, the Provost of Marischal College. He was in early life selected by the Duke of Northumberland as private tutor to his son, Lord Algernon Percy ; and having taken orders, was presented, through the interest of the Percy family, to the living of North Chapel, Essex. He afterwards obtained the Lectureship of Deptford which he held for forty years. His abilities as a pulpit orator are recorded in all the periodical works of his time, and he was pre-eminently successful, as a preacher, in pleading the cause of charity. By his exertions the Royal Kent Dispensary—now located in the Greenwich Road, but formerly in Deptford Broadway—was founded.

He was likewise an eminent botanist, and wrote " Institutiones Botanicæ Linniæ " ; " Indigenous Botany or Habitations of English Plants " ; and in conjunction with Alexander Gordon " Botanical Excursions in Kent and the neighbouring counties." His great work was a botanical dictionary, published in 1788, and dedicated by permission to His Grace the Duke of Northumberland. He also published some sermons.

The following anecdote of him is related by one Saunders, a noted book-maker in London, who was employed in compiling family bibles and histories of England. When he had put together the Commentary, which bears the name of Herries, he went to get Dr. Milne to sanction it by his popularity as the author. " I went twice to Deptford " says he " to solicit the Doctor for his name, but he honestly told me, that although he had no doubt concerning my abilities, yet he would not have his name to what he was not to write." This was in 1773, on which Saunders applied to poor Dr. Dodd who asked one hundred guineas for the allowance of his name, but this was thought too extravagant, and then Herries granted his name for £20.

Dr. Milne died at Deptford in October, 1815, aged 71, greatly beloved and lamented.

Elegiac lines written on the death of the Rev. Dr. Colin Milne,—

" Up to the realms of everlasting day,
Thy soaring spirit, Milne, hath wing'd its way ;
There to behold the glorious Throne of Grace,
And view the great Creator face to face ;
Where Justice by the side of Mercy stands,
And Truth, and Peace and Righteousness join hands,
Whilst saints and angels loud hosannas raise,
And hosts of cherubs join in rapturous praise ;
But Ah ! thy cup on earth was dash'd with gall,
'Twas thine to see thy budding flow'rets fall,

Of beauteous form, in youth's attractive prime,
The mind prepared for sentiments sublime ;
Yet those accomplishments could not withstand
The fatal stroke of Death's vindictive hand.
The King of Terrors to enchance thy cares
Sent thy dear daughters to the grave in pairs ;
Thy sons were brave, still to augment thy tears,
They were not suffered to reach thirty years ;
Nor could thy gifts and graces ward the blow,
That has subdued and laid thy body low.
Arrived almost at Nature's utmost bound,
Studious no more to publish or expound.
No more the sacred page wilt thou explore,
Nor works botanical illustrate more :
Oft have we felt the powers of thy great zeal,
For who that saw thy tears spontaneous flow,
Whilst pleading to alleviate *sad* human woe.
If for the school, where plebeian offspring range,
And native ignorance, for sense exchange ;
Or did'st thou exercise thy oral power,
For suffering females in their trying hour ;
Or for the medical and healing aid,
Where kind humanity her stand hath made ;
Or when the flood hath stopped the throbbing heart,
And life's last spark was ready to depart.
Whenever Charity announced thy name,
Thine energy and efforts were the same.
The niggard hand was opened by thy force
And sceptic coldness glowed with thy discourse.
May thy successor, gifted from above,
Called by thy spirit perfected in love.
With holy rapture see his labours crowned.
The temple filled and gospel grace abound
In every heart God's glory be the aim
And party zeal be only known by name.
May hungry souls be fill'd and amply fed
With living water and eternal bread ;
So may his life and doctrine mark the road
That leads to blissful mansions and to God."

In Showell's MSS. collection there is an anonymous extempore on hearing the two celebrated pulpit orators, Dr. Porteus, Lord Bishop of Chester, and Dr. Milne, Curate of Deptford and Vicar of North Chappel.

" From nature's fountain each derived the art,
Porteus to please and Milne to touch the heart ;
Did genius operate its perfect work.
Milne would be Chester, Chester would be York ;—
Nay further our presumption we may carry,
Milne would be York, Porteus, Canterbury."

Rev. RICHARD CONYERS, LL.D.

" 'Tis open, and ye cannot enter, —— why ?
Because ye will not, Conyers would reply—
And he says much that many may dispute,
And cavil at with ease, but none refute."

COWPER'S "TRUTH."

RICHARD CONYERS was born at Helmsley, in the North
Riding of Yorkshire, February 13th, 1725.

His studies, preparatory to entering Jesus College,
Cambridge, were conducted at a school of considerable
repute, at Cuckwold, near his native town. On leaving
the University he was ordained to the curacy of Over-
Carr, about 12 miles from Helmsley, where he remained
over five years, residing the while with his grandmother,
at Helmsley. As Vicar of Helmsley, " preferring the care
of the flock to the acquisition of the fleece, he thought
himself amply compensated with the prospect of more
extensive usefulness."

In 1765 he married Mrs. Knipe, sister of John
Thornton, Esq., who died in 1774. September 1st, 1775,
his brother-in-law, Mr. Thornton, presented him with
the living of St. Paul's, Deptford. He was so much
beloved by his parishioners that many of them publicly
declared " that they would lay themselves along the road,
and if he was determined to leave them, his carriage
should drive over them." He left Helmsley in the dead
of night for his distant cure. At Deptford he converted
his coach-house and stables into a domestic chapel, and
held four week-night lectures, which were well attended.

On the Saturday before his death he took his servant
with him into the churchyard, and said, " I want to look
out a spot for my grave ; show me Mr. Barker's grave."
Having fixed on a place he drove a stick into it and said,
" If I should live till Monday, I will get the sexton to
come and try whether there is sufficient depth of earth ;
but I do not think I shall hold out till Monday." Next
day he went to church as usual and whilst reading the
second lesson, 20th chap. of Acts, made several pathetic
remarks on that part of it, in which the Apostle calls

I

the Ephesian Elders to record that he had not shunned to declare the whole counsel of God, and intimates they should see his face no more. This proved, in the issue, but too applicable to his own case. He preached from St. Matthew, xxviii., 18. When pronouncing the blessing his voice seemed to falter, and finding himself seized with the stroke of death he said to his servant near him, "I cannot get from my knees." The servant raised him up, being sensible but perfectly helpless. On being removed to the Rectory, he said, "I have no pain, God's will be done, I hope I shall soon be with Jesus." He expired at four o'clock in the afternoon. The Rev. John Newton, Rector of St. Mary, Woolnoth, London, and friend of Cowper the poet, preached the funeral sermon from I. Thess., 11, 8, which he afterwards published.

The person of Dr. Conyers was tall and elegant. His aspect was both mild and majestic. His eyes beamed benignity, and his expressive countenance indicated a mind replete with sympathetic tenderness. His bosom was the residence of the most genuine and diffusive philanthropy. The urbanity of his manners was singularly attractive. The exquisite sensibility of his nature deeply interested him in the joys and sorrows of all his acquaintance. In parlour conversation and scriptural exposition he peculiarly excelled. To the bodies of men he was a father in charity, to their souls he was a servant in humility.

MARLOWE, THE DRAMATIST.

CHRISTOPHER MARLOWE is said to have been the son of a shoemaker at Canterbury, where he was born in 1563-4. He proceeded from King's School to Cambridge, where he took his degree. On quitting the University he became connected with the stage. So little is known of his history that it has been observed of him,

"The sole memorial of his lot
Is this—he was, and he is not."

In a copy of an old book called "The Theatre of God's Judgments," 1597, we are informed of his untimely end in these words :—"But, see what a hooke the Lord put in the nostrils of this barking dogge. It so fell out, that he purposed to stab one whom he ought (owed) a grudge unto, with his dagger, the other party perceiving, so avoided the stroke, that withall catching hold of his wrist, he stabbed his owne dagger into his owne head, in such sort, that notwithstanding all the meanes of surgerie that could be wrought, he shortly after died thereof, the manner of his death being so terrible (for he even cursed and blasphemed to his last gaspe, and together with his breathe an oathe flew out of his mouthe), that it was not only a manifest signe of God's judgment, but also an horrible and fearful terror to all that beheld him."

The scene of this melancholy event was not generally known until a passage in a puritanical work entitled "The Golden Grove Moralized," 1603, gave an account of his death at Deptford, which has since been confirmed by the production of a certificate of Marlowe's burial in St. Nicholas' Church. "1st June, 1593. Christopher Marlowe, slaine by Francis Archer."

In Jonson and Chapman's comedy entitled "Eastward Hoe," 1605, "Sir Petronel Flash" says, "This Captain Seagul : We'll have our provided dinner brought aboard Sir Francis Drake's ship, that hath compass'd the world, where with full cups and banquets we will do sacrifice for a prosperous voyage. My mind gives me that some good spirit of the waters should haunt the desert ribs of her, and be auspicious to all that honour her memory, and will, with like orgies enter their voyages."

The old ship was evidently, therefore, devoted to the purposes of banqueting and feasting, and if it was frequented by "rare Ben" in person, as may be inferred from his introducing it to Captain Seagul, no reasonable doubt can be entertained but that Kit Marlowe (as he was familiarly styled by Jonson) sometimes made one of the party, who took boat at the Temple Stairs and dropped down the river to the "Golden Hind" at

Deptford Yard. On one of these visits the ill-fated Marlowe met his untimely end. Under the influence of wine, he quarrelled with a low fellow named Archer, and at his hand, probably on board the old ship, received his death wound.

Jonson, in his elegy on Shakspeare, makes it one of his highest praises that he had exceeded "Marlowe's mightie line ;" and Peele in his "Honour of the Garter" 1593, calls him

"The muse's darling in his verse.
Fit to write passions for the souls below."

While Heywood styles him " the best of poets." It is something for Deptford to be identified with the subject of these high commendations ; with one whom Shakspeare was proud to emulate, and Jonson extol, and whose sweet verse found an admirer in the pious Izaak Walton.

Marlowe's productions were the link between the plays of Shakspeare and the old " Moralities." The plays attributed to him are " Dr. Faustus," " Edward the Second," "The Jew of Malta," "Tamburlaine the Great," " Lust's Dominion," " Dido, Queen of Carthage," and "Massacre at Paris ;" but he is more generally known as the writer of the following pastoral poem quoted by Izaak Walton in the " Complete Angler :"—

"Come live with me, and be my love,"
And we will all the pleasures prove
That valleys, groves. or hills, or field,
Or woods, and steepy mountains yield ;

" Where we will sit upon the rocks,
And see the shepherds feed our flocks,
By shallow rivers, to whose falls
Melodious birds sing madrigals.

"And I will make thee beds of roses.
And then a thousand fragrant posies,
A cap of flowers and a kirtle,
Embroidered all with leaves of myrtle ;

" A gown made of the finest wool,
Which from our pretty lambs we pull ;
Slippers, lined choicely for the cold,
With buckles of the purest gold ;

"A belt of straw and ivy buds,
With coral clasps and amber studs ;
And if these pleasures may thee move,
Come live with me and be my love.

"Thy silver dishes for thy meat,
As precious as the Gods do eat,
Shall, on an ivory table, be
Prepared each day for thee and me.

"The shepherd swains shall dance and sing
For thy delight, each May morning,
If these delights thy mind may move,
Then live with me, and be my love."

COWLEY, THE POET.

Abraham Cowley was born in London, in 1618, and educated at Westminster School. After passing through various vicissitudes on account of his loyalty to the Stuart dynasty, on the death of Cromwell, he obtained a lease of a farm at Chertsey. Early in life he produced a small volume of poems, called " Poetical Blossoms," which gained him a considerable reputation. His Anacreontics are reckoned his best productions. He also wrote a comedy called " Cutter of Coleman Street," and some pieces in prose, particulaily a " Discourse on the Government of Cromwell." His six Latin Books on Plants were written by him during his residence at Deptford, in which work the fine gardens belonging to John Evelyn, Esq., are supposed to have afforded him great assistance. He died at Chertsey in 1667. Evelyn in his Diary, 1st August, says, " I receiv'd the sad news of Abraham Cowley's death, that incomparable poet and virtuous man, my very deare friend, and was greately deplored," and two days afterwards he says, " I went to Mr. Cowley's funerall, whose corps lay at Wallingford House, and was thence convey'd to Westminster Abby, in a hearse with 6 horses and all funerall decency, neere an hundred coaches of noblemen and persons of qualitie following ; among these all the witts of the towne, divers bishops and cleargymen. He was interr'd next Geoffry Chancer and neere to Spenser. A goodly monument has been since erected to his memorie."

SAMUEL PEPYS.

SAMUEL PEPYS spent so much of his time in Deptford, either in his official capacity as Secretary of the Admiralty in the reigns of Charles II. and James II., or visiting his intimate friend Mr. Evelyn at Sayes Court, that he may fairly claim a notice here.

Pepys' knowledge of naval administration was very large, and by his energy the affairs of the Admiralty were reduced to order and method. His "Memoirs relating to the Navy;" collection of MSS., and library, now at Magdalen College, Cambridge, are an invaluable treasure of naval knowledge. He became President of the Royal Society in 1684, and was Master of the Trinity House Corporation in 1676 and 1685. But his celebrated "Diary" forms his best claim to remembrance. This work, after lying undeciphered in shorthand characters during 150 years, was published by Lady Braybrooke in 1825. He was born in London and was related to the Earl of Sandwich. Died in 1703.

HON. ROGER BOYLE.

The HONOURABLE ROGER BOYLE, eldest son of the celebrated Richard, Earl of Cork, was born in Ireland. He was sent to Deptford, to prepare for the University, in an Academy kept by one Mr. Young. He was a very promising youth, and paid for his proficiency in study by an early death. He died at Sayes Court October 12th, 1617, and was buried in St. Nicholas' Church.

Mr. Evelyn relates the following anecdote in reference to Boyle's monument in a letter dated 1708.

"When King Charles II newly come to his crown, and using frequently to saile down the river in his yachts for diversion, and accompanied by all the great men and courtiers waiting upon him; it was often observed, that when the vessel passed by a certain place opposite to the Church at Deptford ; my Lord Burlington constantly pulled off his hat with some kind of reverence. This being remarked by some of the Lords standing by him, they desired he would tell them what he meant by it. To which he replied," Do you see that steeple there? Have I not reason to pay a respect to the place where my elder brother lies buried, by which I enjoy the Earldom of Cork."

GRINLING GIBBON.

GRINLING GIBBON, the most celebrated sculptor in wood and ivory, of modern times, was unknown to the world, till by chance he was discovered at Deptford, in total obscurity, by " Sylva " Evelyn. Whether he was born here, or indeed in England is a matter of doubt, but it is generally conceived that his father was a Dutchman, settled at Deptford, and that his son Grinling was born here. The circumstances attending the artist's first acquaintance with Evelyn, his future patron and friend, are thus narrated in the Diary, 1760-1, January 18. "This day I first acquainted his Majesty with that incomparable young man, Gibbon, whom I had lately met with in an obscure place by mere accident, as I was walking near a poor solitary thatched house in a field in our parish, near Sayes Court. I found him shut in ; but looking in at the window, I perceived him carving that large cartoon, or crucifix, of Tintoretto, a copy of which I had myself brought from Venice, where the original painting remains. I asked if I might enter ; he opened the door civilly to me, and I saw him about such a work as for the curiosity of handling, drawing, and studious exactness, I never had before seen in my travels. I questioned him why he worked in such an obscure and lonesome place ; he told me it was that he might apply himself to his profession without interruption, and wondered not a little how I found him out. I asked if he was unwilling to be made known to some great man, for that I believed it might turn to his profit; he answered, he was yet a beginner, but would not be sorry to sell that piece ; on demanding the price, he said £100. In good earnest, the very frame was worth the money, there being nothing in nature so tender and delicate as the flowers and festoons about it, and yet the work was very strong; in the piece was more than one hundred figures of men, &c. I found he was likewise musical, and very civil, sober, aud discreet in his discourse. There was only an old woman in the house. So, desiring leave to visit him sometimes, I went away. Of this young artist, together with my manner of finding him out, I acquainted the King, and begged that he would give me leave to bring him and his work to Whitehall, for that I would adventure my reputation with his Majesty that he had never seen anything approach it, and that he would be exceedingly pleased and employ him. The King said he would himself go and see him. This was the first notice his Majesty ever had of Mr. Gibbon."

The following is a copy from an original letter, addressed by Grinling Gibbon to Mr. Evelyn, now in the library at Wotton.

Honred.

Sr, I wold beg the faver wen you see Sr Joseff Williams (Williamson) again you wold be pleased to speack to him that hee wold get me to Case his Ladis sons hous my Lord Kildare for I onderstand it will (be) verry considerabell ar If you haen Acquantans with my Lord to speack to him his sealf and I shall for. Ev're be obliaged to you I wold speack to Sir Josef mysealf but I know it would do better from you.

Sr, Youre Most umbell
Sarvant
G. GIBBON.

Lond. 23. Mar. 1682.

Evelyn's interest at Court, backed by his deserved reputation for taste in the fine arts, quickly advanced the talent and fame of Gibbon and to such a pitch of excellence did he arrive, almost before the years of manhood, that his sculptured flowers, light almost as love, shook to the rattling of the passing carriages. Indeed, so minutely elegant were his performances, so delicately fine were they in their proportions, that even his marble compositions, as well as those in ivory and wood. required the defensive protection of a glass case.

Grinling did not remain long at Deptford after his introduction to the " merrie monarch." From the more minute intricacies of wood enrichments, he soared to the higher region of sculpture in marble. The King appointed him to a place under the Board of Works, and he was employed in ornamenting several of the royal palaces. He carved the foliage in the chapel of Windsor, the choir of St. Paul's Cathedral, and the admirable font in St. James's Church, Westminster. There is some of his carving in St. James's Church, Piccadilly, and King's College Chapel, Oxford. The ornamental decorations in the reredos of St. Nicholas' Church, Deptford, are attributed to him ; but his principal work is said to be at Petworth.

This unrivalled artist died at his house in Bond-street, Covent Garden, August 3rd, 1721.

JOHN CRAWFORD.

JOHN CRAWFORD, born here in 1810, was son of John Crawford, " the humble but aspiring hero that nailed the flag to the mast of the ' Venerable ' after the top-gallant mast was shot away in Lord Duncan's victory over the Dutch off the Texel " on the 1st of October, 1797, when eleven out of the fifteen sail of the line composing the enemy's squadrom were captured ; two of them however being abandoned in consequence of the difficulty of navigation. This fact is recorded on a certificate of the birth of his son taken out in this parish. Whether this gallant tar was himself a native of Deptford is not recorded ; but it is evident that he and his family were inhabitants of the parish for some time, and as such is deserving of a place in the roll of " Parish Worthies."

R. GASTRILL.

R. GASTRILL was boatswain's mate of H.M.S. "Marlborough," of 80 guns, in the memorable engagement between the English fleet, commanded by Matthews and Lestock, and the combined fleets of France and Spain, when the gallant Captain Corwate was killed. He was afterwards boatswain of H.M.S. "Chesterfield," of 20 guns, which was taken possession of by the Lieutenant of Marines, carpenter, and some others of the crew, on the Coast of Africa. Gastrill was the means of recovering the vessel from the mutineers; and after keeping possession of her for six weeks, he delivered her up, together with the prisoners, to the Admiral upon the Barbadoes Station. The lieutenant of Marines, carpenter, and several others were afterwards executed at Portsmouth; when the Lords of the Admiralty, as a reward for his courage and meritorious conduct, appointed him Master Attendant of Woolwich Dockyard. He afterwards removed to Portsmouth Yard, and from thence about 1776 was appointed Lieutenant to Deptford Yard, where he died March 10th, 1783.

ADAM GORDON.

ADAM GORDON, Esqre., head of the old-established firm of Gordon and Co., of Deptford Green, iron-founders, engineers, &c., was a gentleman who took a deep interest in all that related to the welfare of the parish and neighbourhood of Deptford.

As a Justice of the Peace for the counties of Kent and Surrey, he usually sat at the Deptford Petty Sessions, where he gave the highest satisfaction to rich and poor alike. In promoting all the public charities he was always amongst the foremost; he was for some years Treasurer of the Kent Dispensary; and as Chairman of the Deptford Board of Health—to which office he was unanimously elected — during the prevalence of that dreadful visitation, the Asiatic Cholera, from which Deptford suffered so greatly, he not only devoted his best energies in promoting subscriptions in aid of the sufferers, but gave up a portion of his extensive premises on Deptford Green as a depôt for the warm clothing and other necessaries, provided on that occasion. No case of individual calamity or distress was ever mentioned to him in vain.

The death of this worthy man, of brain fever, at the early age of 38, on the 14th of January, 1839, was deeply felt throughout the whole neighbourhood. He was buried on the 21st of January in the family vault at Camberwell, leaving an amiable widow in a state of pregnancy, and seven children.

For this brief memoir we are indebted to Hugh M. Gordon, Esq., of the Courtyard, Eltham, a son of the deceased gentleman, and to Mr. J. T. Prestige, of Wickham Road, Brockley, who was early connected with the firm of Gordon and Co.

JOSEPH HARDCASTLE.

JOSEPH HARDCASTLE, Esq., a descendant of a family at Hardcastle (a) near Masham, Yorkshire, was born at Leeds, December 7th, 1752.

He either took or bought Hatcham House in this parish in October, 1788, where he resided till his death on the 3rd March, 1819. He was buried at Bunhill Fields. It was here that he entertained Thomas Clarkson, Granville Sharpe, and other labourers in the cause of the emancipation of slavery; and here also Clarkson wrote a portion of his "History of the Abolition of the Slave Trade." The Rev. Rowland Hill was accustomed to speak with kindling delight of the pleasure he enjoyed with Mr. Hardcastle at Hatcham, where he often read the MSS. of "Village Dialogues." Dr. Haweis, Revds. John Eyre, John Newton, Melville Horne, John Simmons, of Paul's Cray, Dr. Hawkins, &c., were his frequent guests.

a Hackfall was once theirs.

Hatcham House was at all times open to men of this description, and to the close of his life, the hearty north country hospitality which he delighted to maintain made the name of Hatcham familiar to Christians of every denomination, not only throughout the British Empire, but also in America and on the Continent. Mr. Hardcastle was the first Treasurer of the London Missionary Society. It is said of him that he never, during the whole course of his life, turned a deaf ear to the suppliant for relief of any kind.

PETER ROLT.

MR. ROLT, son of Mr. John David Rolt, by his marriage with Sophia, eldest daughter of Mr. Peter Butt, clerk of the Survey in Deptford Dockyard, was born in Broomfield House (a) in the year 1798. He married in 1820 Mary, eldest daughter of Mr. Thomas Brocklebank, of Deptford, managing director of the General Steam Navigation Company, but his wife died in 1845.

Mr. Rolt was elected M.P. for the Borough of Greenwich, in July, 1852, in the Conservative interest. He was a partner in the firm of Brocklebank and Rolt, timber merchants and contractors. For some years he served as a director of the Commercial Dock Company, and was a past master of the Drapers' Company. He served as Deputy-Lieutenant for Middlesex, and was created an Italian count in 1872. For many years he was connected with the Thames Ironworks Company, in the course of which he took a leading part in the construction of the Warrior, the first British ironclad man-

---

a Broomfield House, which was pulled down in the early part of the present century, stood on the site of the Evelyn Estate Office, Evelyn Street, opposite the Globe Inn, and was the only house then in Broomfield, west of the market gardener's (Busby's) house, and the Cockpit, at the eastern end of Broomfield, near where the turnpike gate formerly stood, before its removal in 1834 to the westward of the Globe Inn.

In this house lived Mr. Rolt's father, John David Rolt, grandfather, John Rolt, and great-grandfather, Richard Rolt.

of war. He died at Trafalgar House, September, 1882, in his 85th year.

"Gallant, jaunty, conversational, and quick in the part of paying pretty attentions and compliments, Mr. Rolt imparted life and spirit to the gravest assemblage. He was a capital dinner-giver, and was exact in the mating of the viands and the wine, his menus being preserved by the curious in such things as the models of gustative propriety. Rarely in one person has the man of pleasure and the man of business been more shrewdly and intimately commingled " (*Daily Telegraph*).

JOHN SWAN.

MR. SWAN—the original inventor of the " Screw Propeller " and " Self-acting Chain Messenger "—was born at Coldingham, Berwickshire. His " Rotative Sculling Wheels " were first tested in 1824, on a sheet of water in the grounds of C. Gordon, Esq., of Dulwich Hill, in the presence of Dr. Birkbeck (founder of the Birkbeck Institute) and a number of scientific gentlemen, when the experiment was eminently successful.

Here is Mr. Swan's own account of his invention in a letter to Dr. Birkbeck, published with three diagrams in the London Mechanics' Register, of January 22nd, 1825 : " According to your request I send you my remarks on the rotative sculling wheels for propelling vessels. First, I would notice their compactness, in not occupying more than one-fourth part of the space the common wheels do. As seen in the plan, they may lay in harbour, with other vessels, without any danger of being injured at all, which is at present a great inconveniency. Secondly, the superior advantage in a rough sea, in which they act the same as in a calm pool, being entirely beneath in the solid dense water ; and besides, their weight, from their situation, as will plainly appear, will be as ballast in the hold, an object at sea worthy of consideration. Thirdly, from their situation beneath the surface, they are not liable to be impeded by floats of ice, or by storms ; therefore, I think they might be suitable to packets for dispatch, and

might be used all the winter. Fourthly, they make no
swell or commotion, either disagreeable or dangerous in
the water, as the common wheels do when lighting in a
fermentation of air and water ; but go on as smoothly as
a vessel under sail, their action being in the solid water
as a lever upon a rock for a fulcrum."

Professor Allen, in a lecture on Screw Propulsion, delivered in 1851, says "The first feasible scheme of which
I can find record is dated 1824, and is the invention of
John Swan. His contrivance was to propel ships by
double-bladed screws, immersed deeply in the water at
the sides of the vessel. The patent taken out by Smith,
1836, was for what he termed an improved Propeller ;
but the chief feature in his improvement consisted in the
propeller being placed in the dead wood of the stern, the
principle of his propeller being the same as that of
Swan's. I consider that with the latter rests the honour
of the invention."

Mr. Swan resided at 35, Deptford Green, and was for
many years manager to Messrs. Gordon and Co., Engineers, and it was whilst in this capacity, in 1824, that he
invented the screw-propeller. From a variety of reasons
he failed to avail himself of the protection afforded by the
patent laws, the result being that other parties speedily
adopted his invention, and having made some minor
improvements, reaped the benefit of Mr. Swan's
ingenuity. As manager, he was universally respected
by the men under his charge—the greatest unanimity
always prevailing between them ; whilst so great
was his opinion looked up to, that many of the most
eminent engineers gladly availed themselves of the
advice of so ingenious and modest an inventor,
which was always freely and obligingly given. Mr.
Swan's "Self-acting Chain Messenger" was introduced
into the Navy in 1831, yet, although it has been frankly
confessed by men of the highest authority that the invention was a very great saving, both of money and men's
lives, neither he nor any of his posterity have ever received the slightest remunerative acknowledgment from a
grateful country.

" Some men labour and others enter into their labours,"
is an appropriate motto on Mr. Swan's tombstone in Abney
Park Cemetery. He died at 82, Mansfield Street, Kings-
land Road, London, in 1869, aged 81.

We are indebted for some of the above particulars to
Mr. Swan's son-in-law, Mr. James Seaward, of New
Cross. We may here mention that Mr. Seaward, at No.
2, High-street, Deptford, in 1843, started one of the first
cheap local newspapers, entitled "The Boro' of Greenwich Pioneer of Progress." He afterwards published
"Seaward's Family Newspaper" with illustrations of
Montagu Chambers, Q.C., M.P., Peter Rolt, Esq. M.P. ;
view of Lewisham High-road Congregational Church, &c.
He likewise established at Greenwich the "Boro' of
Greenwich Free Press," and was one of the first
founders of the Local Permanent Building Societies, &c.
He is the composer of some popular music which has been
sung with great success at the Crystal Palace Fêtes, and at
the principal Musical Festivals throughout the United
Kingdom.

RICHARD ROPER, F.S.A.

RICHARD, son of JAMES ROPER, was born in the parish of
St. Nicholas, Deptford, in 1829. At the age of 14 he was
apprenticed to the General Steam Navigation Company,
at their Home Station, Stowage, Deptford, for 7 years ;
having previously been employed for 3 years in a ship-
yard at Rotherhithe.

Like many men who have risen in life, Mr. Roper seems
to have been indebted to his mother, who was a person
of refinement and education, for the mental training
which he failed to receive at the private school which he
attended until he was eleven years of age. His exemplary
conduct, perseverance, and honest application to duty
and self-improvement during his apprenticeship induced
Messrs. Mare and Co., the eminent ship-builders, to offer
him, at its completion, an engagement as foreman ;
where he remained for several years, until he commenced

business on his own account as a contractor and ship-fitter.

The nature of his employment had made him acquainted with the construction and fitting of ships, and to improvements in connection with these he directed his thoughtful attention. An early result was his invention of a " Pneumatic Drilling Machine " to fix without bolts or drill holes to ships' sides and boilers where no means exist of fastening an ordinary " John Bull," that was found to act efficiently. He afterwards introduced a " composition " for painting iron ships, bridges and iron work in general. This composition prevents fouling of ships' bottoms, and several vessels coated with it, have, after long voyages, returned home perfectly clean. Black-friars Bridge, which was painted with it when built, has never required repainting. It was fully tested at Portsmouth Dockyard, when it was approved of by the Lords of the Admiralty who caused it to be placed in the South Kensington Museum.

To prevent ironclads having to be coated with timber, before sheathing with copper, an expensive process, he invented a method of fastening sheet copper on the iron which would project not more than 3-8 of an inch, thereby increasing the speed with less horse power. His greatest invention, and the one which entitles him to a place in the category of " Parish Worthies," is his " Patent Self-Launching Life Raft. During his apprenticeship and subsequent service with Messrs. Mare and Co., his attention was drawn irresistibly to the urgent necessity existing for the provision of some more trustworthy appliances for saving life at sea, in cases of wreck, foundering, or fire, than the present defective boat systems, by which ship-wrecked passengers, troops, and crews have been so often cruelly mocked in the hour of death. The germ of the " Life Rafts " that he has since elaborated and patented was then formed in his mind.

An adequate supply of " Roper's Rafts " would have floated off in safety, every soul on board the ill-fated Princess Alice, Northfleet, Teuton, and many other ships that have been staved in or wrecked in comparatively smooth water.

A ship may have one or more of these rafts on board without adding top-weight or interfering with the navigation. One should occupy the place and serve the purpose of captain's bridge, others form extensions of poop and forecastle; and arranged to be launched from either side. At each end the bulwarks are constructed to open and let down to a slope for the passage of the raft, or it can be launched over the rail. The launching ways are iron beams descending to the proper slope, but not leaving the ship with the raft; friction rollers being furnished to facilitate the launch, which can be effected in a few seconds by any one; no mechanical skill or experience being required to put it in motion. The raft would be self-floating in case of the ship foundering.

It may be constructed of timber, steel, or other metal; an essential characteristic being the adoption of the air-tight cellular principle to secure buoyancy. The deck, of double diagonal boarding, crossed, is surrounded by iron stanchions four feet high, with the under half closely netted. Water-tight steel lockers opening by screw caps on the top are fitted at the sides and ends for the reception of provisions and other stores requisite for a voyage; masts, oars, rudder, &c., being lashed to the side and end stanchions. The middle rail of the side stanchions is fitted with strong rowlocks for working the sweeps.

Very many high naval authorities, engineers, ship-owners, and practical men have certified to the great merits and utility of this invention; the Lords of the Admiralty have expressed their "high approval of the Raft, and the ingenuity of the invention." Admiral Sir George Sartorius, Admiral of the Fleet, in writing to the *Times*, says: "This Raft will live out any storm, and form a breakwater for boats to hang on to."

Mr. Roper was awarded the first prize silver medal at the Royal Aquarium, Westminster, for his Life Rafts; and at the Naval and Submarine Exhibition, held at the Agricultural Hall, London, in April, 1882, received the first prize of one hundred guineas for his self-launching "Bridge Life Rafts" as affording the readiest means in case of shipwreck, of saving collectively a large number

K

of persons, and supporting them above water for a lengthened period. Two bridge rafts on Mr. Roper's principle have been fitted on board H.M.S. "Polyphemus" at Chatham, and recently tested with the most satisfactory results.

Mr. Roper's exquisite taste and consummate skill as a decorator are well known (*a*), he having been entrusted with the painting and decorating of H.M. steamship, the "Serapis," which conveyed H.R.H. the Prince of Wales to India. The *Times* referring to the ship says : "Superb as are the handsome cabins of the Peninsular and Oriental Company's steamers, the finish and decoration of the "Serapis" far exceed anything to be met with in that Company's world-famous fleet, or any other of the finest vessels afloat."

By making the best possible use of his talents and opportunities ; by his steadiness of conduct and generous disposition, Mr. Roper has achieved an honourable position in business, and earned "a good degree" as a local philanthropist ; being one of those who

> "Do good by stealth, and blush to find it fame."

> "Yet, taught by fame, his heart has learned to glow
> For others' good, and melt at others' woe."

> "To those who know him not, no words can paint
> To those who know him well all words are faint."

Eminent, practical, professional, and scientific men have testified to the successful application of his inventive faculties ; and the day will surely come when Deptford will be proud of numbering amongst its sons the inventor of the "Self-launching Life Raft."

EDWARD ROBERTS, F.R.A.S., F.S.S.

MR. ROBERTS was born in Deptford Broadway in 1845, and educated at the Greenwich Proprietary School, under

a Any one desiring a proof of this need but to pay a visit to his residence in the Lewisham High Road, which is truly a palace in miniature.

the Rev. Thomas Goodwin, LL.D., where he gained many prizes and distinctions, more especially in mathematics and chemistry. On quitting school in 1860 he joined the staff of the Royal Observatory, Greenwich, on the introduction of the Rev. Robert Main, the then first assistant to the Astronomer Royal, G. B. Airy, Esq. (afterwards Sir George B. Airy), M.A., D.C.L. Whilst at the Royal Observatory, in addition to his routine work of computing and observing, Mr. Roberts was employed upon much extraneous work for the Astronomer Royal and Mr. Main, afterwards Radcliffe Observer at Oxford. In 1864 he quitted the Observatory and entered the Nautical Almanac office, taking at once a middle position in the establishment. Here, again, in addition to his official duties, he has been engaged in much work of a scientific nature for many scientists, including Professor J. C. Adams, Sir William Thomson, the Earl of Crawford, &c. But the work with which his name will be, perhaps, more particularly associated is in connection with Tidal Analysis and Prediction, which branch of scientific enquiry has engaged his attention from 1867 to the present time. The success of his harmonic tidal analysis led the Indian Government to ask him to undertake the designing of a Tide-predicting machine for the Indian ports, the tides of which presented many seeming irregularities, and precluded their prediction by the methods generally adopted for other places.

An idea of the saving effected by the Tide Predicter, designed by Mr. Roberts, may be gathered from the fact that the tide curves computed by an expert calculator to include the same number of components as comprised in the machine, could not be worked out in less than four or five months for the year's tides at any port. These can be run off by the machine in about two hours, and then only require the heights and times to be read off.

The value of the machine is very great in any work where the whole tide-curve is of service, and will be of great value in engineering works in which a fore-knowledge of the tides is necessary, such as in constructing

the foundations of quay walls, embankments, dock
sills, &c., the whole time during which the work can be
prosecuted being seen at a glance for every tide.   The
machine has been used for the prepartion of Tide Tables
for several Indian ports, since 1880, with the most satisfactory results ; and its use is being extended to the ports
of China and South Africa.

Mr. Roberts is still a resident of his native parish.   He
was elected a Fellow of the Royal Astronomical Society
in 1871 ; and in 1882 a Fellow of the Statistical Society.

COLONEL JOHN H. ALLEN.

COLONEL ALLEN, who was for many years a resident of
St. John's Terrace, Lewisham High Road, published in
1845 a 4to volume, entitled " A Pictorial Tour in the
Mediterranean, including Malta, Dalmatia, Turkey, Asia
Minor, Grecian Archipelago, Egypt, Nubia, Greece,
Ionian Islands, Sicily, Italy and Spain."   The work
which is dedicated to his H.R.H. Prince William of
Prussia, in grateful and respectful remembrance of his
affability and kindness to the author, is profusely illus-
trated with original drawings of great beauty.

The Colonel was a member of the Athenian Archæo-
logical Society, and of the Egyptian Society of Cairo.

He died in the early part of the present year and was
interred in Nunhead Cemetery.

*Notices of many other Deptford Worthies will be
found in the narrative of the various parochial works
in which they were engaged.*

ECCLESIASTICAL HISTORY.

St. Nicholas Church.

THE Church of St. Nicholas—the mother church of the parish—is situated on the south side of Deptford Green, near the banks of the Thames. There are no records extant of the date of its erection ; but the style of the old tower, which is a fine specimen of Early Kentish architecture, points us to the twelfth century. That the church *was* in existence in the twelfth century is clearly proved by the grant of the advowson by the Countess Juliana de Vere, to the religious order of Premonstratensians, or White Canons. Soon afterwards, perhaps on the removal of the Order from Brockley to Begham, the patronage of the Church seems to have returned to the Lord of the Barony of Maminot, Geoffrey de Say, who granted it to the Knights Templars, in pure and perpetual alms. His son regained possession of it in exchange for the Manor of Saddlescombe in Sussex, and by his deed gave it to the Canons of Begham or Bayham.

"Gualeranus, Bishop of Rochester, appropriated this church about A.D. 1183 to the Abbot and Convent of Begham, which was confirmed by Pope Honorius III. by his bull dated the third year of his Pontificate; as well as by the Cardinal Legate in England; and afterwards by Benedict, Bishop of Rochester; Lawrence, Bishop of Rochester, 1256; the Prior and Chapter of Rochester, and in 1513 by Walter, Archbishop of Canterbury." It remained in the possession of this Abbey till the dissolution of monasteries, when it was granted by the King to Cardinal Wolsey by writ dated 10th of May, 1526, " to appropriate, consolidate and annex to the deans and canons of the College of Thomas Wolsey, Cardinal of York, in the University of Oxford."

By an ancient valuation taken in the reign of Edward I., A.D. 1287, the church was estimated at fifteen marks and the vicarage at six and a half marks. It paid nine pence chrism-rent yearly to the mother church of the diocese, as every other church did within it.

The church remained but a short time in the possession of Wolsey's College, for in 1529 it was again a Crown living; and so continued till 1568, when it was granted by Queen Elizabeth, by letters patent dated 4th May, to Philip Conway. The rent reserved to the Crown in the grants of this vicarage was £5 6s. 8d., which on the 14th of March, 1626, was settled by King Charles I. on his Queen, Henrietta Maria, in dower for life.

The Vicarage in the King's Book was valued at £12 17s. 3½d., and the yearly tenths at £1 5s. 8¾d. Soon after the death of Charles I., a Commission of Enquiry into the value of church livings having issued out of the Court of Chancery, by order of the State, Deptford was returned as a Vicarage with house and five acres of glebe land worth £60. It was granted by the Commonwealth at the above named rent to Edmund Downing and Peter Aston; returning to the Crown again at the Restoration, with whom it seems to have remained till 1737, when we find Mrs. Wickham, of Garsington, patron of the living. The patronage passed into the Drake family, by marriage, in 1780, where it at present remains.

In 1630 the number of inhabitants and communicants had so greatly increased that the church accommodation was found to be totally inadequate to the requirements of the parish ; this was remedied by the erection of a new north aisle, towards the building of which the East India Company contributed largely ; the chancel being at the same time enlarged and beautified, partly at the cost of Sir William Russell, Treasurer of the Royal Navy.

Towards the close of the century, the church was again too small for the rapidly-increasing population, and the nave requiring considerable repairs, it was determined to rebuild it, which was done in 1697, by a voluntary subscription and an assessment of five shillings in the pound. Isaac Loader, Esq., a native of Deptford, was the greatest benefactor, as the following inscription on a tablet erected in the church proves :—

" In thankes to so generous a benefaction and for the encouragement of others to imitate good works and piety and charity, this parish have thought fitt at their own charge to perpetuate the memory of the voluntary contributions of Isaac Loader, Esquire, (a) preasant high sheriff of this county, towards the rebuilding and beautifying this church.

	£	s.	d.
Given by subscription for building the church	125	0	0
For paving the aisles with marble	161	0	0
For the altar	293	0	0
For vestry and portals	50	0	0
For the bells	38	0	0
For the charnel house	194	0	0
For recasting the tenor, with addition of metal	40	0	0
	£901	0	0

An Act of Parliament, passed in 1710, may be considered the primary cause of the dissolution of Deptford as an entire parish, in the state it had existed from the days of William the Conquerer. Power was given, by

a Isaac Loader was probably born at Loader's Court, his father's residence in the Stowage. Speaking of his father Evelyn says "One Loader, an ankersmith, grew so rich as to build an house in the street with gardens, orangeries and other magnificence." Fifty years ago this house was occupied by a baker, who used the old bath room beautifully frescoed, as his bakehouse.

that Act. to build fifty new churches in and near London, whereof Deptford was considered one. Another Act of Parliament was passed in 1730 for making the new district parish of St. Paul, and providing for the maintenance of the minister, £3,500 being vested in the Old South Sea Annuities for that purpose ; the King was to present to the first vacancy, and the patrons of the old church afterwards.

A writer in the *Gentleman's Magazine* of February, 1795, says :—" The Church of St. Nicholas, Deptford, in its present state has a strange disjointed exterior. The tower is evidently of very great age. The earth round it appears to have been raised, as there is a descent of several steps contrary to the usual manner of entrance into such places. Nothing, surely, can exceed the monstrous incongruity of the church, and its tower, stone and brick, Gothic, and a defiance of every order, jumbled together; yet the person employed in rebuilding the church must have been a man of taste, as the inside plainly demonstrates, for that is elegant. The chancel is small and railed off from the church ; it is richly ornamented with carving of foliage, figures, &c. (the work of a parish worthy, Grinling Gibbon), and two paintings of Moses and Aaron ; over the Commandments there is an oval painted glass representing the Adoration of the Infant Jesus, that has considerable merit."

Several bearings in coloured glass were inserted in the windows of the present building, from the old church; amongst which may be mentioned : I. Gules, a cross flory Or, between three trefoils of the second, The Arms of Manning ; II. Sable, a cross ingrailed Or ; The Arms of Paton, III. Quarterly. 1st, Or, three frame saws sable ; 2nd, 3rd, and 4th gules, two battle axes in saltier Or, in chief a helmet of the second. The Arms of Verzelini. These were placed in the east window.

In the north window of the chancel : I. Argent, three escallops azure ; II. Quarterly, 1st Argent, two bends ingrailed, and a canton, sable. The arms of Petley, 2nd--3rd, Argent, a bend azure, between two cotizes sable, 4th azure.

In the south window of the church : Or, a bend ermine.

In the first window on the north side of the body of the church, " A large rose finely coloured in glass, parted per pale, argent and gules, within a glory surmounted with a crown, for the union of the Houses of York and Lancaster.

Local tradition asserts that the old tower of St. Nicholas, like many others around our coasts, formerly served as a light-house, for the guidance of vessels navigating the river by night; which is not at all improbable.

The steeple was repaired in 1780, and the great bell recast. The spiral staircase leading to the belfry is partly formed of Purbeck marble, a material never used for such purposes later than the reign of King Edward II. ; a fact, which, at once, establishes its antiquity. The tower contains a peal of eight bells.

Above the doorway of the Charnel-house, in the Churchyard, is a very curious piece of carving, representing Ezekiel's vision in the valley of dry bones ; now carefully preserved from the action of the weather by a plate of glass. This is generally supposed to be the work of Grinling Gibbon. The gate posts, leading to the churchyard from the Stowage, are surmounted by a skull and cross-bones cut in stone, and apparently very old.

The Church, which has accommodation for one thousand worshippers, was re-opened after restoration, on the 20th of February, 1876. The organ was built by Smith in 1697 ; rebuilt by Hunter in 1868 ; and repaired by Bevington in 1876.

The painting by Sir Godfrey Kneller, of Queen Anne, which hangs in the chancel, was intended for St. Paul's Church, but being sent to the parish before the completion of that building, it fell into the custody of the officials of St. Nicholas, who placed it where it now remains.

LIST OF VICARS.

SINCE A.D., 1561.

———

Rev. Robert Foster, 19th of August, 1561.

Patron, Queen Elizabeth.

Rev. Samuel Page, D.D., about 1603. Buried here on the 8th of August, 1630.
Dr. Page was author of a work on the Psalms.

Patron, Queen Elizabeth.

Rev. Robert Mercer, M.A., 9th August, 1630.

Patron, The Lord Keeper.

Rev. Henry Valentine, D.D., 8th December, 1630. He died probably in 1644.

Patron, The Lord Keeper.

Rev. Thomas Mallory was appointed Vicar in 1644. He resigned in 1659 for the living of St. Michael, Crooked-lane, from which he was ejected by the Bartholomew Act. (*Nonconformist Memorial, vol.* 1, *p.* 133).
"Sylva" Evelyn speaks of him as "a quiet presbyter," but he could scarcely have been a good orthodox churchman, or Mr. Evelyn would not have sought the services of Mr. Owen, the sequestered Minister of Eltham, to christen his children and administer the Blessed Sacrament to him and his family at Sayes Court, during Mr. Mallory's incumbency. This fact is strengthened by an extract from his diary " 1659, January 17th. Our old Vicar preach'd, taking leave of the parish in a pathetical ' *speech*,' to go to a living in the citty."
Calamy says " He hath a sermon in the morning exercise at Cripplegate, On the conceptions we should form of God in Duty."

Patron, The Lord Keeper.

Robert Lytler, or Littler, was presented to the living by John Culter, Esq., in 1659. Evelyn says of him, " One Mr. Littler being now presented to the living of our parish, preach'd on 6 John, 53, a sermon preparatory to the Holy Communion."— (*Diary*, 1659, *April* 10).

Mr. Littler must have died or resigned in 1661, for Evelyn says on Nov. 3rd of that year. " One Mr. Breton preach'd his probation sermon at our Parish Church, and indeede made a most excellent discourse on 1 John, 29, of God's free grace to penitents, so that I could not but recommend him to the patron." He obtained the living.

Rev. Robert Breton, D.D., was inducted in 1661, and died in February, 1671. He was rector of St. Martin's, Ludgate, London ; and Prebendary of Cadington Minor in St. Paul's Cathedral.

Dr. Breton was "a very useful charitable man."— (*See Parish Charities*). Mrs. Evelyn, in a letter to Mr. Bohun, Fellow of New College, Oxford, dated from Sayes Court, says " Should I tell you how full of sorrow I have ben for the losse of Dr. Bretton, you only would blame me ; after death flattery ceases, therefore you may beleeve there was some cause to lament when thousands of weeping eyes witnessed the affliction their souls were in ; one would have imagined every one in this parish had lost a Father, Brother or Husband, so great was the bewailing ; and in earnest it does appear there never was a better nor more worthy man. Such was his temper, prudence, charity, and good conduct, that he gained the weake and preserved the wise. The suddennesse of his death was a surprise only to his friends ; as for himselfe, it might be looked upon as a deliverance from paine, the effect of sicknesse, and I am allmost perswaded God snatched him from us, least he might have ben prevailed with by the number of petitions to have left him still amongst us. If you suspect kindness in me makes me speake too much ; Dr.

Parr is a person against whome you cannot object ;
it was he who preached the funerall sermon, and as
an effect of truth as well as eloquence he himselfe
could not forbeare weeping in the pulpit. It was
his owne expression that there were three for whom
he infinitely greeved, the martyred King, my
Lord Primate (Abp. Usher) and Doctor Bretton ;
and as a confirmation of the right that was done
him in that oration, there was not a drie eye
nor a dissenting person."

Rev. Richard Holden, M.A., " a learned man," succeeded
Dr. Breton, of whom Evelyn says, " This gentleman is a very excellent and universal scholar, a
good and wise man ; but he had not a popular way
of preaching, nor is in any measure fit for our
plaine and vulgar auditorie, as his predecessor was.
There was, however, no comparison betwixt their
parts for profound learning ; but time and experience may forme him to a more practical way than
that he is in of University lectures and erudition,
which is now universally left off for what is much
more profitable." (*Diary*, *Mar*., 1673). He was
Rector of St. Dunstan-in-the-East, and Sub-Dean
of His Majesty's Chapel, and died in 1700. He
published a sermon preached before the Trinity
House. (*Patron the Lord Keeper*).

The Very Rev. George Stanhope, D.D.   (*See Parish
Worthies, p.* 113).

Rev. William Norton, D.D.—The district parish of St.
Paul, Deptford, was formed during Dr. Norton's
incumbency, and he held the Rectory of St. Paul
as well as the Vicarage of St. Nicholas till his death,
May 31st, 1731.

Rev. Isaac Colman succeeded Dr. Norton and exchanged
with his successor for the Rectory of Weston and
Vicarage of Halworth, in Suffolk, in January, 1737.

Rev. Thomas Anguish.—He held the living till his death
in 1762. He published three sermons : " On the
Accession ;" " On the Rebellion, 1745 ;" and " On
the Earthquake."

One of his daughters was married to the Duke of Leeds.

Rev. William Worcester Wilson, D.D., inducted in 1762. He died in 1791.

Rev. John Drake, LL.D., 1791.

Rev. J. Drake, D.D., held the living in 1814.

Rev. John Drake, B.C.L., held the living in 1835.

Rev. Alexander Everingham Sketchley, D.D., of Magdalen Hall, Oxford, was ordained deacon by the Bishop of London in 1828, and priest by the Bishop of Lincoln in 1830. He took his degree of B.A. in 1828, M.A. in 1831, and B.D. and D.D. in 1849. He was Curate of Amersham, Bucks. until his appointment to the Vicarage of St. Nicholas in 1836, which he held until his death, October 6th, 1874. Dr. Sketchley resided in his parish during his incumbency, in the house now occupied by Mr. Richard Trickett, and was much respected.

Rev. John Robert Gregg, M.A., Trinity College, Dublin, was ordained deacon in 1854, and priest in 1855 by the Bishop of Lichfield. His first curacy was at Burton-on-Trent, Staffordshire, from whence he removed successively to St. Lawrence's, Reading; Sandon, Essex; and North Cerney, Circencester, 1866, which latter he held till his appointment to St. Nicholas, Deptford, in 1875. Mr. Gregg (who had but recently returned from a voyage to the Cape of Good Hope, ordered by his physician for the benefit of his health) died somewhat suddenly whilst his family were at church on Sunday, June 11th, 1882, and was buried on the following Friday in Nunhead Cemetery, much regretted by his parishioners. Mr. Gregg was a son of the late Bishop of Cork.

Rev. Joseph Marychurch Vaughan, Theol. Assoc., Trinity Hall, Cambridge, and King's College, London, was ordained deacon by the Bishop of Rochester in 1859, and priest by the Bishop of Ely in 1860. He was curate of Shildon, Durham, from 1859 to 1865; St. George's-in-the-East, London, 1865 to 1869.

He was Chaplain of the Union of St. George's-in-the-East, 1870, and vicar of St. John the Evangelist, St. George's-in-the-East, from 1869 to 1879. For a short period he was Rector of Englishcombe, near Bath, which he resigned on his appointment to the Vicarage of St. Nicholas.

MONUMENTS.

The oldest recorded monument in this church is given by Weever in his "Funeral Monuments," A.D., 1631; the inscription at that date being scarcely legible :—

"Orate pro Anima . . . . Weuer . . . mercatoris et Maioris Stapul.—Ville Calcis qui ob . . . . Februar . . . et pro . . . Joanna x.u. eius, qui ob . . . .

of which he says, ,"Martin the fifth, Bishop of Rome, (who held the Papacy from A.D., 1417 to 1424)," granted by Bull to these Staple merchants, in this Weever's Maioralty at their earnest request, an itinerarie or portable Aulter, which they were to take with them to what place soever they travelled to make any time of aboad ; and with all gave them licence to elect a Priest to say Masse, administer the sacraments, to heare their confessions, to enjoyne them penance, and to give them absolution as the cause should require. The forme of which I hold it, not much amisse here to set down, as I found it in an old M.S. without name or date, in the Earl of Excester's Librarie."

"The ready merchant runs to th' utmost Inde with speed.
By sea, by rocks, by fire, to shun outrageous need."

Horace, Epist. lib. I, *Ep.* I.

On the south side is a grave stone on which were the effigies of a man and woman in brass. The inscription is now gone (in 1766), but is preserved in Weever as follows :—

"𝔒𝔯𝔞𝔱𝔮 𝔭𝔯𝔬 𝔞𝔫𝔦𝔪𝔞𝔟𝔲𝔰 𝔍𝔬𝔥𝔞𝔫𝔫𝔦𝔰 𝔓𝔢𝔩𝔩𝔮, 𝔞𝔫𝔡 ℭ𝔥𝔯𝔦𝔰𝔱𝔦𝔞𝔫𝔮 𝔲𝔵𝔬𝔯𝔦𝔰 𝔢𝔧𝔲𝔰; 𝔮𝔱 𝔍𝔬𝔥𝔞𝔫𝔫𝔦𝔰 𝔓𝔢𝔩𝔩𝔢, 𝔢𝔱 𝔄𝔩𝔦𝔮𝔦𝔢, 𝔢𝔱 𝔗𝔥𝔬𝔪𝔢 𝔓𝔥𝔦𝔩𝔦𝔭𝔬𝔱, 𝔞𝔮 𝔭𝔞𝔯𝔮𝔫𝔱𝔲𝔪 𝔪𝔢𝔬𝔯𝔲𝔪 . . . ."

On a grave stone within the rails were the effigies of a man and woman in brass, with this inscription in Roman capitals :—

Here lyeth buried Jacob Verzelini, esquire, borne in the citie of Venice, and Elizabeth, his wife, borne in Antwerpe, of the Auncient houses of Vanburen and Maes, who having lived together in holye state of matrimonie fortie nyne yeares and fower moneths, departed this life ; the said Jacob, the twentye day of January, anno domini 1606, aged LXXXIIII yeares ; and the sayd Elizabeth, the XXVI. daye of October, anno domini, 1607, aged LXXIII. yeares ; and rest in hope of resurrexion of life eternal.

Beneath are the portraitures of six sons and three daughters. Above the figures are two escutcheons in brass, viz : 1st Coat. Two battle axes in saltier, in chief a helmet. 2nd Coat, Quarterly, 1st Three frame saws. 2nd Two cinque foils, a canton charged with an hour glass. 3rd as the 2nd ; 4th as the 1st. Beneath is another escutcheon, viz., Verzelini, impaling as above.

On a mural monument of Alabaster in Roman capitals.

Monumentum hoc, omnes qui aspexerint inclyti viri Petri Pett, armigeri, famam et laudes benigne audiant. Dic igitur, lapis ; ex his enim tu literis et tanti viri historia, vitam adeptus in multa durabis sæcula, dic cujus sacra ossa juxta te tam quiete custodiuntur illius ;

scilicet qui fuit patriæ suæ decus, patriæ suæ magnum
munimetum ; quippe qui non solum naticam nostram
restituit rem, verum illud eximium et novum navigij
ornamentum, quod nostri frigatum nuncupant, hostibus
formidolosum, suis utilissimum atque tutissimum primus
invenit ; qui archinaupegi munus per viginti et tres
annos tanta cum fide et solertia gessit, ut hinc plane
appareret, se non suum sed bonum publicum corde
habiusse, justus sane vir evit, et sui sæculi Noah ; qui
postquam cum Deo ambulavit, et supradictam illius
inventionem in lucem protulit (que fuit arcæ instar, unde
nostrum maris dominum uraque nostra e naufragio pene
erapta sunt) evocatus fuit ex hujus mundi tempestatibus,
Deo gubernante, atque an. M. illius in Salvatoris sui
gremio tanquam in gloriæ arca reposita. Obijt vero
Julü 31° ætatis suæ anno 60° post Redemptoris nostri
nativitatem, 1652.

EPITAPHIUM.

Quantum antiqua viris tribuerunt tempora magnis,
Utile qui patriæ attulerint vel nobile quicquam ;
Tantum hanc ætatem tibi, Pette. rependere oportet.
Ergo inter veteres tu collaudabere semper ;
Namque tibi hoc proprium est, retro ut tua fama recurrat
Laudibus atque vovis priscorum jungat honores.

Translation.—" Let all who see this monument listen
kindly to the praise of that illustrious man, Peter Pett,
Esquire. Speak, then, stone, who hast won long centuries
of existence from this inscription and the history of so
great a man, speak, and say whose sacred bones so quietly
repose hard by. One who was the glory and bulwark of
his country ; one who not only restored the efficiency of
our navy, but first invented that new and brilliant
addition to it which is called a frigate, so formidable to
our enemies, so useful to ourselves, and so safe an instru-
ment of naval war ; one who for twenty-three years filled
the post of master shipbuilder with such fidelity and
industry as to make it evident that he had in his heart
only the public good and not his own. He was truly a
just man, the Noah of his age, who, after he had walked
with God and brought to light the above-mentioned

invention—which was an ark for the preservation of our
naval supremacy and our land were almost saved from
shipwreck—was called from the tempests of this world by
the ordinance of God, and placed in his Saviour's arms as
in an ark of glory. He died July 31, in the 60th year
of his age, of the nativity of our Redeemer, 1652."

EPITAPH.

Whatever praise the ancient ages gave
To those who could their country serve or save ;
Such praises Pett, this age should give to thee ;
'Mongst ancient worthies thou shalt lauded be.
Thy honors backward run, and add thy name
To th' roll of heroes in an equal fame.

*Beneath is the model of a frigate well expressed in alto
relievo ; on the top of the monument are these arms, viz. :
Or on a fesse gules a lion rampant, Or between three
pellets, Crest a pelican Or, vulned proper.*

On a mural monument of alabaster in gilt letters :—

"M. S. Prope hanc parietem deposuit exuvias carnis
Jo. Turner, armiger navis cui titulus Eboracum, nuper
Strategus, Thomæ Turner & Elizabethæ uxoris ejus,
unicæ filiæ and hæredis Johannis Holmden, militis, filius
natu secundus ; illibatæ fidelitatis erga regem infractus
assecla intemerati erga parentes obsequij ingens sym-
bolum, amicis suada et lenocimo calami, quam apprime
gratus, et in omnes alios facinis et urbanis. Qui cum in
utroque bello Batavico & contra prædones Algerinos
strenuam navaverat operam, causo correptus et eodom
denuo confectus et opressus fortissimam animam Deo
transmisit. 1672 ætatis, suæ 27."

Beneath on a tablet is the following in Roman
capitals :—

Quem non Turca domat, non Belga ferocior illo
  Turpitur, imbellis mors, sine cæde rapis ;
Nilausa in gladio accintum, nec territa navim
  Conscendis tacitum tutior usque forum.
Cur injuste negas meritum virtutis honorem,
  Cum tibi tot Batavas sæpelitavit, apros ?
Pro rege et patria vixit, pugnavit, ovavit ;
  Quam cuperet fortis sic licuisse mori ?

L

On the top of the monument are the arms, viz. : Sable, a fesse between two chevrons ermine.   Crest, a leopard's head erased Or, and spotted azure.

Translation.—Close to this wall are laid the mortal remains of John Turner, Esquire, Captain of H.M. ship "York." He was the second son of Thomas Turner and his wife Elizabeth, only daughter and heiress of Sir John Holmden, Knight.   Firm in his fidelity to his King, a remarkable model of unfailing respect and obedience to his parents, and greatly endeared to his friends by the exquisite charm of his correspondence, kind and courteous to all, after good and active service in both the Dutch wars, and against the Algerine pirates, he was seized with sunstroke, and after severe illness yielded his brave soul into the hands of God, 1672, in the 27th year of his age.

> Whom Turk, nor Belgian fiercer still, could tame
>   Unworthy of his fame
> Unarmed death ! thou mad'st an easy prey,
>   Thou did'st not dare to slay
> The chief with sword in hand, nor board his bark,
>   But with thy mandate dark
> Didst hale him all unconscious to his fate.
>   Why thus unjust, abate
> His honours due, who on Batavia's soil
>   Gave thee so rich a spoil ?
> For country and for King, as warriors ought
>   He lived, he prayed, he fought
> Alone unblest, that for his country's good
>   He might not shed his blood.

On a small monument of Alabaster, is represented in curious sculpture, a man kneeling at a desk in the dress of the times, with an angel holding aside a curtain ; in the back ground is a view of a naval engagement.   Beneath on two tablets of black marble, are the following inscriptions in gilt Roman capitals :—

M.S.,H.S.E., Rogerus Boyle, Richardi comitis corcagiensis filius primogenitus, qui in Hibernia natus, in Cantio solo patris natali denatus, dum hic ingenii cultum capessit.   Puer eximiæ indolis, præcocitatem ingenii

funere luit immaturo ; sic luculenti, sed terreni patri-
monii factus exhæres, cœlestem crevit hæreditatem,
Decessit, A.D. 1617, IV. die., VIII. bris.

Death.—Richardus prænobilis comes corcagiensis,
uxoris suæ patruo.

B.M.P., Memoriæ perenni Edwardi Fenton, reginæ
Elizabethæ, olim pro corpore armigeri, Jano O-Neal,
ac, post eum, comite Desmoniæ, in Hibernia turbantibus,
fortissimi taxiarchi ; qui, post lustratum, improbo ausu,
Septentrionalis plagæ apocryphum mare, et excussas
varüs peregrinationibus inertis naturæ latebras, anno
1588, in celebri contra Hispanos naumachia, meruit navis
prætoriæ navarchus. Obiit Anno Domini 1603.

> Cognatos cineres & amicam manibus umbram,
> O Fentone, tuis, excipias tumulo.
> Usurum tumuli victuro marmore pensat,
> Et red lit gratus, pro tumulo, titulum.

Translation.—Here is laid Roger Boyle, eldest son of
Richard, Earl of Cork, who was born in Ireland, and
died while pursuing his studies in Kent, his father's
native place. He was a boy of unusual intelligence,
and paying for his too rapid proficiency in study by an
early death, lost a splendid inheritance on earth to
obtain a still nobler one in heaven. He died October
12th, 1617. Richard Earl of Cork erected this monument to the uncle of his wife.

This monument is placed to the perpetual memory of
Edward Fenton, formerly Esquire of the body to Queen
Elizabeth, and who afterwards served with great distinction as Brigadier in the civil commotions occasioned by
Shane O'Neil and afterwards by the Earl of Desmond,
in Ireland. He subsequently undertook many bold and
adventurous voyages in the then unknown regions of
the North Seas, where he made many valuable additions
to our geographical knowledge of countries in that
portion of the globe. Finally he commanded the
Admiral's flagship in the famous naval engagement
against the Spanish Armada. He died A.D. 1603.

L2

'Mid kindred dust, Fenton, we lay thee down,
Where kindred shades shall greet thy high renown.
Not that the living marble shall set forth
To future times a soldier's, sailor's worth ;
Recorded but the line " Here Fenton lies "
Shall living marble's self " immortalize."

Above are the following arms : viz., 1st Coat, Parted per bend embattled, argent and gules, a label of three points sable. 2nd parted per bend embattled, argent and gules, a crescent for a difference. 3rd as above, impaling argent, a cross sable between four fleur de lis of the second. 4th argent, a cross sable, between four fleur de lis of the second. 5th as above, impaling argent, three bends wavy sable, each charged with three besants on a chief gules.

On a neat mural monument of white marble—

Near this place lieth the body of Ann, wife of Thomas South, Esq., of Deptford, who died the 15th day of May, anno domini 1732. Ætatis 24.

Also Ann, daughter of the above Ann South, who died the 8th of April, 1748. Ætatis 17.

Above are these arms, viz. : Argent three staples sable, impaling gules. On a bend argent three choughs proper, membered and beaked gules.

Thomas Turner, gent, obiit September, anno domini 1671. Elizabeth his wife, daughter of Holmden, obiit November the 19th, anno 1685.

Above is an achievment with these arms, viz.: Sable, a chevron ermine, between three fer de molines Or, on a chief argent a lion passant gules impaling sable, a fesse between two chevrons ermine. Crest, a lion passant gules, in his paw a branch vert.

On a mural monument of grey marble is the following inscription :—

"Neere this place is interred the body of Jonas Shish, Esq., Master Shipwright to King Charles the 2nd of his Majesties yards Deepford and Woolwich, who departed this life May the 7th, 1680, in the 75th yeare of his age, and in his last sickness did appoint his epitaph in words. to this effect.

"By sin I die, the wages due to all.
By sin, as I, the universe must fall ;
Yet, holy Jesus, bring me to the throne
Of heavenly bliss, where God doth rule alone ;
That I may sacred anthems always sing,
With holy angels to their sovraign King.
Once I was strong, but am intombed now
To be dissolved to dust, and so must you
In health remember still thy latter end
That will *beget* a care nere to offend."

Here also lyeth the body of Elizabeth his wife, who departed this life the 5th of March, 1678, in the 59th yeare of her age, together with eight children and twelve grandchildren, leaving behind them three sons and three daughters."

"Also John the eldest son, Master Shipwright of his Majesties yard of Deptford, obijt October 16th, 1686, aged 43 years ; and Thomas the third son Master Shipwright of his Majesties yard of Woolwich, obiit December the 6th, 1685, aged 37 years ; and Kendrick, the son of John and Marie Shish, who deceased . . . Aged 14 years.

On the top of the monument were these arms, viz. : Argent, three bars wavy azure, on a chief gules, an axe between two anchors Or in pale. Beneath was another coat, viz. : Azure on a sea vert the hull of a ship argent on a chief, argent, a cross gules, charged with a lion passant argent.

On a neat mural monnment of white marble.

In memory of William Boulter, Esq., who dyed the 4th day of January, anno domini, 1714. In memory of Richard Wilkinson, Esq., grandson of William Boulter, Esq., who died the 9th day of December, 1725, aged 28 years.

Above are these arms, viz.: 1st *Party per chevron, gules and argent, two mullets in Chief Or. 2nd Argent, on a chevron gules three dead men's skulls of the first, impaling gules, a fesse varry, argent and azure, in chief an unicorn between two mullets Or.*

On an achievement are these arms in a lozenge, viz.: Quarterly, 1st *Argent, on a fesse counter—embattled sable three escallops argent, a canton, gules and azure charged with a leopard's head Or. 2nd sable, on a fesse nebule argent gutte de sang, between three elephants' heads couped Or. 3rd as the 2nd. 4th as the 1st.*

And beneath is this inscription :—Near this place lyes the body of Mrs. Jane Netmaker; obiit 16th January, 1712. Ætat 70.

On an achievement are these arms, viz.: Quarterly of two coats ; 1st *Argent, a lion rampant gules, between nine pheons sable. 2nd Argent, two lions rampant sable, on a chief of the second, three covered cups Or. 3rd as the 2nd. 4th as the 1st, impaling Or, a lion rampant gules, within a border invected of the 2nd. Crest, a lion rampant gules, holding a bow and arrow.*

And beneath is this inscription :—

"In the middle isle lies interred the body of Sarah the eldest daughter of and co-heiress to George Pomeroy, Esq. ; deceased (late commander of the Katherine yatch) and wife of Nicholas Roope. Esq. ; storekeeper of his Majesty's yard at Sheerness, and son of the late Nicholas Roope of Rotherhith, Esq. She died July 16th, 1742, aged near 30 years, with a most deserving and amiable character ; and had six children by her said husband, but left only one of them living ; viz Mary Pomeroy Roope, born and christened so in July 1736, and is likely to inherit all her said mother's singular virtues."

On a mural monument of white marble :—

"Near this place lyes interred the body of Robert Castell, late of this parish, gent. who lived beloved and

died lamented by all good men, but most by his sorrowful widow Mrs. Margeret Castell, who erected this
monument to his memory, though he himself hath left
behind much better and more lasting monuments ; such
were his piety towards God, affection to the established
Church, loyalty to his king, justice in his dealings,
hospitality to his neighbours, bounty and compassion to
the poor, fidelity to his friends, kindnesse and fatherly
care for his relatives, his considerable benefactions to this
parish, and particularly his zeal and generous contributions for the rebuilding and adorning this church, which
ought to be recorded here in justice to the dead, but
chiefly for the imitation of the living, that they may find
comfort in their deaths, when they shall depart this life,
as he did on the fourteenth day of August, 1698, and in
the sixty-fifth year of his age."

*On the top of the monument are these arms, viz.:
Argent. three castles gules. Crest, on a helmet a castle
argent. Beneath is another coat, viz.:—Sable three
salmons haurient argent, impaling Argent, a chevron
gules, between three cormorants sable.*

On a neat monument of white marble :—

" R. Evelyn, J.F. Quiescit hoc sub marmore una
quiescit quicquid est amabile, patres quod optent, aut
quod orbi lugeant genas decentes non, ut, ante, risus
lepore condit amplius ; morum venustas, quanta paucis
contigit desideratur omnibus ; linguæ Latinæ, Gallica,
quas imbibit cum lacte materno, tacent ; tentarat artes,
artiumque principijs, pietatis elementa hauserat ; libris
inhæsit improbo labore ut sola mors divelleret ; quid
indoles, quid disciplina, quid labor possint, ab uno
disceres. Puer stupendus, qualis hic esset senex si fata
vitæ subministrassent iter ! set aliter est visum Deo ;
correptus ille febricula levi jacet, jacent tot una spes
parentum, Vixit Ann V. M. VIII. super D. Ehew !
delicias breves, quicquid placet mortale, ne placet nimis.'

Translation :—" R. son of John Evelyn, rests under this stone ; and with him rests everything that father's love can cherish, and lament when deprived of. The fair face no longer, as of old, bright with the smile of intelligence ; the unusual grace of manner which few can attain, which all who knew him will miss ; the simple talk in French or Latin languages which he took in with his mother's milk—all silent now. He had begun the study of the arts, and with the principles of the arts had learnt those of piety as well ; and was so fond of his books that only death could tear him from them. His example showed how much natural quickness, discipline, and labor, when united, could achieve. Marvellous as a child, what would he have been when old, had fate allowed him length of life ? But God decreed otherwise. A slight fever carried him off after he had lived five years, eight months, and a few days. He was the only child of his parents, and alas ! how brief was their enjoyment ! What mortals love, let them beware never to love too well."

Mary Evelyn, eldest daughter of John Evelyn, and Mary his wife, borne the last day of September, 1665, at Wooton, in the County of Surrey ; a beautiful young woman, endowed with shining qualities both of body and mind, infinitely pious, the delight of her parents and friends. She died the 17th of March, 1685, at the age of nineteen years, five months, seventeen days, regretted by all persons of worth that knew her value.

Above are these arms, viz.:—*Quarterly of two coats ; 1st Azure, a griffin passant Or, a chief of the second. 2nd Or, a chief sable. 3rd as the 2nd. 4th as the 1st.*

On a mural monument of white marble :—

M. S. Neer this place are deposited the bodies of Sir Richard Browne, of Sayes Court, in Deptford, Knight, and his wife dame Joanna Vigorus, of Langham in Essex, deceased in November 1618, aged 74 years. This Sir Richard was younger son of an ancient family at Hitchin in Suffolk, seated afterwards at Horsley in Essex ; who being student in the Temple, was by Robert Dudley, the great Earl of Leicester, taken into the service of the Crown, when he went governour of the United Netherlands ; and was afterwards by Queen Elizabeth made clerk of the green cloth ; in which honourable office he also continued under King James until the time of his death, May 1604, aged 65 years.

Of Christopher Browne, Esq., son and heir of Sir Richard, who deceased in March, 1645, aged 70 years.

Of Thomazine, his wife, daughter of Benjamin Gonson, of Much Baddow in Essex, Esq ; whose grandfather William Gonson and father Benjamin, were successively treasurers of the Navy to King Henry VIII, to King Edward VI., to Queen Mary and Queen Elizabeth, and died June, 1638, aged 75 years.

Of Sir Richard Browne, Knight and Baronet, only son of Christopher.

Of his wife dame Elizabeth, daughter of Sir John Prettyman of Dryfield in Gloucestershire, who deceased vi. of October 1652 aged 42 years. This Sir Richard was gentleman of the privy chamber to King Charles I. and clerk of the Council to his Majesty, and to King Charles II. and, after several foreign and honourable employments, continued resident in the Court of France, from King Charles I. and from King Charles II. to the French Kings Lewis XIII. and Lewis XIV. from the year 1641 until the happy restoration of King Charles II. anno 1660. deceased 12th of February 1682-3. aged 78 years ; and (according to antient custome) will'd to be interred in this place. These all deceasing in the true faith of Christ, hope through his merits for a joyfull and blessed resurrection. This table was erected by John Evelyn, of Says Court, Esq. ; who married Mary, sole daughter and heir of Sir Richard.

Above are these arms, viz.:—Quarterly 1st Or, a chief azure. 2nd Gules, a griffin passant Or, a chief of the second. 3rd Argent, a fret gules. 4th Quarterly, indented Or and gules.

At the upper end of the sou h side is thus written :—

Sacræ perpetuæque memoriæ Gulielmi Haukyns de Plimouth, armigeri ; qui veræ religionis verus cultor, pauperibus præcipue navicularij munificus, louginquas instituit sæpe navigationes ; arbiter in causes difficillimis æquissimus, fide, probitate, & prudentia singulari. Duas duxit uxores, e quarum una 4, ex altera 7 suscepit liberos. Johannes Haykins, eques auratus, classis regiæ qvæstor, frater mœstissimus posuit. Obijt spe certa resurgendi 7 die mensis Octobris, anno domini 1589.

———

"Near this place lyeth interred the body of Mr. Thomas Shish, late master shipwright of his Majesties yard at Woolwich, who dyed the 6th of December, 1685, leaving behind him his wife, three sons, and two daughters.

Above is an achievement with these arms, viz.:—Argent, three bars wavy azure, on a chief gules an axe, between two anchors, Or in pale, impaling argent, a chevron gules, between three helmets sable. Crest. Or a naval crown, a demi lion rampant gules, holding an anchor, Or.

Against the east wall of the chancel, on the outside, is a tablet to the memory of Susanna, wife of Captain George Shelvocke, 1711. Near it is the tomb of her husband.

Inscription :—" Here lyeth the body of Captain George Shelvocke, descended of an ancient family in Shropshire ; but long an inhabitant of this town. He was bred to the sea service, under Admiral Benbow, and served on board of the Royal Navy in the wars of King William and Queen Anne. In the years of our Lord 1719, 20, 21, 22, he performed a voyage round the world, which he, most wonderfully, and to the great loss of the Spaniards, completed, though in the midst of it he had the misfortune to suffer shipwreck, upon the Island of Juan Fernandez, on the coast of the Kingdom of Chili. He was a gentleman of great abilities in his profession and allowed to have been one of the bravest and most accomplished seamen of his time. He departed this life in London,

November 30th, 1742, in the 67th year of his age. He married Susanna, daughter of Captain Richard Strutton, who died in 1711."

On the north side of the Church.

" Sacred to the memory of George Shelvocke, Esq., late Secretary of the General Post Office and F.R.S., who at a very early period of life attended his father, Captain George Shelvocke, in a voyage round the world ; during the course of which he remarkably experienced the wonderful protection of Divine Providence, and ever retained a grateful remembrance thereof. In his life, he was most amiable ; in his death he is most lamented ; in him , his kindred regret the greatest ornament, his acquaintance their best companion, his intimates their dearest friend. Learned, without pride, pious, without ostentation, he fulfilled the duties of his office with the utmost integrity, and shewed the goodness of his heart in repeated acts of benevolence. He died the 12th of March, 1760, aged 58 years ; and is buried with his father."

This monument is erected by the particular desire of his widow, who did not long survive him.

These ancient monumental inscriptions—many of which seem to have disappeared when the church was rebuilt— have been copied from Thorpe's " Registram Roffense."

The Parish Registers, dating from 1561, contain some highly interesting information.

Extracts :—" 1st June, 1593, Christopher Marlowe, slaine by Francis Archer."

" Richard, son of Mr. John Wells, Paymaster of his Majesties Navy, baptized August 18th, 1619."

John Wells, who was afterwards Treasurer of the Stores, distinguished himself as a mathematician, and published a treatise on " Shadows." He was buried at Deptford. December 7th, 1635. His son Benjamin, of All Souls, Oxon, was an eminent physician, and published a treatise on the Gout. He died at Greenwich.

"Anne, daughter of Sir William Russell—created a baronet in 1628—Treasurer of the Navy, baptized July 5th, 1519 ; Gerard, son, June 13th, 1620 ; Edward, June 8th, 1621 ; Robert, September 10th, 1622 ; John, buried May 31st, 1624 ; Mr. Edward Lukenor, and Mrs. Elizabeth Russell (daughter of Sir William), married November 1st, 1663 ; Thomas Chichley, Gent., and Mrs. Sarah Russell, married August 13th, 1655 ; John Bodville, Esq., and Mrs. Anne Russell, married September 11th, 1638."

"William Shewers, and John Finicho, two children, who, playing together, shut themselves into a hutch and were smothered, buried August 26th, 1631."

"Mr. Ephraim Paget, buried October 27th, 1646." He was rector of St. Edmund's, Lombard-street, and the author of a description of the sundry sorts of Christians not subject to the Pope ; and an account of the heresies of later times. .

"Captain Thomas Pearse and Lieutenant Logan, shot to death for losing the Saphire cowardly ; buried August the 26th, 1670."

"Rebecca, Sarah and Rachel, daughters of Edward Rippington, baptized August 5th, 1688." It appears that these triplets all lived and that the mother recovered.

"Richard, Ellis, and Saul, children of John Powell, mariner, baptized November 28th, 1738." They were all buried December 14th.   "

"Anne Bland, widow, who was the mother of twenty-five children born of· her body, aged 80, having at that date fifteen sons in his Majesty's Army, from a cellar in Butt-lane, buried January 9th, 1710-1."

"October, 1727. Gave for the relief of John Butler, with a permit Pass from Somersetshire for himself, his mother, and two children more, (his Father being Rob'd and Murther'd, and afterwards his house set on fire by ye Rogues that Rob'd him, who also cut and burnt the fflesh of several of the ffamily to make them confess where the money was laid, 3s. od."

"February, 1747. Gave Susannah Brock to ffetch her shoes out of pawn, 1s. od."

A line starting from the middle of the River Thames, passing up the centre of Deptford Creek to a short distance above Creek Bridge ; thence across to the boundary stone inserted in the wall in front of the new houses erected on the site of the Trinity Hospital ; through the centre of the following streets, viz. : Church-street, Union-street, High-street, Old King-street, Dock-street, Prince-street, Evelyn-street, Albert-street, Victoria-road, and across the Victualling yard to the centre of the Thames, and following the stream to the starting point, forms the boundary of St. Nicholas' Parish.

St. Paul's Church.

"May the Banner of Peace and Concord wave for ever on the Standard of St. Paul."—*Mr. Marchant's Address, Nov. 7th, 1825.*

AN Act of Parliament was passed in 1729, 3rd George II., c. 33, authorising the formation of the new district parish of St. Paul, Deptford, and providing for the maintenance of the minister of the new church erected— between Church Street and Butt Lane (High Street)— out of the public bounty, under the Acts passed in the years IX and X of Queen Anne, for the building of fifty new churches in or near London. The Church, which was consecrated by the Right Rev. Edward, Lord Bishop of London, June 30th, 1730, is a handsome stone structure, consisting of a small apsidal chancel, nave and two aisles, supported by Corinthian columns ; being surrounded on three sides by deep galleries. The pews are of Dutch oak. In the central window of the chancel is a fine representation of the patron saint of the Church —St. Paul—in stained glass. Two chairs within the sanctuary were presented by the celebrated Dr. Burney. At the west end is a tapering spire of some beauty, partially supported by massive pillars ; the west end being approached by a semi-circular flight of steps. It is currently reported that all the stones used in the construction of the Church were dressed at Portland, prior to their transportation here. There are sittings for 1,300 persons, 300 of which are free.

According to an advertisement of November 14th, 1843, announcing the sale of the advowson, the living is given thus :—Interest arising from South Sea 3 p.c. stock £101 2s. 8d. ; surplice and other fees, £173 ; rental of vaults, regularly paid by the Churchwardens. £70 ; and rents of pews, £25. According to Crockford and Mackesson the living is now worth £450 per annum.

MONUMENTS.

On the south side of the chancel is a monument to the memory of Dr. Charles Burney, with a bas-relief bust of the great bibliopholist, the inscription on which will be found in his memoir. This monument was erected by his parishioners :—

On the north side is a monument by Nollekens.

"In memory of James Sayer, Esq., Vice-Admiral of the White, son of John Sayer, Esq., and Katherine, his wife, one of the daughters, and co-heiress of Rear-Admiral Robert Hughes, and Lydia, his wife, who all lie buried in the old Church of this town, with many of their issue. He was a man of the strictest honour and integrity ; an active and diligent officer. In the war of 1739 he had the thanks of the Assembly of Barbadoes for his disinterested conduct in the protection of their trade ; and he first planted the British standard in the Island of Tobago. In the war of 1756 he led the attacks both at the taking of Senegal and Goree ; and was Commander-in-Chief off the French coast at Belle Isle, at the time of making the peace in 1763. As his life was most exemplary, he met death with a becoming fortitude, after a tedious and most painful illness, on the 29th of October, 1776, aged 56 years." Arms. Quarterly 1st and 4th Gules, a chevron between three sea-pies, Argent, Sayer, 2nd and 3rd Azure, a lion rampant, Or. Hughes.

On the north side of the Chancel is a sumptuous monument, before which are several steps of black marble inclosed with iron rails. On a sarcophagus is a large urn of statuary marble, in part covered with a mantle; and on the front of the base is the following inscription:—

"Underneath this place lyes the body of Mathew Finch of this parish, gent., who departed this life the 20th of March, 1745, aged 70.
Also the body of Mr. Benjamin Finch, brother of the above-said.

Above the urn, on a back ground of dove-colour marble, are these arms, viz.:—Argent, a chevron between three griffins passant, sable.

On the north side of the Chancel is a large and beautiful monument with an urn of Silician marble, incircled with a festoon of flowers in statuary; and underneath is this inscription:—

"M.S.—Mariæ, filiæ Benjaminis et Saræ Finch, Richardi Hanwell, decivitate Oxon, generosi, conjugis optime meritæ, marito placidæ et amantissimæ, parentibus morigræ, et omnibus jucundæ, quæ, terra relicta, die decimo quinto Novembris, anno domini M.DCC.LIV, et ætatis suæ vicesimo quinto, ad cœlum migravit; quo Maria, filiola ejus recens nata, paucos tantum dies præcesserat."

Translation.—"Sacred to the memory of Mary, daughter of Benjamin and Sarah Finch, and the excellent wife of Richard Hanwell, gentleman of the city of Oxford. She was a loving wife, a dutiful daughter, and an affectionate friend to all around her. She left this world for heaven, November 15th, 1754, in the 25th year of her age, her daughter, Mary, an infant newly born, having preceded her only a few days."

In the Churchyard—which has recently been planted with trees and evergreens by the Burial Board, and made to appear as " God's Acre " should be : a place of beauty —there are many noteworthy tombstones, amongst which may be mentioned :—

Martha, wife of Richard Leake, Esq. (son of Sir John Leake, 1732.

Elizabeth Blake (sister of Richard Leake, 1734).

Thomas Hawtree, aged 95, 1757, and Margaret, his wife, 1734. This stone contained the following epitaph :—

> " She was an indulgent mother, and the best of wives,
> She brought into the world more than three thousand lives."

Lysons says the explanation of this is that she was an eminent midwife, and that she evinced the interest she took in her calling by giving a silver basin for christenings to each parish church.

Thomas Stanton, Esq., 1762.

Mrs. Jane Susanna Desboro, 1766.

John Paul Elers Scott, M.A., 1777.

Captain Stephen Dryden, 1779.

Mr. Archibald Hutton, 1780.

John Barron, Esq., of Woolacre, in this parish, 1786.

Richard Conyers, LL.D., rector, 1786, with the following inscription now illegible :—

" Here is deposited the mortal part of Richard Conyers, LL.D., ten years Rector of this Parish. In his ministry, with singular wisdom and simplicity, with equal fidelity and tenderness. He most successfully displayed and enforced the glorious gospel of the Lord Jesus Christ. his God and Saviour ; and the tendency, and power of it, exemplified in his master's work on the Lord's Day, the 23rd of April, 1786 Ætat 62.

> He was suddenly called away,
> To behold his glory.
> Blessed is that Servant,
> Whom his Lord, when he cometh
> Shall find so doing.

> Sent by the Lord on purposes of grace,
> Thus Angels do His will and see His face,
> With outspread wings they stand, prepared to soar
> Declare their message, and are seen no more.

PECCAVI.

| Resipui. | — | Confidi. |
| Amavi. | — | Requiesco. |

Resurgam.

Ft, ex gratia Christi,

Ut ut indignus,

Regnabo.

Thomas Mitchell, Esq., Assistant Surveyor of the Navy 1790.

Thomas Hicks Esq., 1795.

Mr. Isaac Blight with this inscription :—

"This tomb was erected to perpetuate the memory of Mr. Isaac Blight, who was inhumanely shot in his own house at Rotherhithe, by the hand of a perfidious domestic, the 23rd day of September, 1805, in the 49th year of his age.

> "Have you not seen beneath a darken'd sky,
> Quicker than thought, the vivid lightning fly;
> Equally swift was the invidious blow,
> That pierced my heart and laid my head thus low;
> Merciful God! thou glorious God of heaven,
> Forgive the deed, and may I be forgiven."

Mr. Blight, a ship breaker of Greenland Dock, was killed by a pistol shot, as he was sleeping in his chair in the back parlour. Richard Patch who had been taken into the employment of the deceased, out of motives of charity, about three years before, and was his confidential servant, was tried on suspicion of the murder, convicted upon a chain of the most satisfactory evidence and executed on the 18th April, 1806. Tne culprit's trial and execution excited for some time an uncommon degree of interest.

———

RECTORS.

Rev. William Norton, D.D., Vicar of St. Nicholas, who died May 21st, 1731, was the first Rector.

Rev. James Bate, B.D., 1731, died September 28th, 1775. He was the eldest son of the Rev. James

M

Bate, M.A., Vicar of Chilham, Kent, and published a work called "A Rationale of the Doctrine of Original Sin;" an address to his parishoners on the occasion of the Rebellion in 1745; several sermons, one to the "Order of Ubiquarians in 1738, and other works.

Patron the King.

Rev. Richard Conyers LL.D., September 29th, 1775; died April 23rd, 1786. *Vide* "Parish Worthies."

Rev. John Eaton, 1798, died 19th of September, 1805.

Rev. Henry Purrier, 1809.

Rev. Charles Burney, D.D., died 28th of December, 1817. See "Parish Worthies."

Rev. George Cookson, 1818.

Rev. T. W. McGuire, B.D., died December 5th, 1833, after a protracted illness of several years.

Rev. Benjamin Sanderson Ffinch, M.A., of Trinity Coll., Cambridge, was inducted to the living in 1834. He was ordained Deacon in 1827, and priest 1828, by the Bishop of Rochester. He was likewise Lecturer of St. Paul's, Deptford. In 1842 he was appointed Domestic Chaplain to the Earl of Buchan; and Chaplain to the Trinity House in 1847. Mr. Ffinch who belonged to a Deptford family, was a gentleman of a genial disposition, and much respected by his parishioners and townsmen.

Rev. Frank Owen, M.A., of Trinity College, Dublin, inducted in 1874, and exchanged in September, 1881, with the Rev. Dr. Cundy for the rectory of Miserden. Mr. Owen was ordained Deacon by the Bishop of Winchester for the Bishop of Worcester in 1851; priest by the Bishop of Worcester in 1852. He was Curate of St. Martin's, Birmingham, from 1851 to 1853; St Stephen, the Martyr, Marylebone, from 1853 to 1863; Rector of Dunmore East, Ireland from 1864 to 1872, and Vicar of Christ Church, Nailsea, from 1872 to 1874.

Rev. Henry George Cundy, D.D., of St. Mary Hall, Oxford, the present Rector, was ordained Deacon by the Bishop of Oxford in 1865, and priest by the same prelate in 1866. He took his degree of B.A. in 1865 ; M.A. in 1868 ; B.D. in 1876 ; and D.D. in 1880. Dr. Cundy was Second Master of Christ Church Cathedral School, Oxford, and curate of St. Philip and St. James', Oxford, from 1865 to 1867 ; Professor of Classics in Queen's College, Birmingham, from 1867 to 1870 ; and Rector of Miserden, in the Diocese of Gloucester and Bristol, from 1870 to 1881. He is author of " The Baptism of Water and the Spirit ; or Baptismal Regeneration," the Doctrine of the Church of England and the Word of God ; being a reply to " The Baptism or the Spirit," by the Rev. W. W. Robinson, of Chelsea, 1867 ; " The Apostolical Succession : a sermon," 1870 ; " Members one of Another : a sermon," 1872 ; " Eschatology," 1878, and " How shall we work the new Burials Act," 1880.

———

CHURCH WORK.—St. Paul's Mission, Edward Street Schools. A childrens' service, in lieu of morning Sunday School has been held here ever since the erection of the schools, at 11.15 a.m. In January, 1878, a Friday evening service at 8 p.m. was commenced, and additional services during Lent and Advent. A Sunday evening service at 7 p.m. was begun in October, 1879, which has increased in strength and usefulness, mainly through the indefatigable zeal and untiring energy of the Honorary Lay Preacher, Frederick J. Dickinson, Esq., of 483, New Cross-road, and other laymen associated with him in the good work. The services are choral, and there is a surpliced voluntary choir of about thirty men and boys. There are no paid agencies connected with this Mission, and it is supported entirely by the offertory. A site for a new Mission Church in Edward Street. West, has just been secured at a cost of £1,100 by the Bishop

M2

of Rochester's Fund; on which one of the ten new churches to be built by the said fund, will be erected as soon as the necessary funds have been guaranteed.

Union of Church workers. This Union, of which the rector is president, was instituted September 3rd, 1874, and at the present time numbers about 50 members.

The object of this Parochial Union is to draw together more closely in the bonds of Christian fellowship, all those who are engaged in any way as Church workers in the Parish of St. Paul, Deptford. These workers may be Sunday school teachers, district visitors, superintendents of dorcas, provident, or coal societies, members of the choir, librarians, &c., the only condition of membership being a sincere desire to promote the work of the Church in St. Paul's parish, according to the opportunity and ability of each; all persons so employed being eligible as members.

A branch of the Girls' Friendly Society is in active working order. This society, which numbers about 100 members, holds weekly meetings and a monthly tea. The objects are :—

1.—To bind together in one Society, ladies as Associates, and working girls and young women as members, for mutual help (religious and secular), for sympathy and prayer.

2.—To encourage purity of life, dutifulness to parents, faithfulness to employers, and thrift.

3.—To provide the privileges of the Society for its members wherever they may be, by giving them an introduction from one Branch to another.

The hon. secretary is Miss Grant.

St. Paul's Church Institute.—A club for youths over 14 years is held at the club rooms in the rectory, High Street, under the superintendence of Messrs. Dickinson and E. Layman. Branches of the Church of England Temperance Society for Adults, with weekly meetings every Monday at the Schools, and for girls, senior boys and junior boys, with weekly meetings in the Edward Street school rooms. District Visitors' Society and Fund meets weekly during the winter months. Sunday school library. Christmas Gifts Fund. The St. Paul's Men's club meets every Monday at the Institute club room. St. Paul's Penny Bank, 400 members. Mother's meeting on Monday afternoons.

St. Paul's Rectory, a quaint old house, triangular in shape, and said to have been built from designs by Sir John Vanbrugh, after being unoccupied as a residence for some time was sold July 10th, 1882, for £1,500.

St. James', Hatcham.

THE Hatcham Church Building Committee was formed at a meeting of the inhabitants of Hatcham, on the 10th of May, 1844, at which the Rev. B. S. Ffinch, M.A., Rector of St. Paul's, Deptford, took the chair. A year elapsed before the gentlemen, who desired to promote the spiritual interests of the Hamlet, succeeded in securing this impotant step. The Rev. Augustus Kerr Bezzi Granville, M.A., undertook the charge of this, the first modern ecclesiastical division of the parish of St. Paul, Deptford, at the invitation of a Church Committee. He was licensed Minister of the District of St. James', Hatcham, July 31st, 1845; having received the Bishop's licence, to perform and celebrate Divine Service in Mr. W. J. Cormack's seed loft, on the 17th of the preceding month. This room soon filled to suffocation, and in 1846, Mr. Granville erected, what was known as the Temporary Church, costing £1000; it stood in the Old Kent Road, about the centre of St. James' Terrace, and afforded accommodation for about 700 persons. This hard-working and zealous clergyman not only defrayed the cost of this temporary building, but maintained the services in it also, at his own expense, for a period of eight years; when he was unfortunately compelled by the ground landlord, on account of a defective lease, to

remove it, at a loss of £800.   With the materials of the
Temporary Church, he helped to build the National
Schools ; the foundation stone being laid by the Right
Honourable, the Earl of Shaftesbury on the 31st of
October, 1851.   Meanwhile a temporary room—stables
in Basson-street, at the bottom of a little opening to the
right from the Old Kent Road, and a loft at the Railway
Station, were occupied till the Schools were opened and
services held in them ; with, however, but very
indifferent accommodation for little more than half of his
former congregation.   Mr. Granville laboured hard,
almost single-handed, to build his Church.   He began by
endowing it with £1500, and gave also the sum of £500
towards the building fund.   The site was purchased
from the Govenors of Christ's Hospital for £100, with
the understanding that they would return that sum, as a
grant from the Hospital, to the funds of the Church.
During the period the incumbent was labouring in the
good cause, the venerable Archdeacon Sinclair, was,
through the munificence of a private individual,
enabled to promise a grant of £1000 towards erecting
the Church, on condition that the work was commenced
within twelve months.   However, subsequently, the
Archdeacon informed the Committee that the above sum
could not be paid until sufficient funds were collected to
complete such a portion of the Church, as the Bishop
might approve for Divine Worship.   The funds
previously collected and promised, including grants from
societies, amounted to about £1500.   The estimated cost
of a portion of the Church, fitted for Divine Service, was
£4500, while that of the entire building, intended for
the accommodation of about 1100 people, was £6000.
The foundation stone was laid by the Right Honourable,
Lord Haddo, on the 1st of June, 1853 ; and the building
—which is Early English, decorated—was consecrated on
the 17th of October, 1854, by Bishop Bloomfield.   The
parsonage was built and occupied in 1856.   During Mr.
Granville's incumbency, "a simple musical service, as in
our cathedrals, was the order followed, with surpliced
choir and the offertory, usages which, if a little novel at

the time in a parish church, have since become very general and acceptable." The Church, schools and parsonage—all erected by the first incumbent—out of funds provided mainly by himself—are a fitting monument of his twenty-four years arduous labours, which form, as he himself expresses it "the chief work of my life."

The Rev. A K. B. Granville resigned about the close of 1863, having sold the patronage to R. Tooth, Esq., who appointed his brother, the Rev. Arthur Tooth, M.A., to the living. In defference to Mr. Granville's wish, we refrain from entering into a narrative of the disgraceful scenes which have given to this Church and parish, an uneviable and world-wide notoriety, and which culminated in the imprisonment of the Rev. A. Tooth, for contumacy and contempt of the Court constituted by the Public Worship Regulation Act.

Mr. Tooth was sentenced to imprisonment on the 13th of January, 1877 ; committed to Horsemonger Lane Gaol on the 22nd of the same month, and released on Saturday afternoon, February 17th, 1877.—On Sunday, 24th December, 1876, the Rev. Canon Gee, D.D., Chaplain to the Bishop of the diocese and Vicar of Abbots Langley, Herts, having been appointed by the Bishop to conduct the services during Mr. Tooth's inhibition, presented himself at the Church, where he was met by Mr. Tooth and his churchwardens, who refused to allow him to officiate. During the month of January the Church was closed for several Sundays by order of the Bishop and the then Curate-in-charge the Rev. Richard Chambers. Mr. Chambers who never actually undertook the charge was succeeded by the Rev. Benjamin Dale, who preached his first sermon on the 18th of February, 1877.

Considerable alterations were made in the Church during the incumbency of Mr. Tooth ; notably, the building of a new bapistry and sacristy ; the erection of an elaborate chancel screen, on the panels of which were painted representations of the following subjects, viz.: Vice, Virtue, Heaven, Hell, The Good Angel, The Rebel

Angel (five of them wise) and (five of them were foolish) the Parable of the Ten Virgins ; the removal of the beautiful stone pulpit ; erection of an altar in the " layde chapel," &c.   Several of the windows were filled with stained glass containing the following representations, viz. : chancel window, centre light, Our Saviour, with St. Alban, St. Mary Magdalene, St. John, St. James, St. Mary B.V. and St. Andrew, occupying the remainder lights.

East window in " ladye chapel," the Three Mary's, the B.V.M. and Child occupying the centre light.   Large window in "ladye chapel," upper lights contain—St. Agnes, St. Margaret, St. Raphael, St. Catherine, and St. Cecilia.   Lower lights—St. Lawrence, St. Paul, St. Gabriel, with scroll, " Hail, Mary," St. Peter, and St. Stephen.

In the baptistry are three small windows with two lights each, filled as follows : East window—St. Jerome and St. Bernard ; centre—St. Mary Magdalene and St. John ye Baptist ; west—Jonah and Noah.   Brasses.   1. *On south wall of chancel :* " In memory of Alexander Read, Esquire, formerly of the Madras Civil Service, and the first patron of Hatcham, who died Oct. 8th, 1849, aged 72.

" Blessed are the Pure in Heart for they shall see God."

" This tablet is erected by Ellen Elizabeth, his youngest daughter and her husband Augustus K. B. Granville, M.A., the first Incumbent."   *On the north wall of the Bapistry :* " In Memoriam, Marie Turton. Fell asleep 6th March, 1875.

R. I. P.

Another brass to the memory of some member of the Kirkland family in the " lady chapel " mysteriously disappeared some years ago.

———

CHURCH WORK.—There are in active operation in con-nection with the Church, a Penny Bank, a Coal and Clothing Club, a Children's Boot and Shoe Club, a Slate Club for men and another for women, Bible and Com-municants' Classes, a Band of Hope, a Mothers' Meeting, &c.

LIST OF VICARS.

Rev. A. K. B.Granville, from 1845 to 1863. Mr. Granville is author of the following publications, viz. : "The Divine Hymnal : A Collection of Hymns of Direct Homage for the Use of the Church ;" "The Sores of Lazarus : Five Sermons on Temporal and Spiritual Destitution ;" "The Church Renewing Her Strength, and the Blessings of the Gospel," two sermons ; "Education of the Poor," a sermon on Acts viii., 30, 31 ; "An Order of Preparation for Holy Communion, gathered from the Book of Common Prayer ;" " Deptford Worthies," a lecture, &c.

Rev. Arthur Tooth, M.A., held the living from 1863 to 2nd December, 1877.

Rev. Malⸯlm MacColl, M.A., had sole charge of the parish until the appointment of the Rev. Henry Aston Walker, M.A., who was instituted by the Bishop of Rochester, January 6th, 1879 ; inducted by the Rev. Canon Money on the 15th, and read himself in on the 19th of the same month. Mr. Walker graduated at Oriel Coll. Oxon., B.A., 1856. He was ordained deacon by the Bishop of Oxford in 1857. From 1862 to 1879 he was curate of St. Alban's, Holborn, having been previously engaged in mission work in St George's-in-the-East.

St. John's Church.

ST. JOHN'S owes its origin to the generous and enlightened philanthropy of S. S. Lucas, Esq., and the indefatigable labours of the present Vicar—the Rev. Canon Charles Forbes Septimus Money, M.A. The beginnings of church work in this district were very small. A little school, started and supported by the liberality of the Baroness Burdett Coutts, formed the nucleus of the present parish. The Church, which is one of the noblest Gothic structures in the neighbourhood, is pleasantly situated on the brow of Loampit Hill, in the Lewisham High Road. It was consecrated on the 18th of July, 1855, and consists of chancel, nave, and two aisles. It has a well-proportioned lofty spire at the south-west corner, containing a peal of eight bells. In the west porch is a brass with this inscription :—" The Clock in this Tower was erected by his sisters, nephew and nieces, in memory of James John Seymour Spencer Lucas, of Burfield Priory, Gloucestershire, who died June 14th, 1875, aged 49. He was born in the adjoining vicarage, and through a life of suffering showed the strength of Jesus, made perfect in weakness, and by his forethought and liberality was in a great degree instrumental in the formation of the Ecclesiastical District of St. John's, and in the promotion of various good works in this parish."

On a pillar in the nave is a beautiful white marble monument by Noble, " In beloved remembrance of John Allen, of St. John's Villas, Wickham Terrace, who died 29th May, 1865. And of his Relict, Judith Allen, who died 26th August, 1866."

The fine east and west windows are filled with memorial stained glass.

Canon Money, son of W. T. Money, Esq., formerly M.P., and afterwards Consul General at Venice, by Eugenia, daughter of W. Money, Esq., of Homme House, Herefordshire, was early in life employed in the Colonial Office. Under a powerful and constraining impulse he exchanged the service of the Crown for the service of the Cross. Having been entered at Corpus Christi Coll., Cambridge, he made his B.A. in 1845, and M.A. in 1850. He was ordained deacon in 1845 ; his first curacy being at Cheltenham. He was successively incumbent of St. John's, Derby ; Senior Curate of All Souls, Langham Place and Curate of Upper Chelsea ; and for some time filled the office of Association Secretary of the Church Missionary Society. Mr. Money was appointed Hon.

Canon of Rochester in 1875 ; Chaplain to the Bishop
of Rochester in 1877, and Rural Dean of Deptford in
1879.

He is author of many tracts, sermons and pamphlets,
among which may be mentioned ;—" Have you the One
Thing Needful ?" " God or Baal ?" " All Flesh is Grass ;"
" Hannah's Faith and Samuel's Obedience ;" " Greenwich Fair ;" " Mormonism Unmasked ;" " Retirement
and Prayer ;" " Formation of God's Image in the Soul ;"
" Paraphrase on the Lord's Prayer ;" " The Drying up
of the Euphrates ;" " The Indian Mutiny ;" " Memoir
on the Education of the Natives of India ;" " Revolution
in China and its Bearing upon Missionary Efforts, &c."

The Home Mission work of the congregation of St
John's among their poorer neighbours is carried on in St.
John's Mission Hall,—a Gothic building erected on the
site of Ebenezer Chapel in King-street, which was opened
by licence, June 18th, 1873. Connected with the Church
is a District Visiting Society, Dorcas Society—of which
Mrs. Money is President, Penny Saving's Bank, Women's
Provident Society, Mother's Meeting, St. John's Temperance and a Branch of the Church Missionary Society.

The Patron is Mrs. Whidborne. Value of the living
£800 per annum.

Christ Church.

The Ecclesiastical District Parish of Christ Church
originated with a mission started by the present Vicar, in
a room over the old saw pits, near the Tide Mill, in
Church-street, in 1859.

The Church, which is a handsome brick building, with
stone facings of Byzantine Gothic architecture, was consecrated on the 27th of December, 1864, by the Bishop
of London. The cost of the building, including the site

was £7000. The reredos is a stone representation of
Leonardo da Vinci's famous picture of the Last Supper
The pulpit and reading desk are also of stone richly
carved.

The Rev. John Polkinghorne Courtenay of King's
Coll., London, received his M.A. degree from the Archbishop of Canterbury in 1867.   He was ordained deacon
in 1857, by the Bishop of London, and priest in 1858 ;
his first and only curacy being that of St. John, Deptford.   In 1875 he received the appointment of Chaplain
to Queen Elizabeth's College, Greenwich. The patronage
of the church is invested in the Archbishop of Canterbury and others.

Attached to the church is a commodious iron school-
room in Reginald-road, where much parochial work of a
practical character is being carried on, including
Provident Sick Clubs with 800 members ; Mother's
Meetings ; Blanket Club ; Maternity Society ; Parochial
Library and a Provident Dispensary.

All Saints' Church,

HATCHAM PARK.

ALL Saints' Church was erected in 1869, at a cost of
£5,629.   The Architects were Messrs. Newman Billing.
It is built in the decorated style of Foreign Gothic, and
consists of nave, aisles, transepts and choir ; but the
tower and spire are not yet completed.

It was built to seat 936 persons, one-half of the sittings
to be free. The patronage is vested between duly
appointed trustees, and the Worshipful Company of
Haberdashers.

The church was erected through the labours of the
Rev. Edward Wynne, who first entered the district as a
Missionary clergyman in connection with the Bishop of

London's Fund, and the London Diocesan Home Mission.

Mr. Wynne collected a congregation in a small damp room in Besson-street, and laboured there until he got a church built, consecrated, and a separate Ecclesiastical District assigned.

The Church was opened on the 1st of December, 1869 ; consecrated on the 1st of November, 1871, and a separate Ecclesiastical District assigned it out of the parish of St. James,' Hatcham, in 1872. The funds for building the church were raised through the liberality of the Worshipful Company of Haberdashers who gave the Freehold of the site and £1,500; the leasehold interest in the site being given by J. A. Hardcastle, Esq., M.P. ; together with grants from the Bishop of London's Fund, Bishop of Rochester's Fund, &c., and donations from friends and residents in the neighbourhood, with contributions from various other sources.

The name of All Saints was chosen, owing to the church being built in Hatcham Park, in which formerly stood the residence of Mr. Hardcastle, the friend of those earnest philanthropists—who then resided at Clapham— and who assisted them in many of their noble religious works, meeting together often for the purpose at Hatcham Park.

The anxiety, labour and difficulties connected with the formation of the parish and erection of the church, so seriously affected the health of the first Vicar, Mr. Wynne, after being here thirteen years, that he was compelled to seek a change, and he consequently exchanged the living for that of St. Mark's, Manningham, Bradford (a smaller parish with more bracing air) with the Rev. R. Gardner Smith, the present Vicar, who entered on his duties in January, 1878.

Adjoining the Church is an Institute, which was erected in 1877, at an expense of about £1,859; including fixtures, fittings, and other incidental expenses. This sum was met by a handsome donation of £500 from the Bishop of Rochester's Fund, also of £155 from the National Society for the Education of the Poor, and of liberal donations from private gentlemen, together with other donations of smaller amounts, and a balance of £352 then still remaining unpaid was realised by a bazaar held in the Institute in November, 1878, under the sanction, council, and presidency of the present vicar (the Rev. R. Gardner Smith), when the debt was paid off. The Institute is used for various purposes in furtherance of the well-being of the district of All Saints parish, one of which is—its primary object—a Sunday school, and the building affords accommodation for about 700 children, which number, under the judicious organisation of the Vicar, aided by christian members of the congregation, assemble under its roof. During the current year (1882) an adjunct building has been erected between the institute and the church at an expense of upwards of £400, for the purpose of giving additional accommodation for the Sunday school, and to meet the wants of the choir. To defray the expense of the building a bazaar was held in January of this year, and provision made for the payment of the whole amount.

St. Peter's Church, Brockley.

THE Ecclesiastical District Parish of St. Peter, Brockley, was formed out of St. John's Parish in 1870. The Church—a noble Gothic structure of the Geometrical Period, consisting of chancel, nave, aisles, and two transepts, with galleries over the transepts and western part of nave—was consecrated on the 13th of August, 1870. It is situated in the Wickham Road—one of the finest and most fashionable thoroughfares in the Parish of Deptford—in close proximity to the site of the old Premonstratensian Monastery, which existed in the latter part of the 12th century. Previous to the erection of the Church, services were held in a temporary iron building, which was opened for that purpose n 1866.

The Church is seated for 1,100, about 170 of which are free. The income is derived from pew-rents.

The patronage of this church, together with St. Paul's, has been recently conveyed to the Bishop of Rochester.

LIST OF VICARS.

REV. Joseph M'Cormick, M.A., of St. John's Coll., Cambridge, was ordained deacon in 1858, and priest in 1859. His first curacy was at St. Peter's, Square, London; he was afterwards Rector of Dunmore East, Waterford; Assistant Minister of St. Stephen's, Marylebone, and was appointed to the Perpetual Curacy of St. Peter's, Brockley, in 1867, which he held uutil his appointment to the Vicarage of Hull, 1875. He was recently appointed Rural Dean of Hull. He is author of "The Matterhorn Accident: a sad Holiday;" "Ruth;" "Bill Edmonds," &c.

Rev. John Cordeux Wetherell, M.A., of St. John's College, Cambridge, was inducted to the living in 1875. Mr. Wetherell was ordained priest in 1862 by the Bishop of Chester. He was curate of Cheadle, 1861-62; Lymm, Cheshire, 1863; Camden Church, Camberwell, 1863 to 1867; Chaplain to the Camberwell Hospital Asylum from 1863 to 1875; Morning Reader at St. Giles, Camberwell, from 1865 to 1867; Curate of St. John's, Clapham, from 1867 to 1869; Senior Curate of Lambeth, from 1869 to 1871, and Perpetual Curate of Verulam Chapel, Lambeth, from 1871 to 1875.

CHURCH WORK.—St. Peter's Hall, Cranfield Road; this noble building, which originated in a scheme propounded by the present Vicar in 1877, and completed some two years afterwards at a cost of upwards of £3000, has become the centre of church agencies in the parish, and amply fulfilling the objects for which it was designed.

On Sunday at 3.30 p.m. there is a Children's Service ; a Bible Class for Youths ; a Bible Class for Elder Girls and Domestic Servants. A Prayer Meeting is also held on the 2nd Sunday in the month at 10 a.m. It is also used for Confirmation and other classes. Monday, 7.30 p.m., Young Men's Bible Class in connection with the St. Peter's Young Men's Society. Tuesday, Committee, Debating, and other meetings in the evening. Thursday, fortnightly series, Readings, Concerts, Lectures, Entertainments, &c. ; also Microscopical Society's meetings. Friday, Prayer Meeting of Teachers and others, and occasional meetings in large hall. Saturday, Practice of the St. Peter's Orchestral Society, 7.30 p.m. to 9.30 p.m. during the season, *i.e.*, from October to March. The Book Club of the St. Peter's Young Men's Society is in connection with Messrs. W. H. Smith and Sons' Library. Books are issued and exchanged to members at the Hall on Monday and Thursday evenings from 7 to 8 o'clock. A new Circulating Library has been commenced, and is in good working order.

The Hall is open to youths with certain reservations, every evening.

St. Luke's Church,

LOWER ROAD, DEPTFORD.

THE St. Luke's Mission was established by the Bishop of London's Fund and the London Diocesan Home Mission in 1867, in the north-western portion of St. Paul's Parish, the population of the district being at that time about 5000.

That great results often arise from small beginnings is well exemplified in the history of this church. In one of the occasional papers issued by the Bishop of London's Fund is an interesting account of how Mr. Malcolmson

—the present much-respected Vicar—began the work of the mission. He says, "On my first Sunday here I met with seven lads, of ages varying from 14 to 18, behind a brick-kiln, playing at 'pitch and toss,' and smoking tobacco. As soon as they saw me coming up to them, they pocketed their pence, but continued smoking. Dirty and in rags, I asked them if they wished to ruin their health." The answer was "No." "But you are doing so by smoking away at this rate," I observed. "Yes," exclaimed one boy, "that chap (pointing to one of his fellows) smokes an ounce a day." "He may well be in rags, then," I continued ; and this was readily assented to by most of the boys. I then inquired, "Did you ever go to any school?" "Yes," answered most. "Then why did you give it up?" "Because the others in school laughed at us on account of our ragged clothes," they replied. "Would you like to go to a school now, if I could get one for boys like yourselves?" To this they said, "Yes." On this, I asked, "Do you know of any room near here where we could meet?" "Yes, there is our woodshed, in Penny Bundle-lane," said one of the smartest of the lads ; "I dare say you can have that, only mother uses it to wash in some-times." I was shown the place, and secured the use of it for the following Sunday morning. The next Sunday I found 8 boys assembled in the wood-shed, which is *ten feet by six* in area. At first they seemed to regard my coming amongst them to teach them with derision ; but I proposed to read to them the account of St. Paul's voyage. When we came down to the part about "the south wind blowing softly," and the tempest immediately succeeding, picturing it out as a representation of life, one lad exclaimed, "That is just like what it has been at our house ; for we were better off, but two of us were sick, and one died." From that moment the boys were softened, and I had thenceforth no difficulty with them."

In March, 1867, the disused Bethel Independent Chapel, near Black Horse Bridge,—a building affording accommodation for about 400 persons—was secured, and used as a temporary Church. It was, however, soon

N

found to be quite inadequate to the wants of the neighbourhood. A committee was formed in October, 1867, for the purpose of obtaining a permanent building capable of seating 1,100 persons ; and through the generous grants from the Bishop of London's and Bishop of Rochester's Funds, and other Societies—through the self-denying efforts of the people in the Mission district, and the timely assistance of many Christian friends—this good object was attained.

The foundation stone of St. Luke's Church was laid on the 19th of July, 1870, by W. J. Evelyn, Esq., who kindly gave the site. It was consecrated by the Bishop of Rochester, on the 30th of July, 1872, and although there was a considerable debt upon the building, the whole of it, through the exertions of Sir Antonio Brady and the kind liberality of many friends, was cleared off before the 31st July, 1873.

The new parochial district was assigned to St. Luke's, by H.M. Order in Council on the 26th of June, 1873.

During the first decade of the Church's existence an annual average of £1,000 has been raised for church and charitable purposes.

The Church is a Gothic stone structure, consisting of apsidal chancel—well-lighted with stained glass windows—nave and two aisles seated with open pews.

The tower which rises over the chancel contains a peal of eight bells, which were obtained chiefly through the exertions of Mr. Malcolmson's first Curate, the Rev. Henry Small and Mr. Morris, of the Grand Surrey and Commercial Docks.

There is a good voluntary choir, but no organ.

To supply accommodation for the fast increasing Sunday schools a large Parish room is much needed.

There is a large band of church workers and the Provident Clubs and Band of Hope are in a flourishing condition.

During the past summer an "Invitation Band," headed by the vicar, has visited every street in the St. Luke's District, holding out-door services, which have done some good.

The Rev. James Malcolmson was educated at St. Bees'
College, Cumberland. He was ordained priest by the
Bishop of Chester in 1860. His first curacy was St.
Thomas', Hyde. Cheshire, 1859—60, from whence he removed to St. John's, Dunkenfield, the senior curacy of
which church he held for three years. From 1863 until
his appointment to his present incumbency in 1866 he
was London Diocesan Home Missionary and Evening
Lecturer at St. Peter's, Walworth. Mr. Malcolmson is
author of "Post Mission Letters" and "Youthful
Responsibility."

The present curate is the Rev. Henry Wells, B.A., of
the University of London, who has held the curacy for
over four years, but is about to leave to take charge of a
mission district in Camberwell.

St. Barnabas Church,
EVELYN STREET.

THE foundation stone of this Church—which is in connection with the South-Eastern Auxiliary of the Royal
Association in Aid of the Deaf and Dumb, of which Her
Majesty the Queen is patron—was laid on Saturday,
May 13th, 1882, by W. J. Evelyn, Esq. (a). Owing to
the narrowness of the site, the Church is long in proportion to its width, and does not maintain the orienta-
tion usually adopted. What should be the east end is
apsidal, with an ambulatory round the chancel to enable
the minister to reach the vestry at the rear. The church
being a missionary one, the front part will be divided
from the chancel end by a moveable screen, so that the
part devoted to divine service can be enlarged when

a The beautiful silver trowel used on the occasion bore the following inscription :—" Presented to W. J. Evelyn, Esq., on the occasion of laying the foundation stone of St. Barnabas Church for the
Deaf and Dumb, Evelyn-street, Deptford, May 13th, 1882."

N2

necessary. It will accommodate about 200 persons, and as it is necessary that all members of the congregation should see the hands of the minister, the floor will be constructed on an incline.

It is built of brick with Bath stone dressings. Mrs. Evelyn gives the stained glass windows, and some members of the committee the reredos. In the south-east corner of the building is a very interesting relic from Glastonbury Abbey—the gift of James Austin, Esq., the present owner of the ruin. It is an ornamental stone from one of the great doors of the Abbey, and is built into the wall of St. Barnabas to form a book shelf.

In 1874 the Rev. James W. A. Sturdee—a native of Deptford—undertook the charge of the deaf and dumb in the South-Eastern District, numbering about 250, of which anxiliary he is likewise secretary. Services had, however, been carried on especially for the deaf and dumb, by a deaf and dumb gentleman, in the St. Paul's schools, Edward Street, Deptford, for some years previously.

The services, Bible classes, a Penny Bank, and a Debating Society are at present held in the Reading-room, St. John's Mission Hall, King-Street.

The following clergy have been ordained specially for work amongst the deaf and dumb :—

Rev. Samuel Smith, Chaplain of St. Saviour's.

Rev. William Stainer, now superintendent of deaf and dumb under the London School Board.

Rev. W. A. Sturdee, of Deptford.

Rev. Charles Rhind, chaplain of the Association.

St. Cyprian's Church, Brockley.

THIS is an outlying mission church of the parish of Lewisham, but, skirting upon a district of Deptford in which the church accomodation is very insufficient ; a

very large proportion of the congregation being inhabit
ants of Deptford. Indeed, the movement which ended
in the church being built began in the parish of Deptford,
but, difficulties arising, the church was finally built in
its present position, almost on the borders of both
parishes. The foundation stone was laid in October,
1881, by the Hon and Rev. Canon Legge, vicar of
Lewisham. Archdeacon Daykin was then expected to take
charge of the mission, but, though much against his will,
circumstances prevented his doing so, and the work was
eventually undertaken by the Rev. J. G. M. Stretton,
who acts as assistant curate to the vicar of Lewisham in
charge of the church and surrounding district. The church
opened on May 6th, 1882 ; and so great has been the
success of the mission, that in less than six months, it
has ·been found imperatively necessary, to accommodate
the overflowing congregagation, to enlarge the building
to the full extent of the available ground, which gives
some 200 more sittings. The church, which is only a
temporary one (and owes its origin to the christian zeal of
two ladies residing in Deptford) is a plain brick building ;
but inside it is very pretty and effective. The seats are
all free and unappropriated. The services, which are
choral, are very hearty and congregational.

The Sunday schools, Bible classes, and other parochial
agencies are in a very flourishing and promising
condition.

THE CATHOLIC CHURCH
OF THE
Assumption B.V.M.,
HIGH STREET.

FROM the abolition of the Papal power in England in
1534, to the establishment of the present Hierarchy in
1850 (when the See of Westminster was rounded under

the late Cardinal Wiseman), the Roman Catholics of this country were under the jurisdiction of Bishops, in partibus, nominated to ancient Sees in the territories of the infidel Burks. Deptford was under the Bishop of Olena. From the 17th Century it formed a portion of the Greenwich Roman Catholic congregation, which was included in the London District and governed by a Vicar apostolic. For some time this congegation was served by priests from the Mission in St. George's Fields which began after the Gordon riots in 1780. One of the first missioners was the Rev. Father Green who laboured in the district from about 1795 to 1815. He was succeeded by the Rev. Father Stewart, who died in 1823; and then by the Rev. Father McCabe, who only held the charge for four years, being compelled in consequence of ill health, to retire to the Isle of Wight. The Rev. Richard North, D.D., brother of the much, and deservedly respected Canon North, undertook the charge of the Greenwich Mission in 1827, and held it until his death, September 27th, 1860. Dr. North was a generous benefactor to the Catholics of Deptford. He gave the temporary church and school-house in Old King Street, which was used until the erection of the present Church in High Street. The Old King Street School had accommodation for upwards of two hundred children.

Deptford was made a distinct mission on Whitsun Day, May 15th, 1842; the Rev William Marshall being appointed Missioner. He left on the 12th of May, 1850, and was immediately succeeded by the Rev. Joseph Edward North, who was appointed by His Eminence Cardinal Wiseman. On the 30th of August, 1856,— when the See of Southwark was founded—Father North became the first Rector of the Church of the Assumption, which he held until January, 1860; when he removed to the Church of "Our Lady the Star of the Sea," at Croom's Hill, Greenwich, rendered vacant by the death of his brother, Dr. R. North. He was elected a Canon of Southwark in 1866.

The second Rector was the Rev. J. Norris, who was appointed 29th January, 1860, and resigned 25th August,

1862. He died at Buckland, 24th June, 1880, and was buried at Brockley, 30th June, 1880.

The third Rector was the Rev. J. M. Glenie, who was appointed after an interregnum of some three or four months in December, 1862, and left October 28th, 1871; being succeeded by the present Rector, the Rev. M. P. Fannan, who had been his Missionary Coadjutor since the 26th of May, 1865. Buried at Brockley.

The Missionary Coadjutors at present are :—

The Rev. W. B. Alexander, appointed 14th July, 1877, and

Rev. Edmund Carroll, 20th February, 1880.

The Church was built by the Rev. W. Marshall at a cost of over £2000. The foundation stone was laid on the 22nd of June, 1844; and the sacred edifice was opened for Divine Service in 1846. The extreme plainness of the interior has been relieved by the erections of a chancel, twenty-eight feet long, which is very richly decorated. The chancel, which was designed and built by the Rev. Canon North, was opened on the 15th of December, 1859, by the Right Rev. Dr. Grant, Lord Bishop of Southwark; the sermon on the occasion being preached by the Right Rev. Dr. Morris, Lord Bishop of Troy.

The Altar and reredos (a) are of stone, and very rich. On the front of the Altar are carved representations of the "Nativity;" the "Annunciation" and "Assumption, B.V.M."

In the reredos is a fine statue of the Blessed Virgin, with two angels on either side bearing scrolls and mystic symbols; and over these are four shields, on which are painted the "Purple robe," "Crown of thorns," "Nails and scourges," and the "Spear and sponge." Running across the chancel on both sides of the reredos is this inscription :—"Assumpta est Maria in Cœlum;" and

a This reredos was presented to the Church by the late Rev. Dr. Richard North, after being shewn at the Paris Exhibition, where it was awarded the gold medal.

The carved archway leading to the side Chapel was exhibited at the same time, when a prize medal was awarded to the Architect for the design.

above is a fine wheel window—filled with stained glass
in 1880, the centre light representing the "Assumption
of Our Lady." On the pillars supporting the chancel
arch are statues of the Blessed Virgin and St. Joseph,
four of the lancet windows, on the south side of the
Church, were filled with stained glass in 1881, representing St. Joseph, St. Peter, St. Paul, and St. Patrick;
and the centre light of the triple lancet window, above
the gallery, is a memorial window containing a representation of the "Madonna and Child":—

"In memory of the Very Reverend John Melville
Glenie, Canon of the Diocese of Southwark, and
sometime Rector of this Church, who died at Weybridge
in the County of Surrey, on the 23rd day of June, A.D.
1878, aged 62 years; on whose soul God have mercy."

On the north side of the chancel is a side Chapel with
an "Altar of the Rosary;" the doorway of which is a
splendid work of art, and said to have cost about £100.
The subject is the "Descent of our Blessed Saviour into
Hell" with the legend "Descendit ad Inferos" inscribed
underneath.

The interior of the Church has, during the present
year, been thorougly renovated and beautified. The
ceiling has been ornamented with a chaste stencilling
and a rich dado added to the lower part of the walls.
The space above the apex of the chancel arch has been
covered with a mural painting of the Crucifixion in
bright colours on a gold ground; and it is proposed as
funds come to hand to fill in the remaining blank spaces
on either side of the arch, with other mural paintings;
that on the south side is to be the "Ascension of Our
Blessed Lord;" on the north the Assumption of the
B.V.M., with the Apostle looking into the empty tomb,
out of which lilies are growing. This subject is taken
from the description given by St. John Damascene.

The Chancel Arch (a) is decorated with Cherubs in gold,
grapes, and the passion flower; and around it on a scroll
is painted the legend "Terribilis est locus iste hic

a Some important improvements in the chancel, costing about £500,
are in contemplation, including a new altar.

Domus Dei est, et porta Cœli et vocabitur aula Dei "
(*Gen. XXVIII.* 17).

In the Sacristy, on the south side of the Chancel is a
Spanish painting of " The Annunciation," of some merit,
presented to Dr. North by the Countess Dillon, and by
him to the Church at Deptford. Other paintings
belonging to this Church are " The Entombment " by
Mr. Fryer, after Titicus ; "St. Patrick banishing the
Snakes " by Mr. Kenelm Digby, an amateur and author
of some distinction ; the Fifteen Mysteries of the Rosary,
&c.

Around the walls of the Church are some fine bas-
relievos of the stations of the Cross : and under the
gallery near the entrance doorway is a large crucifix.

The pulpit is of oak, richly carved, of the latest period
of pointed architecture, already sliding into the
Renaissance, and apparently of Flemish workmanship.

The Vestments now in use are of Gothic design and
very rich. There are two silver chalices, the larger
one which belongs to the Church is gold plated and
finely chased It bears six engravings of the following
Scriptural subjects, beautifully executed, viz. :—" The
Crucifixion ;" The Sacrifice of Isaac ;" " Christ
blessing little Children ;" " Assumption B.V.M. ;"
" Return of the Spies with bunch of Grapes ;" " Binding
the Lamb at the Altar for Sacrifice." On the bottom is
inscribed, " Ora pro anima Thomæ Toomey, Deptford,
A.D. 1875. This chalice cost the sum of £40. Several
other sacred vessels are of considerable value.

The Congregation consists of about 6000. The annual
number of baptisms averages about 250, and marriages
about 60.

The district assigned to this Church comprises the whole
of the parish of Deptford, to the eastward of the London,
Brighton and South Coast Railway.

The Presybtery, which adjoins the Church on the south,
is a fine commodious building, with stone dressings. It
is four storeys high, with a castellated parapet, and har-
monises well with the Church.

The Chapel of St. Michael and All Angels in the Catholic cemetery, Deptford, of which the first stone was laid by the Right Rev. Thomas Grant, Bishop of Southwark, on the 17th of December, 1866, and the altar consecrated on the 7th of May, 1868, the chapel having been blessed by authority of the said Bishop by the Rev. J. M. Glennie, missionary rector of Deptford, on the 6th of May—the relics being those of Saint Valentine and Saint Urbica. The chapel in extreme length is in the interior about 26ft. by about 11ft. wide, and is built of stone; has an apse at the east end. under which is a small vaulted sacristy with three windows. The body of the chapel is built over the vault, where lie the bodies of Elphege Stuart and Anne Knill. The eastern portion of the vault, with the exception of the space occupied by the above-named bodies, is made over to the priests of Deptford for their burial; the rest being the property of Stuart Knill. The entrance to the vault is under a stone in front of west end of chapel. The altar is of stone, and has its table and super-altar of marble. The reredos consists of three panels carved with Saint Michael separating the Good from the Damned to Hell. Round the chapel is a string of carved foliage by Earp. The roof is supported by Corbels of Angels in stone, by Boulton, and is painted on panel, with the monograms of Elphege and Anne Knill, and over the altar, with the motto of Saint Michael, "Quis ut Deus," and his arms, the Plain with Cross on the red ground. The east window, of two lights, represents, in painted glass, Saint Michael weighing souls before Our Blessed Lord, enthroned, and the quatrefoils on either side, the Archangel Gabriel with the Lily, and the motto, "Ave Maria Gratia prena Dominus;" and Saint Raphael with the Fish and the motto "Quiæ Angelis suis mandavit de te." The nine single windows round the chapel divided by marble columns represent the nine Choirs of Angels. The Cherubim on Wheel; Denominations with Orb and Sceptre; Virtue with book; Principalities with two crowns; Angels with Thurible; Power with Sword; Throne with Fald; Archangels with the Suir, and

Seraphim glowing with love. The west window, which is the dedication window, represents in the upper part Our Lady Star of the Sea, in whose parish the Founders live, and on either side the deceased children offered by their angels ; below is the Founder and his son with motto "Ave Maria Stella," and the Foundress and her daughter. In the centre is a west view of the chapel. The whole of the glass is by Hardman & Co., of Birmingham, and designed by Mr. John H. Powell. On the Gospel side of the Chapel is a recess for vesting lined with wainscot and with a series of drawers in polished oak lined with cedar, made by Friend and Vinte of Ramsgate. Above are oak shelves and small Aumbry for mundatories ; and above is an oak bracelet supporting a picture painted on plaster. The two light windows are filled with the Arms and Monogram of the Founder. A recess in Chapel at west end contains a stove with an iron flue running into the wall which is hollow. The west front runs up into a large Calvary with metal figures of Our Blessed Lord, Our Lady, and St. John by Mayer, and stone angels adoring by Farmer. On the buttresses on either side are large stone figures of angels holding the deceased children of the Founder, carved by Boulton of Cheltenham. Below the Calvary is a belfry containing three bells by Mears and Stainbrook which were blessed at the Church of Our Lady Star of the Sea, Greenwich, by the Bishop of Southwark, with the names of the Archangels Michael, Gabriel and Raphael. The hinges of the door torm the motto of the Founder " Nil Desperandum."

Inscription on first stone.

Sanctus-Michael-Signifer et Angeli Militiiæcelestis repræsentate in lucem sanctam animas hic in Christo quiescentium.
Die XVII Decembris MDCCCLXVII. Pontificatus Pie IX, Anno XXI. Thoma. Epsco. Suthwarc. Lapidem imponente.

Inscription in copper gilt box with coins of the year in first stone, laid on Monday, 17th December, 1867, by Bishop of Southwark. Mass by Rev. J. M. Glenie.

Propre hoc Sacellum Extructum Anno MDCCCLXVII. beatum resurrectionem exspectant Anna et Elphegus Stuart Knill quibus lux æterna lucescebat Mense Januarii MDCCCLXV. Eos hoc inloco consepeliendi parentis amanter lugent. Stuart et Maria Anna Rosa Knill petentis ut fideles velut Orare pro ipsis pro patre Johanna Mortuo dir VIII Jan: MDCCCLIV. et pro matre Elizabeth MDCCCLXII, decessit, Necnon pro omnibus defunctis ut in Christo requiescant Æt uno cum Sancto Michæli Principe et Angelis Militæ Calestis tætentur   STUART KNILL. MARY ANNE ROSA KNILL.

Inscription on parchment, with relics in altar.

MDCCCLXVIII. die VII. Mensis Maii. Ego Thomas Episcopus Suthwarcensis Consecravi Altare hoc, in honorem Sancti Michaelis Archangeli et omnium Angelorum et Religuias Sanctorum Martyrum Valentii et Urbicæ in co inclusi, et singulis Christi fidelibus, hodie unum annum, et in die Anniversario consecratioris hujusmodi ipsum visit antibus quadraginte, dies de vera indulgentia in forma ecclesiæ consueta concessi.   THOMAS GRANT.

Baptist Chapel,

CHURCH STREET.

WILSON in his "History and Antiquity of Dissenting (a)

a Nonconformity appears to have been introduced into Deptford about the middle of the 17th century : indeed, during the Commonwealth, the pulpit of the parish church was occupied by a clergyman of whom, "Sylva" Evelyn, apparently speaks, "January 30, 1653," as "somewhat of the Independent."

Two chapels are supposed to have been erected during the reign of Charles II. ; one in Butt Lane, by a small congregation of Quakers and the other in Church-street. by a society of general Baptists. Mr. Evelyn, who was a loyal churchman, refers to the latter place when describing the state of affairs in the "Declaration of Indulgence." granted by James II.

1687, April 10.—" In the last week there was issued a dispensation from all obligations and tests, by which Dissenters and Papists especially had public liberty of exercising their several ways of worship, without incurring the penalty of the many laws and acts of Parliament to the contrary. This was purely obtained by the Papists thinking thereby to ruin the Church of England, being now the only church which so admirably and strenuously opposed their superstition. There was a wonderful concourse of people at the Dissenters Meeting House in this parish, and the Parish Church left exceedingly thin. What this will end in, God Almighty only knows."—*Evelyn's Diary, vol.* I, *p.* 639, *4to.*

Churches" published in 1814, says " At Deptford there
had existed a church of the General Baptist persuasion
ever since the days of Charles II." He gives the following
list of ministers ——

Rev. John Clayton, 16— to 1688.
Rev. Richard Adams, 1688 to 1689.
Rev. George White, 1690 to 1702.
Rev. Nathaniel Foxwell, 1703 to 1721.
Rev. Ralph Gould, 1721 to 1722.
Rev. Benjamin Ingram, 1723 to 1736.
Rev. Jas. Richardson and Assistants, no dates.
Rev. Samuel Fry, 1738 to ——
Rev. Joseph Brown, 1766 to 1803.

According to Timpson in his Church History of Kent
this list is not strictly correct, as the Rev. Mr. Baron was
minister for some time previous to Mr. Brown, who was
succeeded by

Rev. Mr. Moon, 1803 to 1823.
Rev. E. Chapman, 1823 to 1833.
Rev. Mr. Squiers, 1833 to 1853.
Rev. Michael Castle Gascoigne, the present minister,
1853.

" There were four general Baptist churches in London,
that experienced great vicissitudes ; but they co-operated
in building a new chapel in Worship-street ; and they
dedicated it to the service of God, June 24th, 1781.
Three of the congregations united in their attendance at
that place ; but the Rev. Mr. Brown, continued minister
of the church in Fair-street, Horsleydown, Southwark :
he removed, however, with his congregation, to Deptford,
at Lady-day, 1801.

During the ministry of Dr. Foxwell, the celebrated Dr.
John Gale resided at Blackheath. He was then assistant
to the Rev. Joseph Burroughs, Barbican, from the year,
1718, and preached every other Lord's day morning, and
afterwards every Sabbath morning, to the general Baptist
congregation at Deptford. His health declining, he
preached here only once a fortnight after April, and died
in December, 1721.

From the church-books of 1802, it appears that part of this congregation consisted of a secession of certain members of the general Baptist Church at Shad Thames, London, in 1674. They assembled in a building in Winchester-park, Southwark, until March 7th, 1683, when they removed to Dock Head; from this they removed to a building in Fair-street, Horsleydown, June 6th, 1692, taken on a lease for 31 years. They again removed, in 1772, to Pinner's-hall, Broad-street; thence to Dr. Savage's Meeting House, in Bury-street, in 1779; afterwards June 24th, 1781, to Worship-street; and thence, March 1, 1802. to Church-street, Deptford.

Dr. Brown, who was minister of the United General Baptist churches at Deptford, was a gentleman of superior learning. He had been five years a student under Dr. Doddridge; and was for many years secretary to the general Baptists. He died, May 21, 1803, aged 73, and was buried in the Meeting House, Deptford. His last discourse was on Luke xxii., 15.

His funeral sermon was preached by his successor, the Rev. Mr. Moon on Rev. xiv., 13 (*Wilson's History of Dissenting Churches, vol. iv., pp.* 257, 263; *Dr. Evan's Tracts, pp.* 154, 163, 418.

Hitherto the principles of the general Baptists at Deptford are believed to have been Trinitarian, but Mr. Moon is regarded as a Unitarian. He died 8th June, 1823, aged 48. (*Timpson's " Church History of Kent,"* pp. 346, 357).

There is a permanent endowment of about £80 per annum belonging to this Chapel. This endowment is paid out of certain farms, comprising some five or six hundred acres of land, near Malling, in Kent, left in the last century by Captain John Pearse, the rents being equally divided towards the maintenance of the ministers of the following Baptist Chapels, viz.:—Boro' Road, Worship Street; Commercial Road; Peckham and Deptford. After the donor's decease these estates were for some time in Chancery.

Some eminent men are said to have attended the services here; notably the late Earl Beaconsfield when a youth at an Academy on Blackheath, Mr. Moon, being at that time, minister ; Milner Gibson, Esq., M.P., for Manchester ; and Thomas Hollis, one of the regicides of King Charles I., who fled to America, at the Restoration, where he died. There is a tomb in the chapel yard to his wife, who was buried here.

The present trustee is Samuel Brent, Esq.

Quakers' Meeting House,

HIGH STREET.

THIS building, which is a pattern of plainness both externally and internally, was first erected during the latter half of the 17th century ; but as no records have been kept, at least as far as can be ascertained, its history is involved in obscurity. The only historical incident connected with it seems to be that recorded by Dr. Mackay in his " Thames and its Tributaries," who says : " William Penn visited the Czar from Stoke Togis, and conversed in Dutch. Peter conceived from his manners and conversation such formidable notions of the Quakers that during his residence here often attended their meetings, conducting himself with great decorum and condescension." The form, on which Peter the Great is supposed to have sat, is now used as a support to a small library cupboard, in which is a curious old illustrated Bible, of the time of Queen Elizabeth, of which the Society seems to be very proud. There is a small burial ground at the back of the building.

Congregational Church,

HIGH STREET.

THE Rev. Henry Goodman, M.A., who was ejected from Radmill, in Sussex, in 1660, was the first settled minister at this chapel, and previous to this no history is recorded beyond the fact that the first "Meeting House" was built in 1702, which was rebuilt and probably enlaged in 1756.

The present structure was erected in 1861, and opened for Divine Service in 1862. It is seated for 886 persons.

LIST OF MINISTERS.

Rev. Henry Godman, M.A. He was esteemed as a preacher, and published a sermon while at Deptford, preached at the funeral of Mrs. Kilbury. He died January 29th, 1702.

Rev. John Beaumont, M.A. Mr. Beaumont accepted the pastorate in 1696, and held it for thirty-two years. It appears, by inscriptions on some of the Communion-plate presented to him that he was esteemed a successful minister of Christ here in 1707-8. Dr. John Evans calls him a Presbyterian. He died in 1736.

Dr. Abraham Taylor. He became minister in 1728, and was ordained here January 1st, 1731. In addition to his pastoral duties, Dr. Taylor undertook the tutorship of the Protestant Dissenters' Academy from May, 1735 to March, 1740, which was then kept at a house in Church-street, then called "The Great House." Among Dr. Taylor's students may be mentioned the Rev. Messrs. Brewer and Towle, popular ministers of the Independents, in London. The seminary itself was afterwards removed to

Mile End, London, and thence to Homerton. Deptford is therefore the birthplace of Homerton College. Dr. Taylor was an author.

Rev. Mr. Pickersgill. He held the pastorate for six years.

Rev. Jenkin Lewis. He died in November, 1751. " He appears to have been specially concerned," says Timpson, " for the support of Evangelical doctrines, which was then being denied by many, through the prevalence of Arianism. He drew up, therefore, a declaration of the principles held by his people, and entered it in their Church-book." The chief points are as follows :—

" Whereas, our lot is fallen on an age wherein the important doctrines of revealed religion are denied, and the precepts of it neglected by many, we, therefore, the members of the Church of Christ who assemble in Butt-lane, Deptford, believing ourselves obliged to bewail and, as far as we can, to prevent the present infidelity and profaneness—in order, hereunto, we do renew, and enter into a solemn engagement to Almighty God and one another, to maintain and continue in the profession and practice of the reformed religion, which is contained in the Scriptures of the Old and New Testaments ; and summarily expressed in the following proposition :—

" 1. That there is One God, of infinite, absolute, and incomprehensible perfections.

" 2. That in this One God there are Three Persons, Father, Son, and Holy Ghost, the same in substance, equal in power and glory.

" 3. That the Second Person assumed human nature, and is True God and real man in one person.

" 4. That there was a covenant of redemption from eternity, whereby Jesus Christ was made under the law, to obey and suffer as our surety, and in our room, that He might perfectly redeem and finally save all that the Father gave Him (*i.e.*, all that come unto God by Him ; and him that cometh, He will in no wise cast out).

o

" 5. That all the natural posterity of Adam sinned to him, and fell with him in his first transgression, whereby they are become guilty, unclean, and corrupt in all the powers of their souls, and members of their bodies..

" 6. That Jesus Christ did and doth execute the offices of a Prophet, Priest, and King, both in His estate of humiliation and exaltation.

" 7. That the righteousness in and for which we are pardoned, justified, and have right to glory, is the righteousness of Christ's active and passive obedience received by faith alone.

" 8. That the inward and efficacious power of the Holy Ghost in and upon the soul, is absolutely necessary for our regeneration, conversion, sanctification, perseverance, and eternal salvation.

" 9. That we under the moral law, contained in the Ten Commandments, as a rule of life (or of conduct), and not as a covenant of (life or of) works.

" 10. That God hath made and revealed a covenant of free grace in Christ, which contains all the blessings that are necessary for life and godliness, to which God requires our consent aud submission.

" 11. That Christ has appointed and settled in His Church many holy ordinances as His Word, Prayer, Communion of Saints, exhorting, reproving, and comforting one another ; Baptism and the Lord's Supper.

" 12. Finally, that there will be a resurrection of the dead, at which Christ will judge all mankind, openly declare the justification of all His Saints, and receive them into eternal glory, and punish the wicked with everlasting wrath.

"These are the great doctrines of revealed religion, which we profess, and which we hope and trust will be continued in this church to the glory of our God and Saviour, for our spiritual good, and the comfort of our posterity. To which we set our names in the presence of Almighty God.

"Approved and subscribed for by us, the seventh day of January, 1746-7.

"JENKIN LEWIS, Pastor."

Rev. John Olding. Mr. Olding, who was a pupil of the celebrated Dr. P. Doddridge, came from Gloucester and commenced his pastorate September 16th, 1754. His name is found subscribed to the Articles of Faith, drawn up by his predecessor. In 1776 he published a funeral sermon, preached by him after the death of his daughter, Ann Olding—a pious and amiable young lady, who wrote some hymns and verses during a long and painful illness. A memoir of Miss Olding accompanies her father's sermon, "Seeking the Lord while He may be found." After his death a tablet was erected in the chapel to his memory, bearing the following inscription :—

" Beneath this building are interred the remains of the Rev. John Olding, endeared to his affectionate flock by the faithful discharge of the duties of his office, by his attachment to the great principles of the Gospel, and an unblemished and exemplary life. They record this humble but sincere testimony to the veneration in which they hold the memory of their beloved Pastor, who, after having for 31 years, with great acceptance and usefulness, spoken unto them the Word of Life, fell asleep in Jesus October the seventh, 1785, in the 64th year of his age." Mr. Olding's funeral sermon was preached by the Rev. Dr. Addington.

Rev. John Theodore Barker. He was assistant to Mr. Olding from the 12th of December, 1784, when he preached his first sermon at Deptford. He was ordained March 6th, 1785, and succeeded to the pastoral office in the following October ; which he filled for nearly half a century ; his ministry being highly acceptable. A tablet bearing the following inscription was placed against the wall of the chapel :—

" Sacred to the memory of the Reverend John Theodore Barker, forty-seven years Pastor of this Church, who died on the 3rd day of April, 1833, aged 73 years. He was endeared to the people, alike by the zealous fidelity of his ministry, the holy consistency of his character, and the habitual devotion of his life to God. As a man, he was distinguished by singular simplicity of manners and kindness of heart ; as a preacher, by purity of doctrine, fervour of spirit, great plainness of speech. Disciplined in the school of Christ, he was pre-eminently fitted to deal tenderly with the sorrowful in heart, and to speak a word in season to the weary. And meekly taking up his Cross, he followed his Master with cheerful submission, until called into His presence to receive his reward. This tablet was erected by his people as a testimony of their affection."

Rev. John Pulling. Mr. Pulling was a native of Ottery St. Mary, Devonshire, the birthplace of Samuel Taylor Coleridge, poet, philosopher and theologian. He was prepared for the work of the ministry under the Rev. Flavel Stenner, of Dartmouth, a descendent of quaint John Flavel, the eminent Nonconformist divine. Thence he proceeded to Highbury College, where he gained the lasting friendship of his tutors, Dr. Halley, Dr. Henderson, and Dr. Henry Foster Burder. He succeeded to the pastorate of Deptford at the death of Mr. Barker, whom he had been assisting for some months, on the unanimous invitation of the Church. · His ordination took place on the 16th of October, 1833, when the charge was delivered by Dr. Collyer, of Peckham. The other ministers taking part in the service were the Revs. Messrs. H. B. Jeula, W. Chapman, and Belsher, of Greenwich ; Thomas James, of Woolwich ; Hope and Timpson, of Lewisham ; Slatterie, of Chatham ; and his College tutors, Drs. Henderson and Halley. The present spacious and elegant chapel in High Street owes its existence mainly to the persevering exertions of Mr. Pulling ; the cost, upwards of £5,000, being raised by him and sympathising fellow-helpers from the denomination. He resigned the pastorate in 1872, having held it for nearly forty years. In 1868 he was elected Vice-Chairman of the Congregational Union, and delivered the address, and he was also for some years member of the Council of New College. He filled the office of Secretary to the Greenwich District Association of Ministers and Church for many years. In 1858 he published a volume of vacation travels entitled, "Travels in Southern Europe and the Crimea," the proceeds of which were devoted to the erection of the new church ; and three years later "Memorial Sermons," giving a historical sketch of the church in High Street, Deptford, from the passing of the Act of Uniformity under Charles II. ; and later still, a "Funeral Sermon for Mr. Joynson, of St. Mary Cray." He died at Hampstead May 5th, 1880. A tablet containing the following inscription has recently been erected in the church :—

"IN MEMORY OF

"THE REVEREND JOHN PULLING.

"EIGHTH PASTOR OF THIS CHURCH ;

" WHO for forty years cheerfully devoted himself to the faithful discharge of the duties of the Christian Ministry and adorned the doctrines of his Lord by a life of Piety, Honor and Integrity.

" He was of genial presence, and loving disposition, faithful in friendship, warm in sympathy, decisive in action.

" This building stands a monument to his persevering labor, the cost of its erection having been mainly procured by his personal influence ; materially aided by his own liberality.

" Seven years after retirement from active duty he passed away, 'As a shock of corn cometh in, in his season.'

"May 5th, 1880—aged 73 years.

" Erected as a tribute to his memory by members of the Church and friends."

Mr. Pulling was assisted for about a year by the Rev. John W. Ellis, late of South Shields and now of Walthamstow.

Rev. Samuel Holmes. Mr. Holmes—who was a native of Deptford, being the son of a grocer in the town —succeeded to the pastorate on the resignation of Mr. Pulling. He was educated at Hackney College, and ordained July 8th, 1873, in the presence of the Rev. Dr. Parker of the City Temple, Holborn Viaduct, the Revs. John Pulling, Samuel McAll, Principal of the Hackney College, and other ministers in the neighbourhood ; the charge being delivered by the Rev. Morlais Jones, of Lewisham. He published a sermon to children, "Little Foxes and Tender Grapes," "Jesus Only," and several others. He died October, 1874, aged 31 years, and was buried at Nunhead Cemetery, on the 14th of the same month. His funeral sermon was preached by the Rev. Dr. Halley, Principal of New College.

Rev. S. Sabine Read. The Rev. S. S. Read accepted the pastorate in April, 1875, and was ordained on the 20th October following, on which occasion the Rev. John Pulling presided. The ordination prayer was delivered by the Rev. Joseph Beasley, of Blackheath ; the charge by the Rev. Samuel McAll, Principal of Hackney College, and an address "On the Nature of the Christian Church by the Rev. G. Lyon Turner, M.A., of Hackney College ; the Rev. R. T. Verrall, B.A., of Greenwich Road, being also present. Mr. Read's labors have been greatly acceptable in the neighbourhood ; and not only has the church increased its membership during his ministry, but also the various charitable and other institutions have increased in strength and usefulness. A Theological Class for the young, and a class for the study of Bishop Butler's "Analogy of Religion have recently been commenced.

Dr. Halley, the Principal of New College, and Mr. Paxton Hood were formerly teachers in the Sunday School connected with High Street Chapel.

In 1730 an estate in the Broadway—known as the Wingrove Estate—was left by Thomas Wingrove, as an endowment to this church.   The purport of the will is given in these words :—

"The Trustees are to have and to hold for ever in trust, nevertheless for the maintenance and support of the minister and clerk of the Meeting House in Butt Lane, and their successors for the time being for ever."

Owing to a Chancery suit, the church will not receive the full benefit of this endowment until the year 1922. It realizes at the present time about £40 per annum, ground rent.

The principal Christian and charitable agencies carried on by the congregation are :—

The three Sunday Schools, viz. :—

(1). High Street School which has been in existence for 82 years.

(2). New Street School, established 43 years ago.

(3). Queen Street School, which has been connected with this church since 1874.   Besides the morning and afternoon schools held here, there is also an evening Sunday School with an average attendance of about 60. The class of children are of the poorest order, rough, ignorant and difficult to manage ; still, there is something good and genuine about most of them.

> The rough hewn stones from out the mire : unsightly, and unfair
>   Have purest veins of marble hid beneath their roughness there.
> Few rocks so bare, but to their height some tiny moss plant clings ;
>   And around the crags most desolate, the sea bird soars and sings.
> Believe me too, that rugged souls beneath their roughness hide
>   Much that is soft and beautiful : they've all their angel's side.

So the teachers of Queen Street have found ; and it is this that draws them Sunday after Sunday, at the risk of their health to a small, overcrowded, badly ventilated room.   There is a library in the New Street School, which needs replenishing. *The Ladies' Benevolent Society* established to aid poor persons in obtaining suitable clothing &c., by means of their own savings, supplemented by a grant from the subscriber's fund.   Blanket Society.   Dorcas Maternity Society.   Sickman's Friend Society.   Penny Bank, and a Mutual Improvement Society, which numbers about 76 members, who pay a subscription of 1s. per annum.

𝔚𝔢𝔰𝔩𝔢𝔶𝔞𝔫 𝔐𝔢𝔱𝔥𝔬𝔡𝔦𝔰𝔱 ℭ𝔥𝔲𝔯𝔠𝔥,

MARY ANN'S BUILDINGS, HIGH STREET.

METHODISM is supposed to have taken root in Deptford at the commencement of the 18th century ; but the earliest authentic record of its existence in the parish is in the year 1739. At that date, Fetter-lane, City—according to Wesley's Journal—seems to have been the head of the London circuit of which Deptford was a member. The area then comprised in this one circuit is at the present time divided into 83 distinct circuits. In this year we find the Rev. John Wesley here, preaching at a place called Turner's Hall. Some two thousand people had assembled to hear him ; and just as the reverend gentleman was commencing his sermon, the floor of the hall gave way, and sank some two feet, until it rested on some hogsheads of tobacco stored in the vault beneath. Some confusion ensued, which was soon suppressed by Mr. Wesley's continuing his discourse. Wesley seems to have frequently visited Deptford, and to have met with considerable annoyance. In June, 1757, he says, "I preached at Deptford, and, even this wilderness does at length bud and blossom as the rose ; never was there before such life in this little flock." Again, in 1762, he says, " Deptford Society seems more alive than ever, a sure sign of which is their constantly increasing numbers." In 1770 he preached a funeral sermon here for the Rev. G. Whitefield. It would seem from the following entry that Mr. Wesley's intention was never to separate from the Church of his fathers : " I met the various classes at Deptford, and was vehemently importuned to order the Sunday service in our room, at the same time with that of the Church. We fixed all our services all over England at such hours as not to interfere with those of the Church, with this very design, that those who preferred it might attend both, but to fix it at the same hour is obliging them to separate either from us or the Church, and this I consider to be inexpedient." Visiting Deptford again about a fortnight afterwards, he says, " it seemed I was got into a den of lions. Most of the leading men were mad for separation from the church. I endeavoured to reason with them, but in vain ; they had neither sense nor even good manners left. At length, after meeting the whole Society, I told them if you are resolved you may have your service in Church hours, but remember, from that time you will see my face no more. This struck deep, and from that hour I have heard no more of separating from the Church." Up to 1793 the Society does not appear to have had any fixed meeting room. The first building was erected in Loving Edward's Lane, at the corner of Edward Street and Wellington Place, and known as the " Pantile House," where John Wesley often preached.

In the course of five years this building was found inadequate for the rapidly increasing attendance ; and the upstairs part of a tobacconist's shop, which stood on the site of the premises now occupied by Carter, Paterson, and Co., in High Street, were hired, and used for three or four years, when it was decided to erect a permanent chapel in Mary Ann's-buildings, High Street, which was finished in 1803. One of the first collecting books for the building fund is still preserved ; it runs thus :—" A subscription for building a chapel in Butt-lane, Deptford, for the use of the Methodists, late in connection with the Rev. John Wesley ; the Methodists having long occupied a small chapel in Deptford, on lease, the lease being expired, an application was made for a renewal, but this could not be obtained but at a high rent, and as the chapel would require a considerable sum to put it in good repair, and it being thought too small for the congregation, it was thought most advisable to build a large and more commodious place. With some difficulty a piece of freehold land was met with in Butt Lane, and purchased, upon which a chapel is now erecting, capable of containing between 800 and 1000 persons. To complete this building, including the purchase of the ground, about £1.400 will be wanted, to raise which the Society feel that the greatest exertions are necessary ; but they flatter themselves that their endeavours will be aided by the friends of religion.—Signed, REV. JOSEPH BENSON, of the New Chapel, City Road."

On the breaking out of the Scotch rebellion, in 1745. some troops, lately returned from the continent, lay encamped on Deptford Heath, awaiting orders to proceed to the North.   Many of these soldiers were devout Methodists, and obtained an extension of their parole, which confined them within a radius of one mile from the camp, to attend the preaching of Mr. Wesley, twice a week at the old Foundry, in London, and during their six months' stay here, when not on duty, were wont to meet twice a day to read the Scriptures, and to pray and praise God in the old preaching room at Deptford.   One of their number, James Staniforth, a Yorkshireman, then about 25 years of age, became the chief stay and support of Methodism here, in its early stages of progress.   On leaving the army in 1746 he settled in Greenwich as a baker, and soon attained a prominent position in the Methodist Society at Deptford, being a local preacher, steward, sick-visitor, class-leader, and leader of several band meetings.   He commenced a Thursday evening service, sometimes reading one of Mr. Wesley's sermons himself when no other preacher came.   He built here a neat little chapel, with galleries, in 1757, at a cost of £225 ; being solely responsible for the funds ; but we are unable to ascertain in what part of the parish it was situated.

In October, 1750, he was made Constable.   On being summoned to take the oath in the prescribed form, one of the magistrates said "fine him £20 and he will swear anything," upon which Staniforth replied that he would not take it for twenty worlds.   Instead of the usual oath, the chairman suggested the following, which he accepted, viz. : "Sampson Staniforth, of the parish of Greenwich, is by us appointed to serve the office of Constable for one year, in the best manner he can according to his own way of thinking." This was a very trying year, but he gave general satisfaction to the parish.

At this time he walked to London for orders where to preach, every Sunday morning before breakfast, preached five or six times a week, besides attending class and band meetings. His wife's health failing in 1781, he was compelled to give up much of his missionary work ; he then commenced preaching in his own house. On his death in 1799, one of his friends wrote the following lines :—

"Sampson in youth, like the unbroken steed,
   With British soldiers flashed his flaming red ;
   To Flanders marched to meet the Gallic foe.
   'Twas there the youth first learnt himself to know,
   Back to his native country he returns,
   A different flame now in his bosom burns,
   Discharged from royal William's loyal band,
   Enlists in Jesus's nobler ranks to stand.
   Changeless, he firmly stands in his Master's cause,
   A Bible Christian, subject to its laws ;
   A soldier, christian, husband, man of worth,
   Such died the venerable Staniforth."

When the present chapel was opened in 1803, the circuit included the following places, viz. : Deptford, Woolwich, Bromley, Greenwich, Erith, Lewisham, Chislehurst, and many more outlying places, and the local preachers had to defray their own travelling expenses.

The Chapel records up to 1839 have been lost. In that year the total number of members in the circuit was 1073 ; in Deptford alone, 250. The highest total reached at any time for Deptford was 490. Some thirty or forty years ago Deptford Chapel was crowded to excess, people walking miles to attend the services. The late celebrated preacher, the Rev. William Morley Punshon, was nominated for the ministry from this circuit, and it was in Deptford Chapel he preached his first sermon. The Rev. Joseph Spencer, father of the late resident minister, was also recommended from this place; as likewise Mr. Carlyan, in 1868, who was master of the Day School. About A.D. 1850 that eloquent preacher, the Rev. Mr. Ingle was the resident minister here,

Branches from the Parent chapel have been successfully established in Brockley Lane and Windmill Lane, Lower Road. The services at Brockley were at first conducted in an iron building, until the completion of the school room under the Church in 1876. The memorial stone of the Church was laid October 11th, 1876.

The mission in Windmill Lane was opened in two rooms on the 1st Sunday in May, 1875, and the iron building at present in use was removed from Brockley Lane in November, 1876.

In connection with this Wesleyan cause is a Benevolent and Stranger's Fund Society (undenominational in its actions); a Church Poor Fund; Bands of Hope, Libraries, and four Sunday Schools besides other christian agencies.

Midway Place Chapel.

MIDWAY PLACE CHAPEL, was built by the Rev. Thomas Beck, in 1790. It is situated at the extreme western boundary of the parish, and was erected for the evangelization of the inhabitants of the neighbourhood, who were at that time in a most deplorable condition of ignorance and religion. He also established a day school in 1794.

Mr. Beck was a minister in the Rev. G. Whitefield's connexion, London. In 1780 he became minister of the Chapel at Gravesend; and eight years afterwards accepted the invitation of the church to succeed the Rev. Dr. Savage, at the chapel of the late Dr. Watts, in Bury Street, St. Mary's Axe, London. He frequently preached at Midway Chapel; but the pulpit was chiefly supplied by preachers from the Tabernacle, and ministers of the London Itinerant Society, until about 1825, when Mr. Beck's son-in-law, the Rev. John Kingsford took the superintendence of the congregation, as the settled minister, though a Baptist.

Mr. Beck died at the advanced age of ninety-five years, on the 11th of April, 1844, and was buried at the Independent Chapel, High Street, Deptford, by the Rev. John Pulling.

Mr. Kingsford continued minister until his death; and as the population increased greatly, a noble school-house for the district was erected in 1843; the foundation stone was laid by D. W. Wire, Esq. (afterwards Lord Mayor of London) on the 4th of April, and the building was opened on the 23rd of June. Mr. Kingsford, however, was too feeble to preach often, and he was aided chiefly, from October 15th, 1843, by the Rev. G. C. Smith, when the congregation increased, and a new chapel, more commodious, was projected. But differences arose as to the denomination of the new chapel; and it was at length agreed that the Independents should branch off, and form a new church. This was done in February, 1855, when they opened another place of worship, at a short distance, but within the parish of Rotherhithe, where Mr. Smith and his friends proceeded to erect a commodious new chapel, the foundation stone of which was laid, June 10th, 1857.

Mr. Kingsford died June 15th, 1855, aged 85 years, leaving the Rev. R. R. Finch, the pastor of the Baptists, at the old chapel, where he was chosen in March of that year.

Three youths connected with this chapel, viz.: Messrs. Paxton Hood, B. Wale, and T. Ruegg, have since distinguished themselves in the walks of literature.

New Cross Chapel.

THIS chapel, built in 1805, through the zeal of several active members of the church in High Street, aided by

Joseph Hardcastle, Esq., of Hatcham Park, treasurer to the London Missionary Society, was situated in the west side of Lewisham High Road, about midway between the Royal Naval School and the "New Cross House" Inn.

The Rev. Mr. Purkis was the first settled minister, the pulpit having previously been supplied by preachers from Deptford and Greenwich, the London Itinerant Society, and students from the Colleges. He was succeeded by the Rev. Mr. Hughes and the Rev. Mr. Davies, who afterwards removed to Daventry. A new lease of the chapel was taken by Joseph Hardcastle, Esq., junr., and Mr. Slous, and the Rev. W J. Hope, master of the Congregational School, Lewisham, succeeded to the pastorate. He was ordained September 21st, 1831, and held the office until 1853, when he resigned the school, and emigrated to Australia. His successor at the school, the Rev. J. B. Lister, engaged as minister of the chapel, which he relinquished at Christmas, 1854, after the opening of the Chapel of St. David's Congregational Church. This chapel was then occupied by the New Connexion Methodists until the expiration of the second lease at Michaelmas, 1855, when it was demolished. In the graveyard of this chapel was one tombstone :—" In memory of Mary Purkis, daughter of the Rev. Isaac Purkis. She was born at Lechlade in Gloucestershire, 17th, Feby. 1812. Fell asleep in Jesus Oct. 6th, 1820, aged 9 years."

> " Cropt in the bud the fragrant flower,
>   No more on earth is seen ;
> Faded its leaf, its beauty gone,
>   As if it ne'er had been.
> Gone but not lost, this opening flower,
>   This lily of the vale,
> Placed by the side of Sharon's Rose
>   Shall never, never fail.
> Transplanted to the realms above
>   Its beauty it retains,
> And e'en along earth's thorny path
>   Its fragrance still remains.
> However young the Christian dies,
>   To heaven he takes his flight ;
> To realms of everlasting bliss—
>   To scenes of pure delight.

There, Mary now securely lodged
  Sings to her Saviour's praise,
That Saviour whom she sought,
  In childhood's early days.
Let every youthful reader learn
  To choose the better part
To live to God and do His will
  With pure and perfect heart."

Ebenezer Independent Chapel.

'EBENEZER Chapel, King Street, arose through a difference of sentiment among the friends of the cause of Christ at Greenwich Tabernacle. That sanctuary being erected in the year 1800, it was at the time when the Calvinistic controversy was still carried on with considerable zeal. Many in this vicinity entered into it ; and parties were formed of those who held high views, distinct from their brethren who were regarded as moderate in doctrine. Those who cherished the high Calvinistic sentiments at Deptford and Greenwich, left the Tabernacle and assembled for worship in the large building since used as a Theatre in Deptford. They obtained preachers chiefly from London, and such generally as were in connexion with that celebrated preacher, William Huntington." (Timpson). The chapel was built and opened in 1806. Mr. Thomas Burgess was the first settled minister who held the pastorate till his death, April 19th, 1824. After his decease no resident pastor was appointed for a period of six years, when Mr. Kirkness was chosen, who resigned after holding the office for about ten years. His successor was Mr. George Stringer, who was ordained October 19th, 1842, and resigned in October, 1849. No other pastor was appointed till 1854, when Mr. Clarke was chosen.

Various changes arose in the congregation of Ebenezer Chapel ; sometimes the cause of religion appeared to flourish in the place, and then to be depressed. It suffered also by the secession of those who were Baptists, yet holding the same doctrinal sentiments ; and these having united with zeal and activity, left their first place of meeting, which was a small chapel in Giffin Street, for a new and commodious sanctuary, which they erected near the New Cross Road 1846, under the pastoral care of the Rev. Thomas Felton. which was named Zion Chapel.

When Ebenezer Chapel was removed for the erection of St. John's Mission Hall, two iron coffins were found in a vault under the pulpit, containing the remains of the Rev. T. Burgess and his wife, which were re-interred in Brockley Cemetery.

Bethel Independent Chapel.

BETHEL Chapel originated in the open air preaching of the Rev. Isaac Purkis to the workmen employed in the Royal Dock and Victualling Yards. In 1814 it was resolved to erect a chapel to accommodate about 500 persons, and a piece of ground near to Black Horse Bridge, having been obtained on lease, the foundation stone was laid by the Rev. Dr. (then Mr.) Alexander Fletcher, of London, on the 14th of September ; and the building opened for service March 24th, 1815, on which occasion three sermons were preached—by the Rev. Dr. A. Fletcher, the Rev. R. Stodhart, and the Rev. Dr. Collyer, the collections amounting to £57. Many of the congregation, being mechanics, gave personal labour in laying the flooring and fitting up the interior. During Mr. Purkis' ministry, which terminated in 1821, he was assisted by itinerant preachers and students from Homerton College, among whom was Dr. Halley, President of

New College, who preached his first sermon at this chapel. The Rev. John Mackenzie, M.A., became minister in 1821, and left in 1823 ; he was succeeded by the Rev. Mr. Miller, and then by the Rev. W. Woodlands, who afterwards removed to Union Chapel, Woolwich.

Bethel Chapel has just been pulled down, and some cottages erected on its site.—(*See article on St. Luke's Church*).

New Street School and Preaching Station.

This building was erected in 1838, at a cost of £800. I arose from the preaching on Sunday and week-day evenings, in an old mansion, formerly the residence of Admiral Hughes, in Hughes' Fields. The trust deed requires it to be used as a Day and Sunday School, and for preaching on Sunday evenings by the City Missionary. Of the trustees of this school elected in 1838, two only now survive, viz., W. Agutter, Esq., and Mr. Seaward.

Baptist Chapel,

OCTAVIUS STREET.

In July, 1867, a school-room was opened with accommodation for 250, where services were held by the present minister, the Rev. D. Honour, until the erection of the permanent Chapel in 1878.

P

Welsh Independent Church.

A congregation of Welsh residents at Deptford were accustomed to assemble for worship in the old Methodist Chapel, Loving Edward's Lane (Edward Street East) their Pastor, being the Rev. Arthur Jones ; who was succeeded by the Rev. James Hughes, a Calvinistic Methodist ; and then by the Rev. Job Thomas.

In 1836 the congregation removed from the Methodist Chapel to a commodious school-room in the Lower Road ; and their Minister in 1859 was Mr. Flower.

The services were held alternately in English and Welsh. A copy of the Welsh hymn-book used by this congregation may be seen in the British Museum Library.

St. David's Congregational Church,

LEWISHAM HIGH ROAD.

St. David's Church originated in the efforts of the Christian Instruction Society of Greenwich, Deptford, and Lewisham. The committee projected a commodious building on Tanner's Hill, New Town, to be occupied as a Sunday School, day school, and a chapel for Sunday evening services. The foundation stone was laid by M. W. Attwood, Esq., M.P., September 9th, 1840, and, after an expenditure of £374, it was opened by a public meeting, T. L. Hodges, Esq., M.P., presiding, when addresses were given by the Rev. Messrs. Chapman, Jeula, Pulling, Timpson, and other Independent and Baptist Ministers.

The designs of the building were carried on, but with feebleness, after a short time, and the day school declined.

But Mr. Alderman Wire, having come to reside at Stone House, in the immediate vicinity, joined the committee in February, 1842, and a new order of things was soon established. A large portion of the debt was paid off; the Sunday School was revived and a sermon in the afternoon was added.

Mr. Wire erected a gallery at one end of the building to afford increased accommodation for the people; and the gratuitous services of the neighbouring Ministers, with those of others, personal friends of Mr. Wire—who himself was accustomed to read sermons and conduct the services, when no other Minister could be found—continued until the erection of the Evening Chapel, where services were conducted until the completion of the present noble Gothic structure—the corner stone of which was laid October 13th, 1859, by Mr. Alderman Wire, at that time Lord Mayor of London. The top stone on the spire was laid in December, 1860, by Mr. Travers Wire, the only son of the Alderman, who died 9th November, 1860. The building was opened February 14th, 1861, when sermons were preached by Revs. Thos. Aveling and Geo. Smith.

The first resident Minister was the Rev. George Martin of Chelmsford, whose recognition service was held August 15th, 1851.

Mr. Martin, who was highly appreciated by the members of his congregation, resigned the pastorate in August, 1881. He has been succeeded by a very earnest and devoted Minister, the Rev. I. Morley Wright, late of Leicester, whose Recognition Service took place on the 21st November, 1882.

The Missionary labours of this congregation are being vigorously carried out in the New Mission Hall, Napier Street, and the other Christian agencies, including besides, three Sunday schools, a Mutual Improvement Association, Clothing and Infants' Friend Society, Blanket Society, Ladies' Bible Class and Working Society, Christian Instruction Society, Mothers' Meetings, &c., are being prosecuted with a most commendable and exemplary zeal.

𝕭𝖆𝖕𝖙𝖎𝖘𝖙 𝕮𝖍𝖆𝖕𝖊𝖑,

BROCKLEY ROAD.

THIS handsome Gothic chapel was built in 1867 by the present Pastor, the Rev. J. T. Wigner, and opened for worship 20th May, 1868. Under the chapel is a fine lecture hall.

The mission work of this congregation is extensive, being carried on at the Creek Street Hall and New Street, Deptford, Lewisham Bridge Schools, Brockley Road Lecture Hall, and at the Relieving Office, Waterloo Place. The Sunday Schools and other agencies, including Dorcas Society, Blanket Society, Young Men's Association, Aged Pilgrims' Fund, Poor Clothing Fund, and Maternity Society, Foreign and Home Missionary Societies, &c., are all in prosperous condition.

𝕻𝖗𝖊𝖘𝖇𝖞𝖙𝖊𝖗𝖎𝖆𝖓 𝕮𝖍𝖚𝖗𝖈𝖍, 𝕭𝖗𝖔𝖈𝖐𝖑𝖊𝖞.

THIS noble Gothic edifice with its handsome spire 170 feet high just approaching completion, is the outcome of a temporary building erected in 1876.

The first settled minister, the Rev. M. Macaulay, A B., was inducted in February, 1879, and died deeply regretted some 14 months afterwards. After an interregnum of two months the pastorate was accepted by the present minister, the Rev. Hugh McIntosh, formerly of the London Road Free Church, Glasgow.

The new church accommodates one of the 48 congregations constituting the London Presbytery, which is one of the ten Presbyteries into which England is divided.

It may be interesting to know that the general design of the enrichments of the noble western doorway is taken from Jedburgh Abbey. On the memorial stone in the tower is a representation of the Burning Bush, the symbol of the Presbyterian Church, with the legend: " Nec tamen consumebatur."

Brunswick Chapel.

WESLEYAN METHODIST FREE CHURCH.

THIS congregation is an offshoot from the Wesleyans at the disruption of 1836. Until the erection of the present building in 1841, they worshipped in a neighbouring room, now used as a Sunday School.

THE other Methodist congregations in the Parish are the New Connection in Victoria Road, established in 1857, and the small Primitive Methodist Chapel in Napier Street.

Zion Chapel.

THE origin of this place of worship will be found in the account of Ebenezer Chapel. The present minister is the Rev. Mr. Anderson.

THERE is a small Baptist Chapel on the western confines of the Parish in Lausanne Road.

Wesleyan Methodist Church,

NEW CROSS.

THIS is one of Sir Francis Lycett's chapels, and arose from a mission carried on for some years near the Clifton Road Board Schools.

It is a fine Gothic building, having a large school room underneath.

New Jerusalem Church.

THE Swedenborgians have a commodious building in Warwick Street, but the cause, judging by the attendance, is but weak.

A Chapel belonging to the Calvinists in Malpas Road, and another belonging to the Christian Brethren in Wilson Street, have disappeared.

ECCLESIASTICAL SYNOPSIS.

Name of Church.	Denomination.	Date of Erection.	Sittings.	Sun. Scholrs	Popula- tion.
St. Nicholas'	Estab. Church	12th cen.	1000	290	7,850
St. Paul's	do.	1730	1300	738	16,779
Do. Mission Room ...	do.	......	300		
St. James'	do.	1854	900	357	15,816
Do. Mission Room ...	do.	......	30		
St. John's	do.	1855	1550	440	11,703
Do. Mission Hall ...	do.	·1873	500		
Christ Church ...	do.	1864	1200	459	6,761
Do. Mission Room ...	do.	......	400		
All Saints'	do.	1869	857	700	12,909
Do. Institute	do.	......	400		
St. Peter's	do.	1870	1100	400	5,459
St. Luke's	do.	1872	1100	450	7,313
St. Barnabas	do.	1882	200		
St. Cyprian's	....	1882	450	80	
R. N. School Chapel	....	1853	300		
Assumption B.V.M. ...	Church of Rome	1846	700	770	
Church Street Chapel	Unitarian Bap.	17th cen.	200		
Midway Place ...	Baptist	1790	200		
Zion Chapel	do.	1846	600		
Brockley Road Chapel	do.	1867	850	507	
Do. Creek St. Mission	do.	1877		620	
Octavius Street ...	do.	1878	550	550	
Lausanne Road ...	do.				
High Street Church ...	Congregationalist	1702 rebuilt	......	341	
Do. New Street School	....	1756 rebuilt	......	220	Church rebuilt only
Do. Queen St. School	....	1862	886	130	
Lewisham H. Rd. Ch.	Congregationalist	1860	1200	442	
Do. Napier St. Mission	do.	1881	......	320	
Do. Tanner's Hill ...	do.	......	......	244	
Meeting House ...	Soc. of Friends	17th cen.	230		
Mary Ann's Buildings	Wes. Methodist	1803	563	190	
Do. French's Fields ...	do.	......	250	125	
Do. Brockley Road ...	do.	1876	1060	280	
Do. Windmill Lane ...	do.	1877	150	100	
New Cross Chapel ...	do.	1877	1050	570	
Brunswick Chapel ...	Meth. F. Church	1841	220		
Napier Street... ...	Prim. Methodist	......	80		
Victoria Road ...	Meth. N. Con.	1857	315		
Blackhorse Bridge ...	Lon. City Mis.	1857	100		
Evelyn Hall	do.	......	200		
Church Street ...	do.	......	40		
Presbyterian Church...	Presbyterian	1882	1000		
New Jerusalem ...	Swedenborgians	......	200		
Hatcham Park Road...	Free C. of Eng.	1881	100		

CHARITIES.

1563.—SIR John Scampion, Scrivener of London, by will, dated August, 1563, and the same was established by a Commissioner of Charitable Uses in 1609, gave 12s. per annum towards the Relief of the Poor of Deptford, to be paid out of lands in it.

1640.—William Sewers gave 26s. yearly, distributed at Lady-Day and Michaelmas, in Bread, for which four acres of land and two tenements in Upper Deptford, are charged.

1658.—Abraham Colfe, vicar of Lewisham, gave the yearly sum of 6s. 8d., now 8s. 8d., to buy two sweet penny wheaten loaves weekly, for two of the godliest and poorest householders, payable by the Leathersellers' Company in London. He also gave to eight poor boys of this parish, from time to time, the privilege of being freely taught, and entitled to all the advantages belonging to any scholar educated in the Grammar School founded by him at Lewisham, one of which is a presentation to the University of Oxford.

1672.—Dr. Robert Bretton, late vicar of St. Nicholas, Deptford, gave £400 for maintenance of a

Grammar School, free for 24 poor children, of which there only remains now £190, the rest having been long lost by being placed out upon deficient securities. The interest of this £190 is applied to teaching twelve children, six from each parish.

1678.—Left by a person unknown, Pea Straw, for the use of the Church, charged on an estate, in the parish ; half a quartern of wheat on Good Friday, and now received 10s. ; half a load of Rushes at Whitsuntide, and load of wheat straw now received 21s.

1678.—Mrs. Esther Pope gave to the Vicar of St. Nicholas, Deptford, 20s. per annum, to be by him distributed to the poor at Christmas, charged on two tenements in Lower Deptford.

——.—John Riches, gift of bread, distributed weekly, after morning and evening service every Sunday, charged on estate at Upper Town.

——.—Robert Stout, gift of 26s. 8d. yearly, charged on the " Crown " public house.

1709.—Mrs. Elizabeth Wilshaw gave, by her last will, the sum of £120 ; the yearly product whereof is distributed yearly on the day of her death, viz., November 11th, to such poor widows as frequent the parish Church of Deptford.

1713.—Judith Fiott gave to this parish, by her will, £130 ; the yearly product whereof to be disposed in putting out apprentice one poor child born in the parish of Deptford.

—Edward Boulter, Esq.. by his will, bearing date 1707, gave the parish of Deptford a right of presenting one pensioner to a certain almshouse, which he directed should be built near Oxford ; the pensioner to have an annual sum of £7 and a good warm gown with a silver badge. This benefaction has been determined to belong exclusively to the parish of St. Paul, on account of its connection with the Brockley estate.

———.—Mr. Joine (on reference to the Vestry order books supposed to be Josias Joyner, at what time unknown) gave, to be distributed in bread on December 24th, a sum of 20s. yearly for ever.

———.—Walter Bevan Knott, £200, 3½ per cent. int. ; to repair tomb ; residue to be distributed in bread and coals in the week before Christmas.

By Act of Parliament 3, George II., anno 1730, for providing a maintenance for the new Parish Church of St. Paul's, built in the Parish of St. Nicholas, Deptford, in the counties of Kent and Surrey, and for making the same a distinct parish, " It is enacted that all gifts, charities, &c., before given to the Parish, and then the property of it, should, after the consecration of the new Church, be equally divided ; one moiety for the benefit of the old parish, and one for the benefit of the new one."

This parish has a right of a presentation of one poor person to Queen Elizabeth's College, in Greenwich, founded by Edward Lambard, vested in the Leathersellers' Company.

1741.—Thos Jennings, a blacksmith, who died at Buenos Ayres, 1742, gave, by will, 1741, to be distributed by two parishes of Deptford, £50, the interest to be distributed to poor widows on Candlemas day ; vested in trustees.

1749.—Sir John Evelyn, Bart., in 1749, gave. by deed, for the use, benefit, and support of the poor of the parish of St. Nicholas, Deptford, land presumed to be vested in his heir, and now (1751) of the annual value of £11 16s. By consent of the donor, the two trustees, and an order of Vestry, the Churchwardens sold to the trustees of the Kentish Turnpike Road about 20 rods of the said land for £10 in money, which was vested in Bank Annuities, in Trust. And at the same time to the poor of St. Paul's Parish a piece of land let at £6 per annum.

1752.—Thomas Fellowes, Esq., gave, by will, in 1752, the interest of £1000, to be appropriated to the educating of as many poor children—boys and girls—as it would afford, in the three per cents., in the Account-General of the Court of Chancery, out of which the parishes did not receive any benefit till about 1790.

1758.—Mary Wiseman (widow), by will gave the sum of £20, Old South Sea Annuities, to be annually laid out and distributed to poor widows and housekeepers of St. Paul's, Deptford, who do not take alms, but are real objects of charity and members and communicants of the Church of England (on February 19th), yearly vested in trusts, and of the annual value of 12s.

1767.—Richard Brook, in 1767, gave by will the interest, to be distributed to such three poor men and three poor women, housekeepers, not receiving alms, as the minister and Churchwardens should think fit, equally share and share alike the sum of £100 Consols Bank Annuities, annual produce of £3.

1796.—Isaac Wall. The interest of £1,000 three per Cents., to purchase bread and coals for inhabitants for ever. One half in bread, and the other half in coals.

1801.—Mary Curry, died 1801, left, by will, £100 to the Parish, to be distributed on the day of her death (12th October), annually in bread and coals, the yearly product being £4 3s.

1822.—Francis Lambourne, died 21st November, 1822, left, by will, to this Parish, at the decease of his son, £100, Four Per Cent. Annuities, the interest of which to be applied in the purchase of buns and ale to the poor inmates of the Workhouse of this Parish every Good Friday. The money was transferred, the stock reduced to 3½ per cent., and applied to the purpose in 1829.

DR. PRICE'S GIFT.—On the 14th day of February, 1872, £100 was paid to the Official Trustees of Charitable Funds, and was subsequently invested by them in the New £3 Per Cent. Bank Annuities ; the interest arising from the investment thereof to be applied in giving on the 1st day of January in every year for ever, the sum of 5s. each to 12 poor widows of the Parish of St. Nicholas, Deptford ; the selection of the recipients to be in the discretion of the Vicar of the said Parish for the time being, preference being given to the aged, infirm, or afflicted, and any surplus remaining of the said interest to be laid out in the purchase of bread to be equally distributed amongst the said recipients.

LAUS DEO.

A.D. 1853. Mr. John White, by will, gave £200, Three Per Cent. Consols, the interest to be given away in coals annually on the 21st December.

Extract from the will of F. West, of Cove Cottage, Ventnor :—

" I give and bequeath unto my good friend, Canon Money, Vicar of St. John's Church, Lewisham High Road, in the County of Kent, the sum of £1,500 in trust, to invest the same in the public funds of Great Britain in his own name and the name of the Churchwardens for the time being of the said church, to relieve, at the Christmas season of each and every year, such of the necessitous and deserving poor, as the said Rev. Canon Money and his successors to the living in his and discretion shall see fit ; but it is my express desire that a portion of such dividends, interest and annual proceeds of such invested money be set apart for and applied to the expenses of the services of the said church ; but the amount to be so applied and its purpose I leave entirely in the discretion of the minister for the time being of the said church, and I direct my executors and trustees hereinafter appointed to pay the said sum of £1,500 free of all legacy duty in respect hereof."

CHARITABLE INSTITUTIONS.—John Addey's Charity. On the outside wall of St. Nicholas' Church are affixed two tablets with the following inscription :—

I.—" Near this place rests the body of JOHN ADDEY, of this Parish, one of the King's Master Shipwrights, who departed this world in assured hope of his Resurrection, the 16th of April, Anno Dm. 1606, Ætatis Suæ 56.

" His tomb being demolished, this stone was erected at the expense of the Parish, January, 1788.

II.—The above-named John Addey, by his will, gave to his executors two hundred pounds " to procure a perpetuale annuity towards the reliefe of the poor people of Deptford to last for ever." Therewith was purchased a piece of ground on the east side of Church Street in this town ; the rents and profits therefrom, and from the buildings thereon, exceed in this present year, £650. From this fund, 40s. each are annually given to 100 poor parishioners of Deptford and large schools for the poor children of the town are maintained.

This tablet was erected by the Trustees of the Charity to commemorate the good deed of a good man."

The executor mentioned in Addey's will was William Stevenson, the Overseers, Samuel Page, *Vicar of Deptford*, John Kind, *Vicar of Greenwich*, and Ma thew Baker, of Deptford.

At an inquisition taken at the New School House, East Greenwich, on the 24th September, 1679, it was ascertained that the property had so much improved as to produce a yearly rental of £50 9s. 6d.

The following gentlemen were then appointed Feoffees of the Charity, viz. :—Sir Richard Browne, Bart., John Evelyn, Esq., Richard Holden, Vicar, Francis Wilshaw, Thomas Turner, John More, Thomas Wilshaw, John Shish, John Sneare, Francis Hosier, Richard Gibson, Robert Castell, William Edgall, Henry Wilson, Richard Evelyn, Thomas Pitcher, Robert Longridge, Thomas Stere. Robert Walker, William Case, Henry Cremer and Nathaniel Douse, Gent., all of them inhabitants of Deptford, and their heirs.

Full particulars of the Decree, issued from the Court of Chancery, regulating the management of this Charity may be found in a pamphlet published by Order of the Vestry of the Parish of St. Nicholas in January, 1817.

In 1821, a Charity School for boys and girls was erected on the estate in Church Street, which was enlarged in 1862.

A.D. 1698. Mr. Robert Castle, by his last will gave to the Feoffees of the Gravel Pit estate for the benefit of the poor of this parish, the sum of £200. (Not yet paid).

A.D. 1708. Mr. Joseph Fownes, Clerk of the Checque left by will to the Feoffees of the charity the sum of £50, as also did Mr. Francis Atfen, the sum of £10, in 1713.

THE SUBSCRIPTION CHARITY OR DEAN STANHOPE SCHOOL was founded about A.D. 1715 by the exertions of the pious and learned Dean Stanhope ; whose plans were afterwards in 1722, confirmed and enlarged in consequence of a legacy from Mrs. Gransden.

This Charity, provided for the clothing and educating of fifty boys and thirty girls from the age of eight to fourteen. The sons of shipwrights, carpenters and joiners were bound out apprentices ; the girls being instructed in useful needlework and domestic duties. An annual donation of £5 in money, and £1 in books bequeathed by Dean Stanhope to two boys successively, and to one girl every three years upon leaving the school.

Each subscriber was entitled to put a boy or girl into the school by rotation ; the sum of thirty shillings for a boy, and twenty shillings for a girl being required as a security for their clothing, which was deposited in the Savings Bank for the benefit of the child, and returned with the interest accumulated to the person holding the receipt on the child's leaving school.

The first Trustees,—appointed 9th June, 1722, were :— Gransden, Dean Stanhope, Edward Jennings, Joseph Pink, Henry Hoar, Rev. Wm. Sherlock, John Skeat, Richard Wilkinson, Captain William Moses, Captain Richard Hughes, Captain Robert Watkins, Rev. Henry Archer.

By the new scheme brought out by the Charity Commissioners—acting under the Endowed Schools Acts, 1869, 1873, and 1874, and approved by the Committee of Council on Education—the schools have been closed, the teachers pensioned — master receiving £70 and mistress £42 per annum for life, and the name of the charity changed to the "Stanhope Foundation at Deptford."

The governing body of the Foundation to consist of twelve persons, of whom two are to be called ex-officio governors, four representative, and six co-optative governors (a).

The income of the Foundation, after necessary outgoings and business expenses, to be applied in the maintenance of exhibitions, each of a yearly value of not more than £20, tenable at any place of education higher than elementary approved by the governors, and to be awarded in as nearly as may be equal shares to boys and girls who are being and have for not less than two years been educated at any of the Public Elementary Schools in the Parishes of St. Paul and of St. Nicholas in Deptford, and who on examination show proficiency in knowledge of the Liturgy and Catechism of the Church of England. Every exhibition to be given as the reward of merit, freely and openly competed for and tenable only for the purposes of education.

The chief benefactors to this charity besides the founder have been :

Mr. Robert Gransden, who gave during his lifetime the inheritance of the ground in High Street, upon which the school was built ; and his daughter, Mrs. Mary Gransden, who died in January, 1719, leaving by will to the use of this charity her farm of Plaistow, at Halsted in Essex, the ground rent of two tenements in St. Bartholomew's Lane, London, and £80 in money.

The tenements in St. Bartholomew's Lane were afterwards sold to the Bank of England for £1,300.

1714.—Isaac Loader, Esq., gave £200, only £100 of which appears to have been paid.

1717.—W. Hosier, Esq., a sum of money to be applied for educating poor boys ; now producing £9 per annum.

a The following gentlemen were appointed trustees under the new scheme :—Revs. Dr. Cundy and J. R. Gregg, and Messrs. T. W. Marchant, F. G. Skinner, T. Watson, E. Wilkinson, S. Lewes, W. B. Higham, W. T. Hunt, Jr., A. Clifford, A. J. Dickinson, and T. Reeson.

1727.—Dr. Stanhope, by will in 1727, gave, for putting out boys apprentice, and. every third year, for clothing and fitting girls for service, and pious books, £6 per annnm, being at that time South Sea Annuities £150 at four per cent., now £250; the same being increased by a gift of £42 9s. 6d. by W. Sherwin and William Collins, and a donation of Wm. Holt about 1767 of £10, to be added and applied to the purpose of Dean Stanhope's donation, vested in trustees and of the annual produce of £1 10s. od.

1752.—William Sherwin and William Collins, in 1752. gave money to purchase lands, the rents of which to be applied to the educating and clothing seven poor boys of the two Parishes of Deptford, of shipwrights, joiners, or house carpenters, and, if none such, then other boys, and putting out one apprentice to one of those trades, but not to exceed £14 in clothing and apprenticing ; which money is vested in Old South Sea Annuities, being £1.060, and is of the annual produce of £48, which is indiscriminately appropriated to the use of the two Parishes.

1758.—Mary Wiseman (widow), by will, gave £200, the interest to be laid out annually for clothing six poor boys of St. Nicholas, Deptford, and St. Paul's, Deptford, to be clothed in grey, which money has not been received, it being not thought sufficient for the purpose.

1768.—William Reynolds. in 1768. gave, by will, for the support of the Charity Schools in Deptford and the benefit of the children therein, four leasehold houses, subject to a ground rent of £2 4s. per annum, vested in trustees, of the annual produce of £27 10s. per annum.

1783.—John Chester, in 1783, gave, by will, to be transferred to Feoffees of the Gravel Pits. rents in Deptford, the interest to be applied every year to one poor boy out of the Subscription Charity School, a bricklayer's son to have the preference, £300 Four Per Cent. Annuities, vested in his executors : annual produce £12.

1784.—Richard Phillips, in 1784, by will, for the use of the Subscription Charity School, in Deptford, for educating poor children, £50, Three Per Cent. Consol Annuities, value £1 10s.

Benefactions and legacies amounting to £960 were given to the Building Fund of the school, which was opened on May 28th, 1723.

The premises were sold by order of the Charity Commissioners 10th November, 1881, for the sum of £2,450 to Messrs. J. G. Thomas and W. Wright, who have just erected handsome business houses on the site.

ROYAL NAVAL SCHOOL, NEW CROSS.—The primary object of this school, which was projected in 1831, by the late Captain W. H. Dickson, R.N., is to board and educate the sons of naval and military officers in needy circumstances, giving a preference to the orphans of those who have fallen in their country's service. The school was opened in temporary premises at Camberwell in 1833, and ten years later the foundation stone of the present building at Counter Hill, New Cross, was laid by the late Prince Consort. Since the opening, some 3,000 pupils have partaken of its advantages ; and many of these have distinguished themselves in the naval and military services. The building is of the plainest and most substantial character ; the cost of its erection, including the purchase of seven acres of freehold land, is about £42,000. Another sum of £10,000 is required to complete the original design. Alfred Eames, Esq., has been secretary of the establishment for upwards of 50 years.

ASKE'S HATCHAM SCHOOLS were established in accordance with a scheme under the Endowed Schools Acts, on the 9th Aug., 1873, out of the Trust called "Robert Aske's Hospital" at Hoxton. So great has been the success attending these schools that it is proposed shortly to make some additions. Alderman Aske died in 1688.

W. J. Spratling, Esq., is head master, and Rev. R. J. Griffiths, M.A., LL.D., second master.

THE ROYAL KENT DISPENSARY was founded by Dr. Milne in Deptford Broadway, 1st Dec., 1873 ; and afterwards removed to Greenwich Road. The intention of this charity is to give assistance not only to the lowest class of the people, but to poor housekeepers and others whose income will not enable them to pay for it, excepting only such as are receiving parochial relief.

THE DEPTFORD AND GREENWICH PHILANTHROPIC SOCIETY which was founded by Mr. P. J. Shelley for the purpose of assisting the fallen tradesmen, also the deserving and necessitous poor, but not the habitual pauper, is a society whose objects are most commendable and well deserving of support.

Q

SCHOOLS.—There are, besides the schools already mentioned, many Middle Class Educational Establishments, most of them being situated in the neighbourhood of New Cross and Brockley, amongst which may be mentioned, Montagu House School, New Cross Middle Class School, and New Cross Grammar School, three well established schools which have done good service. Brockley High School started some two years ago in connection with Trinity College has rapidly increased in numbers. Of Public Elementary Schools, the town is well supplied, and the efficiency well maintained, the average percentage being over 90. Since the passing of the Education Act, ten large Board Schools have been erected ; one is in process of erection, and another shortly to be built in place of the temporary iron school in Brockley.

The oldest Denominational School is that of St. Nicholas, in Wellington Street ;—a brick building, ornamented in the centre with a pediment, with the date 1680 ; above which is an acorn well carved. This School was incorporated to the National Society in 1818.

St. John's National School and St. James's, Hatcham, are the other two schools belonging to the church ; besides which there is a Day School in connection with the Wesieyan Methodists in Mary Ann's Buildings.

St. Paul's Schools have been transferred to the London School Board at a peppercorn rent.

St. Joseph's School—a large two storey building—belonging to the Roman Catholic Church of the Assumption, is situated between Crossfield Lane and the Railway.

LOCAL INDUSTRIES PAST AND PRESENT.—The Town of Deptford renowned for its Shipbuilding may almost be said to be the cradle of Steam Navigation, for although the first experimental boat was started on the Clyde, yet a Steamboat Company was formed here a short time after the "Comet" ran on the Clyde ; the late Mr. Thomas Brockelbank of Westcombe Park, built a small Steam Vessel at Deptford, and shortly afterwards induced a number of Capitalists and gentlemen of position and influence to join him about the year 1822, which Company was enlarged and incorporated by Act of Parliament in 1824, and is known by the name of the General Steam Navigation Company, and is probably the oldest Steamship Company in existence in the whole world.

The "Harlequin" and "Columbine" Steamships were built on the banks of the Deptford Creek, and at this date their fleet consisted of about 20 ships, every one of which has now disappeared, and their fleet has trebled in number, and much more than trebled in tonnage ; the Works of this Company are situated on the spot that in former years contained the store rooms and rigging sheds, mast-sheds, and sail-lofts of the East India Company, and the street where they are situated called originally "Storage" remains under its modern name of Stowage to this day, and the "Stowage House" is the residence of the Company's present Superintendent, H. J. Jackson, Esq., formerly known as "Jackson Bey," who for several years had charge of the Egyptian Navy at Alexandria.

The town contained several private ship-building firms, and the names of Gordon, Barnard, Colston, and Ive, and more recently of Langley and of Walker, are well known in the commercial world ; Ditchburn and Mare, too, about the year 1837, commenced that career, which afterwards obtained for their ships such a worldwide reputation. Their building yard before they removed to Blackwall was on the spot now known as Deptford Wharf, a depôt of the L. B. & S. C. Railway.

Messrs. Gordon and Co. carried on an extensive business for more than half a century on Deptford Green, as engineers, anchor smiths, &c., and were amongst the earliest manufacturers of marine engines. After the death of Mr. Adam Gordon, who was the sole representative of the firm in 1839, the business gradually diminished, and finally closed in 1842. Messrs. Gordon and Co. were also lessees of Dudman's Dock, where many East Indiamen were built between 1816 and 1835 ; and where

the first steam vessel belonging to the East Indian Co.
—"The Enterprise"—was built and equipped for sea.

On the shores of the Creek are the old Tide Mills (the
manufacture of biscuits here has been discontinued),
several coal and other wharves. Mr. F. C. Hills' (*a*)
extensive chemical works have been in existence about a
century; Gas Works, Board of Works Yard; Wheen's
Soapery, formerly a pin factory; and a Barge building
yard. Abutting on Deptford Green we find Bray's
Steam Wheel Works; Tayler, Tayler, and Co's. Kamp-
tulican factory; Walker's engineering and ship building
yard, with spacious dry dock; Hood and Co.'s iron and
brass foundry, the present proprietor of which is Mr. S.
Jennings, who succeeded Mr. Hood in October, 1873.
Some portions of these premises are very old and were
formerly used as an anchor foundry by Messrs. Gordons,
and, probably, earlier still, by Mr. Loader.

The engineering works of Messrs. Tennant, Humphrey,
& Co., occupy a considerable portion of the property acquired by Act of Parliament, by the Deptford Pier and Improvement Company, about 1839 (whose designs were
never carried out); the remaining portion being occupied
by the marine boiler works of Messrs. John Penn & Son,
In connection with these works is an Accident and Burial
Fund, which provides—for a small monthly subscription
—weekly relief in cases of accident, and a sum for burial
in event of death of either a member or member's wife.

The business of coach and cart wheelwright at 77,
Evelyn Street, and 1 and 2, Duke Street, was established
by Mr. William Skudder in 1801, and has been carried on
by his son, Mr. Job Scudder, since 1852.

Mr. Eddy, furrier, commenced business in 1843, in
Wellington Place; and Mr. Mowbray, smith and wheelwright, started about 1870, in Grove Road, as engineer

a Mr. Hills was the inventor of a steam carriage which was made and
run upon the public roads in 1839. It performed several trips to
Sevenoaks, Tunbridge, and Hastings, and was stopped simply because
limited liability could not be secured for it.

and boiler maker. John Pound, Son, and Hutchins, packing case makers, decorated tin-box manufacturers, &c., an old-established City firm, opened their new works on the bank of the Surrey Canal in March, 1880.

Messrs. J. Stone and Co's Brass, Copper, and Iron Works, recently removed to new and more commodious premises at the junction of the Greenwich and North Kent Railways, Deptford, were first started by the late Mr. Josiah Stone (formerly of Messrs. Gordon & Co.) in the railway arches and premises, previously the Company's workshops at the Deptford Railway Station, in the year 1842. These new works are a perfect model of what such an establishment should be. The multitud-inous articles manufactured by this firm find their way to almost every part of the world. The firm possesses many useful patents, and their patent navy, portable, steam and other pumps, and fire engines, as supplied to the Royal Navy, Foreign Governments, the P. and O. Co., the Royal Mail, and nearly all the principal shipping companies and ship builders in Great Britain are generally acknowledged to be the handiest and most powerful in use. The harmonious relations between masters and men, existing at Messrs. J. Stone and Co.'s works are most exemplary, and speak volumes for the success of the business. The present proprietors are Messrs. Preston, Prestige and Preston.

The firm of Messrs. Frederick Braby and Co., Limited, iron barge builders and manufacturers of galvanized iron water cisterns, zinc roofing, &c., was first established in 1839 at the Fitzroy Works, Euston Road, London. Their Works at Ida Wharf, Black Horse Bridge, Deptford—an extension of the London business—commenced July 27th, 1867, and the Victoria Works, Victoria Road, Deptford, in 1869, and at the present time give employment to some 360 hands. The various influences at work, in this firm, for raising the moral tone and well being of the employés are most commendable, and a practical illustration of what can be done to improve the intellectual and social condition of the working classes (*a*). There is a Library and Club, of which F. Braby, Esq., is President, and Mr. Geo. R. Humphery Librarian and Hon. Sec. and a Committee of Management, one of whose duties it is to organize Saturday afternoon excursions during the summer months, to the various museums and other places of interest in and about the metropolis. The Library was commenced in May, 1870, with about 100 books, which has steadily increased year by year, and now numbers upwards of 1500 vols. of standard works. There are also classes for instruction, and lectures and entertainments are given during the winter months; a Brass Band, a Dramatic Class, a Sick Benefit Club, on the Slate Club principle, Boys' Benefit Society, a Benevolent Fund, Prize Fund, and a Coal Club, also a Building Club.

Messrs. Bunnett and Corpe, New Cross Road, revolving shutter manufacturers, were the inventors of a concentric steam-engine, with an entirely new arrangement of the cylinder, piston, and piston rod.

Hills and Sons, Tallow, Soap, and Candle makers, Regent Street. This business was commenced in 1822 by the late Mr. John Hills (*b*), a gentleman who took great interest in parish matters, filling the office of Churchwarden of St. Paul's for many years. His son, Mr. Benjamin Hills, has likewise been Churchwarden for two years, in addition to having passed every parish office with distinction.

Although Messrs. Hills make the Kent composite candles, soap is their principal trade. Much of the tallow formerly used for candles, is now made into butterine.

The Neptune Chemical Works, Surrey Canal, established in 1864, by A. J. Dickinson, F.C.S., F.J.C., &c.,

a As a proof that working men appreciate the efforts made by this firm to improve their moral and mental condition, it may be mentioned that they presented a handsome testimonial to their hon. librarian a few months ago.

b Mr. John Hills was churchwarden when Mr. Josiah Bratt. overseer of Hatcham, on December 21st, 1841. presented the parish with a snuff-box, which is required to be produced at all Vestry meetings.

manufacturing chemist, for distilling tar and resin, and manufacturing benzoline and anthracene—bodies forming the bases of the aneline and madder dyes. The manufact ures of this description by Hills, Dickinson, Worringham, Catchpole, Correll, &c., form a considerable item in the trade of the town. In Trundley Lane are Torr's animal charcoal factory, established about 1820; and Mr. Adams' Southwark Park Brewery, established in 1869.

Mr. Norfolk's Deptford Brewery is situated at the corner of Mill Lane, facing the Broadway, on what was formerly a timber yard; and adjoining, on Deptford Bridge, is Holland's Distillery, established in 1779. and now occupied by Mr. Kirby, of Fairlawn, New Cross. Mr. Lacy's Pottery (a) adjoining the old Saw Mills, now the Tyne Foundry, is an old-established business ; the other pottery is situated in Copperas Lane. There is but one manufacturing firm in Brockley, viz. : Messrs. Johnson and Co., iron fence and conservatory makers.

The greatest employers of labour in this portion of the parish are Messrs. J. Martin and Sons, farmers, dairy-men, market gardeners, hay and straw merchants, &c., who have an extensive dairy farm at Brockley Rise.

Eno's Fruit Salt Works, Hatcham.—Mr. J. C. Eno, the sole manufacturer of that refreshing, cooling, and health preserving beverage known as Eno's Fruit Saline, opened his works in this parish, 8th July, 1878, the business having been started at Newcastle some few years previously.

The manufacture of the Fruit Salt—which is an ex-tract of sound, ripe fruit, embodying in a most pleasant form the saline virtue of the richest fruit juices—gives employment at the present time to some fifty people, and if the consumption increases in the same ratio as during the past few years, considerable additions will soon have to be made to the already extensive premises.

a The Deptford Ware for which the town was noted in the last century is not now made.

Eno's Fruit Saline, as a drink, both refreshes and invigorates. It gives immediate relief in such monitory symptoms as heartburn, sourness of stomach, or light headaches, but its salutary power goes much deeper.

THE KENT MINERAL WATERS COMPANY. — The business premises of this Company, are situated in Dixon Road, near the Royal Naval School, New Cross. The business was originally carried on by a Mr. Chapman who was joined by Mr. Bratt, whose father was a well known resident of New Cross. The present proprietors are Messrs. Bratt and Cormack.

The superiority of the Non - Intoxicating Drinks manufactured by this firm is, in a great measure, due to the purity of the water supplied by the Kent Water Works Company, from their deep artesian wells, so highly spoken of by Professor Frankland, D.C.L., F.R.S.

KENT WATER WORKS.—On the 11th December, in the 13th year of the reign of William III., a Royal Charter was granted to William Yarnold and Robert Watson, their executors, administrators, and assigns, empowering them to take water from the River Ravensbourne, and to break up the roadways within the Royal Manors of Sayes Court and East Greenwich, and to lay pipes for the supply of water to the inhabitants of the said Manors for a period of 500 years, and prohibiting any other person from breaking up the roads for supplying the inhabitants; and conferring upon the holders of the patent the sole power and privilege of supplying them with water from the Ravensbourne or elsewhere during that period. This was the commencement of the Ravensbourne Water Works. A water mill was erected in Mill Lane, formerly Dog Kennel Row, the machinery being made by that eminent engineer, Smeaton, who built the first Eddystone Lighthouse, on principles of his own invention. There were two wheels, one for grinding corn and the other for raising water. On the 20th June, 1809, extended powers were obtained by Act of Parliament (49 Geo. III., cap. 189), and the Ravensbourne

Water Works then became merged into the company of proprietors of the Kent Water Works.

At the present time the Company supply an area of about 120 sq. miles in the County of Kent. Its limits having been extended by subsequent Acts, now includes the district from Rotherhithe, down the Thames as far as Gravesend, and inland as far as Dartford, Greenhithe, the Cray Valley, and Orpington, Deptford, Greenwich, Woolwich, Lewisham, Bromley, Chislehurst, &c., and its supply of water is unequalled for its purity by any company within the metropolitan area.

Steam power is now used for pumping, and about 9,000,000 to 11,000,000 gallons are supplied daily.

The information under this heading is not so full as was desired, but it could not be readily obtained.

During the Commonwealth a project was set on foot by Sir Nicholas Crispe, of making a mole at Deptford for the harbour of two hundred sail or more to ride in seventeen or eighteen feet of water without cable or anchor. The demesne lands of the Manor—about 200 acres, now lying in St. Paul's Parish—were purchased for that purpose at the price of £6,000 ; and a considerable sum of money was expended in erecting storehouses and setting up a sluice. After the Restoration, Sir Nicholas Crispe, the Duke of Ormond, Earl of Bath, and others who were embarked with him in this undertaking, petitioned King Charles II. to grant them the land in fee-farm. It was stated in the petition that Sir Nicholas Crispe had formed the project principally with a view of ingratiating himself with the then ruling powers, that he might the better watch a favourable opportunity of bringing about his Majesty's restoration. Sir Charles Harboard, the King's surveyor, to whom the petition was referred, advised his Majesty by no means to grant the land in fee-farm, but to offer a lease of thirty-one years at a rent of £160 per annum, with a fine of £2000. These terms, it is probable, were not accepted, for it does not appear that the projectors proceeded any farther with their design.

Another project was started about 1838, to construct two docks, which, if carried out, would have occupied the greater portion of St. Nicholas Parish as well as that portion of Christ Church Parish to the northward of the railway.

RAILWAYS. — Deptford, doubtless, owes its rapid increase in population and importance to its extensive railway facilities, being intersected by the L.B. & S.C. , the North Kent (opened in 1849) ; the L. C. and D. ; and the Greenwich lines — the latter being the oldest in the metropolis. The first train was run from Spa Road to Deptford (a) 28th February, 1836 ; from Bermondsey to Deptford about October, 1836 ; from London Bridge to Deptford 14th December, 1836 ; and from London Bridge through to Greenwich in 1838. There are no less than seven stations in the parish, with just as many more within almost a stone's throw of its boundaries. The Croydon Railway was worked in the first instance by atmospheric pressure, and was built on the site of the old Croydon Canal, with its numerous locks and lock houses, one of which is still standing in Brockley.

PAST AND PRESENT ASPECT.—The growth of Deptford has been so rapid that it is almost impossible for strangers to realize the changes which have taken place during the past 40 years. There is a pen-and-ink sketch map of Lower Deptford in the British Museum—drawn by " Sylva " Evelyn 1623—of which Mr. J. Liddiard and Mr. W. Gurley-Smith have copies, which shows the town at that date to be pretty nearly confined within the limits of the present Parish of St. Nicholas—not more than half of that

a It is not, probably, generally known that the pepper-box entrance to the down platform of Deptrord (High Street) Station is modelled after one of the most elegant,exquisitely proportioned edifices bequeathed to us by the art-loving Athenians, viz. : the Choragic monument of Lysicrates. A more striking example of the utter degradation of the perfection of art by its misapplication could hardly be produced. The original is a small delicate structure, richly decorated with highly-finished sculpture and formerly crowned by the tripod, which commemorates the fact of Lysicrates having been Choragus, or the person who defrayed the annual expenses of the Chorus, or Tragic Entertainments for the year.

area even being covered with buildings. The streets there given correspond to Wellington Street (Flagon Row), The Stowage, The Green, Butcher Row, and Old King Street. A lane to Crane Meadows passed through Broomfields, between Sayes Court and the Dockyard ; two other lanes, bordered with meadows, connected the old town with the Broadway, viz. : Church Street and Butt Lane (re-named High Street, August 13th, 1825). The intervening space between Old King Street and The Green was meadow land—indeed, this locality is to this day known as Hughes' Fields and French's Fields. Deptford Green was a fine open greensward, planted with trees, on which abutted noble mansions, the residences during Elizabeth's reign of the Lord High Admiral, the Earl of Nottingham, and other officers of dignity. It was approached by a pair of handsome gates surmounted with the crest of the noble family of Howard. Queen Elizabeth, who spent much of her time in her native town of Greenwich, was a frequent visitor at the Howard's.

Some of these ancient mansions have only disappeared during the past 50 years ; as for instance, Benbow's house in Hughes' Fields, said to have been inhabited for a short time by Sir Cloudesley Shovel ; the large house on the Green, occupied by E. G. Barnard, Esq.—one of the first M.P.'s for Greenwich ; another large house—stood at the corner of Church Street, and Creek-road, which had a good garden and orchard leading down to Broom-stick-Alley, Flagon Row in former times, was *the* business street of the town, and it was probably here that the " rag and bone shops" or " marine store dealers " first sprang into existence. M. Esquiros in his " English at Home" asserts that the original marine store dealer was a little negress thrown as a waif into Deptford and brought up by the parish. On arriving at womanhood, she commenced business in this line, amassed a competency, and started branch establishments with the sign of her own effigy (a black doll) as she appeared when first consigned to the tender mercies of the parochial officials.

A curious pamphlet,—only two copies of which are known to exist, one in the Ashmodean Coll., Oxford, and the other in the library of W. H. Diamond, Esq.— relating to this street was published in 1685 with the following title (which is here given as an instance of the superstitious absurdity of our forefathers in the 17th century) :—" Strange and Wonderful News from the Town of Deptford, in the County of Kent, being the sad Relation of one Anne Arthur, dwelling in Flaggon Row, who according to her own Report, had divers Discourses with the D—on the 3rd of March, who offered her gold and silver, telling her many strange and wonderful things, and, in the end, carried her into the air a quarter of a Furlong ; folio, half-sheet, London, 1865." It would be interesting to know if a copy exists of " A Miracle of Miracles, wrought by the blood of King Charles I., upon a Yayd at Deptford, foure miles from London, 4to., London, 1649." The title only is given in the Bibl. Cant. :

Mr. Trickett's shop—at one time called the Grass-hopper—was in former days the most noted tea-shop in the town and neighbourhood, the tea being smuggled from the East Indiamen in the river, in sacks of saw-dust.

One hundred and twenty years ago the Broadway was a country green, surrounded by tall, stately, luxuriant elm trees, beneath which the few surrounding shop-keepers were to be seen in pleasant weather with their wives and friends, pleasantly enjoying their pipes and nut-brown ale, on common benches, whilst the good dame's eye, still directed to the main chance, heedfully watched the step of any casual customer who happened to approach the shop-door, near which the group was assembled. Not often, however, was her vigilance re-warded by chance custom, for the Broadway was a place of secondary resort for trade in those days, Flagon Row, Hughes' Fields, and the Green, in the then flourishing old parish, being the principal marts for buying and sell-ing. In the centre of the greensward might be perceived a draw-well, to which the neighbourhood, then unaccommodated with artificial supplies from the Kent Water Works, resorted for water, whilst, but slightly removed from it, near the present Deptford Brewery in Mill Lane, were the stocks (the ancient "little ease") which Shakespear tells us was a

> "purpos'd low correction,
> Such as the basest and the meanest wretches
> For pilferings and most common trespasses
> Are punished with."

The stocks and cage were only removed some thirty or forty years ago, and the old pump (a) erected over the village well of former days, has just disappeared in the improvements carried out by the Board of Works for widening the approaches to Deptford Bridge.

Casting his eye around, the curious observer of 1760 would have been delighted to notice the neat old-fashioned irregularity of the dwellings about him. Detached groups of chevron-roofed dwellings, with whitened fronts, moss-covered yellow tiles and low descending eaves, presented a rich and captivating contrast against the umbrageous gloom of the surrounding elm-trees.

The portions of the parish known as Hatcham, New Cross, and Brockley, were, until modern times, but sparsely inhabited, and contained some of the finest nursery grounds and market gardens in the south of London. In Myatt's gardens at Brockley the first rhubarb taken to Covent Garden market was grown; and it was here that the strawberries for which Mr. Myatt is so justly renowned were produced. Deptford was likewise noted for its celery, asparagus, and onions. The *caryophyllus pratensis* was named by the old botanists the Deptford Pink. But the gardens have all but disappeared, giving place to some of the finest streets in south-east London.

a A statue of some one of Deptford's worthies, occupyidg the site of the old pump, would heighten the rapidly-improving appearance of this ancient thoroughfare.

As a proof of how local history may be written in street nomenclature may be mentioned that Evelyn Street, formerly Broomfield Place, speaks of the ground landlord of a considerable portion of Deptford proper :— Wotton Road, the name of the family residence at Wotton, in Surrey ; Milton Court, the name of a house built by John Evelyn, in Surrey ; Arklow Road commemorates the birthplace of Mr. Evelyn's grandfather ; Victoria Road commemorates a visit of Her Majesty Queen Victoria, to the Victualling Yard in 1858. The family of Drake is well represented in New Cross and Brockley. The Rev. William Wickham, of Garsington, Bucks, who owned the estate now known as the Drake estate, had two daughters, who married two brothers of the name of Drake, bringing the Deptford property into the Drake family. Hence we have Wickham Road and Wickham Park. Thomas Drake, in accordance with the testamentary injunction of Sir John de la Fountain Fountain-Tyrwhitt, assumed the name of Tyrwhitt in 1766—Tyrwhitt Road. The principal residence of Mr. Drake is called Shardeloes—Shardeloes Road—situated in Amersham Vale, near Amersham, Bucks—Amersham Road, Vale, and Park Road and Villas. Another residence is St. Donnatt's Castle, Glamorganshire—St. Donnatt's Road. A member of the family is, or was, rector of Malpas, in Cheshire—hence Malpas Road ; they own some property at Breakspeare, Oxfordshire, the birthplace of the only Englishman that ever sat upon the Papal throne, Pope Adrian IV.—Breakspeare Road.

Sayes Court Museum, New Cross Public Hall, and the Lecture Hall, in High Street, are the only public buildings of which the town can boast. The last-named is the oldest, and when first erected, was of great service. The late Messrs. David Bass (a zealous local philanthropist) and John Wade took an active part in its erection.

The oldest hostelries are the " Dover Castle " in the Broadway, where the Canterbury Pilgrims probably made their first halting after leaving the Tabard ; the

'Globe," in Evelyn Street, and the King's Head, (*a*) in Church Street, the two latter being mentioned in Pepy's Diary.

The toll-gate in High Street, before its removal to Evelyn Street, stood opposite the " Red Cow "—another old inn, formerly constructed of wood, with a ponderous red cow perched on a pole, bearing a bunch of grapes in its mouth. The Deptford stage coaches started from the " White Swan," at the corner of Loving Edward's Lane, in which a century ago, stood two farm houses and a solitary cottage, still in existence, which, singularly enough, is, and always has been, inhabited by a member of the Musgrove family. The New Cross toll-gate, before its removal to the end of Deptford Lane (Queen's Road), stood at the top of Clifton Hill, near the New Cross House, from which the surrounding district has taken its name. The last toll to be removed was the Creek Bridge, which was accomplished some two years ago, mainly through the exertions of Mr. Gurley Smith. A levy had been charged here, not only on vehicular traffic, but also on foot-passengers, since the first opening of the bridge in 1815.

The Deptford and New Cross Amateur Floral Society, of which Mr. Steere is hon. secretary, has been in existence about three years.

POLITICAL ASSOCIATIONS.—The Deptford Conservative Association, of which W. J. Evelyn, Esq. is president, Mr. Wallbutton, chairman, and Mr. Werter Smith, secretary, is a branch of the Greenwich Association.

a Mr. Salter, the present proprietor, has a copper token of this inn dated 1619 ; and it was here that in 1684 lived Mary, who figures prominently in a pamphlet of that date, and reprinted in 1787 in the " Harlein Miscellany," which bears the following title : " The She-Wedding ; or, a Mad Marriage, between Mary, a seaman's (Charles Parsons) mistress, and Margaret, a carpenter's wife, at Deptford. Being a full Relation of a Cunning Intrigne carried and managed by two women, to hide the Discovery of a great —— and make the parents of her sweetheart provide for the same ; for which Fact the said Parties were both committed ; and one of them now remains in the Round House at Greenwich, the other being bailed out. 1684."

The Brockley Liberal Club, established for the advancement of liberal principles and social intercourse, is presided over by Mr. Cooke Baines, Mr. George Kemp being secretary.

NOTABLE EVENTS.

THE GREAT INUNDATION.—A terrible storm from the north east swept over this district on January 1st, 1651, causing an inundation of the Thames of unparalled magnitude. Deptford suffered greatly. About 2 p.m. the storm became so violent that the waves forced down the piles of wood, and entered the merchant shipping yards, removing great trees and pieces of timber, that twenty horses could scarcely move. By 2.30 p.m. there were seven feet of water in the streets of the Lower Town, which rose three feet more during the next half-hour. Most of the inhabitants fled to the Upper Town, leaving their goods and chattels to the mercy, " as the old chronicler states," of the merciless waves. Those inhabitants who did not effect their escape in time had to be rescued by watermen in boats from their chamber windows ; some are said to have perished. The flood forced its way into one Gammer Farthing's house, " who, being turning the spit, laden with a gallant goose, and having two children, one in the cradle and another out of it, ran forth to call her husband, but before their return, the house was about three feet deep in water ; the cradle floating with the child in it ; the goose swimming ; and the other child saved itself by getting on the top of a high table, which sad spectacle, the father perceiving, rushed up to the middle in water, and brought forth his two children." The waters began to subside about 4 p.m. Besides the damage done to the various shipping yards and dwellings, some two hundred sheep, cows, bullocks, and other cattle were drowned in the Deptford meadows and other fields adjacent. The old chronicler of this event concludes by humbly imploring his readers in the future to bear in record this observation : "That when you discern the sun to be eclipsed and the appearing of three black clouds, then expect great inundations, loss of cattel, changes and dreadful revolutions, even as a signal from heaven ; to purge nations and Commonwealths from oppression and tyranny and to restore to the Freeborn their just Freedom and Liberty, that so peace may abound within the walls of Sion and each man enjoy their own again."

It appears that three black clouds were seen in the firmament at Deptford on the evening preceding the day of this great flood.

Innkeepers' Petition to Parliament, 1698.

" The case of many inhabitants of the Towne of Deptford, in the County of Kent, many of whom are Innholders and Victuallers.

" To the Hon. House of Commons in Parliament assembled :—

" That the said inhabitants have from time to time as often as occasion hath been, entertained sick and wounded seamen, sent on shore from the men-of-war ; and have furnished them with all necessaries for their subsistence.

" That the said inhabitants have by such subsistence run themselves into very many and great debts with their Brewers, Bakers, Butchers, and other Tradesmen.

" That the inhabitants are brought so very poor, that they cannot any longer give subsistence to the said poor seamen ; and the said inhabitants and their families must unavoidably perish, if not timely relieved ; several of them having been arrested by their said creditors, and others withdrawn for fear, having left their families to Ruin.

" Wherefore the said Inhabitants most humbly beg that this Honourable House will be pleased to take their miserable case into your serious consideration ; and to give them such Relief therin, as your Honours shall think convenient, that thereby they may be enabled still to supply the said Sick and Wounded."

R

THE PLAGUE began its ravages in Deptford about July, 1665, when two houses were shut up. Its progress during August was more desolating, as may be seen by an extract from Mr. Evelyn's letter to Lord Cornbury, Lord Chamberlain to the Queen, dated from Sayes Court, September 6th, 1665 :—"After 6978 (and possibly half as many more concealed) which the pestilence has mowed down in London this week, near 30 houses are visited in this miserable village, whereof one has been the very nearest to my dwelling ; after a servant of mine now sick of a swelling (whom we have all frequented) and which we know not where will determine, behold me a living monument of God Almighty's protection and mercy. It was Saturday last ere my courageous wife would be per-suaded to take the alarm ; but she is now fled, with most of my family ; which my conscience, or something which I would have taken for my duty, obliges me to this sad station, till His Majesty take pity on me." The contagion raged in the town during the next twelve months, and it was not deemed safe to venture to any place of promiscu-ous resort. Mr. Evelyn says, December 31st, 1666 :—" Now blessed be God for His extraordinary mercies and preservation of me this year, when thousands and tens of thousands perished, and were swept away on each side of me, there dying in our parish this year 406 of the pestilence." On the 28th of October we find entered in the diary :—"The pestilence, through God's mercy, began now to abate considerably in our towne. During 1666 there were 522 persons died of the plague in Dept-ford, making a total of 928 for the two years, which must have been a large proportion of the inhabitants of the town at that period."

In the parish registers are lists of persons who had been touched for the King's Evil during the years 1684-5-6-7-8. In 1686 the number amounts to 82.

The subjoined letter, giving an account of an affray here during the cival wars, August 1, 1647, was written by a gentleman residing at Greenwich to a friend in London.

" DEAR SIR,—I have a sad subject to writ unto you of which makes me tremble, it is briefly thus, that Collonel Sir Robert Pie's Troope quartered at Deptford within a mile of the Towne, and at some other villages, a party of Horse came upon them (as it is said they came over Henley Bridge, and so into Kent, and wheeled about this way) they came to parley with the souldiers, intending (as it is believed to have taken them prisoners) but upon the parley some of them came to such high words, they calling them Runaway Rogues, the other retorted to them again, and meanwhile some got to horse, but at last it came to blows, some they took in pursuit, four were slain in the pursuite and divers wounded by Sir R. Pie's men. Here is blowes struck, here is bloodshed, the Lord direct the Parliament, and the City and the Army to study how to compose these fresh divisions least poor England bee whelmed in the Redde Sea of sub-division."

A much more serious fight took place at New Cross on the 26th of May, 1648, between the Kentish-men under the Duke of Lenox and other lords, and the Parliamentary Force under Colonel Rich, when the Royalists were victorious.

A DUEL was fought here on the morning of August 1, 1803, between Lieut. Sturge of the Militia and a Mr. W. B. Douglas, R.N. The second fire took effect, Lieut. Sturge being wounded in the right shoulder, and Mr. Douglas dangerously, in the groin. The dispute had been of a year's standing.

The Deptford Local Bench was established in 1813 ; and the County Magistrates, who sat for some years at the " White Swan," High-street, the " Roman Eagle," an old wooden structure in Church Street, now used as a Temperance Hall, and at the " Fountain " in Broadway, made short work of the numerous bands of footpads who infested the town and neighbourhood.

CASES OF LONGEVITY, &c.—Maudlin Augur, buried December, 1672, aged 106 ; Catherine Perry, buried December, 1676, aged 110 ; Sarah Mayo, buried August, 1705, aged 102 ; Elizabeth Wibrow, buried December,

1714, aged 101. Mrs. Ann Neale, relict of Captain Neale, died in the Old Trinity Ground, November 25, 1771, aged 101 ; Mrs. J. Gunthorpe, died July 6th, 1774, aged 99 years and 10 months ; John Brinkwell, Esq., R.N. and J.P., died October 11th, 1764, aged 91 ; Henry Selby, R.N. and J.P., died February 16th, 1765, aged 82 ; Margaret Browne, of Butt Lane, buried February 27th, 1714, aged 94 years ; Mary Eden, buried December 18th, 1721, aged 98.

On the 18th of April, 1835, Deborah Wybrow, aged about 103, residing in Crossfield Lane, near St. Paul's Church, came to an untimely end by falling down stairs and dislocating her neck. This old lady, at the time of her death, was in the perfect enjoyment of all her faculties, and could converse freely on topics within her recollection, ranging over a period of ninety years. She was an excellent knitter, and up to the day of her death, partly gained her livelihood by her needle. It had been arranged with the directors of the Greenwich Railway that Mrs. Wybrow should be their first passenger.

In February, 1774, there were living in St. Paul's parish, a labouring man and his wife, whose ages, together with that of their daughter, who was single, amounted to 214 years.

Of the living octogenarians of Deptford, may be mentioned Mr. G. Slous, 88, late vice-chairman of the Board of Guardians :—Mr. G. Roome, retired master sailmaker, 85 ; Mr. T. Watson, timber dealer ; Mr. Roberts, leather-seller, Wellington-street ; Mr. Green, butcher ; of nonogenarians there are Mr. Slous, of Morden Terrace, 90 ; Mr. R. Reugg, 95 ; and Mr. Sturdee, grandfather of the Chaplain of St. Barnabas' Church, Evelyn Street, who has attained the age of 96, and is not only in the enjoyment of good health, but can read very small print without spectacles.

John Greenleaf, commonly called Lord Greenleaf, a fiddler, who, by playing country dances at hops, fairs, &c., died at Deptford in October, 1774, having amassed a fortune of £3,000

Geo. Bryant, of Deptford Bridge, malt distiller, died September 13th, 1768 ; worth £100,000.

Mr. Giles, an eminent attorney, in which capacity he acquired a fortune of £10,000, died at his house at Deptford, December 9th, 1744.

DEPTFORD HALFPENNY.—Mr. Haycraft is in possession of a Kent Halfpenny issued by his forefathers, bearing date 1795. On one side it bears the legend "Kentish Liberty preserved by virtue and courage," and on the other "Prosperity to the wooden walls of Old England." Round the edge is inscribed "Payable at Thos. Haycraft's, Deptford."

Omitted from "Parish Worthies."

John Wade was born at Blackheath Hill on October 21st, 1800. In 1811 the family removed to 245, Evelyn Street, Deptford, then known as 43, Broomfield Place, in which house he spent the remainder of his useful life.

As a young man he became conspicuous as the leader of the Anti-Church Rate Party in St. Paul's, Deptford, and after a series of defeats, which only served to strengthen his invincible courage, he eventually triumphed, and from the year 1840, no church-rate was levied in that parish.

He defended his own cause in a trial instituted by the Church Party, subscriptions being sent in from all parts of England to cover his defence, but having succeeded in throwing the costs of the prosecution upon his opponents, the sum subscribed was spent in a testimonial to him.

On another occasion he received a testimonial which embodied the admiration of persons of all shades of religious and political opinion.

In the year 1854, Deptford was visited by an epidemic of cholera. He visited the homes of the stricken, and brought help to many a death bed by his kindly ministrations. Hundreds of widows and orphans were saved from utter despair during the ensuing winter by his exertions in raising a large sum of money for their relief. In connection with this subscription it may be interesting to note that Vice-Admiral Dundas, then in command of the Mediterranean fleet operating against Sebastopol, saw Mr. Wade's appeal for assistance in the "Times" newspaper and immediately forwarded him a cheque for £10. This truly Christian devotion to the necessities of others earned for him the soubriquet of The Good Samaritan of Deptford.

The fearful mental and physical strain to which he was subjected told upon his constitution, and laid the foundation of the illness to which he eventually succumbed.

As one of the prominent leaders of the Liberal Party in the Borough he exercised great influence, and by the clearness with which he expressed his views, secured many a wavering voter to the side which he espoused.

He was the uncompromising opponent of all civil and religious tyranny, and his pen was ever ready in advocating all social reforms and in denouncing all social abuses.

One year, after a very bad harvest, when food of all kinds was extravagantly dear, he succeeded in obtaining for the Dockyard labourers, for many weeks a rise in their wages.

Literally sacrificing himself for others he died on May 30th, 1863, leaving behind him so good a name that even his most determined opponents admitted that the motives by which he had been actuated through life were pre-eminently pure.

When the funeral procession passed through High Street, Deptford, the flag on the church was half mast high, showing that in death the admiration for the man out-weighed all party dissention.

SPECIMENS OF POETRY WRITTEN IN DEPTFORD.

ON VIRTUE.

Fair virtue, should I follow thee.
　　I should be naked and alone ;
For thou art not in company,
　　And scarce art to be found in one.

Thy rules are too severe and cold,
　　To be embrac'd by vigorous youth ;
And Fraud and Avarice arm the old
　　Against thy Justice and thy Truth.

He who, by light of reason led,
　　Instructs himself in thy rough school,
Shall all his life-time beg his bread,
　　And, when he dies, be thought a fool.

Though in himself he's satisfied
　　With a calm mind and cheerful heart,
The world will call his virtue, pride,
　　His holy life, design and art.

The reign of Vice is absolute,
  While good men vainly strive to rise ;
They may declaim, they may dispute,
  But shall continue poor and wise.

Honours and wealth are made by Fate
  To wait on fawning Impudence,
To give insipid coxcombs weight,
  And to supply the want of sense.

Mighty Pompey, whose great soul
  Design'd the liberty of Rome,—
In vain did Cæsar's arms control,
  And at Pharsalia was o'ercome.

His virtue, constant in distress,
  In Ptolemy no pity bred,
Who, barely guided by success,
  Secur'd his peace with his friend's head.

Brutus, whom gods ordained
  To do what Pompey would have done,
The generous motion entertain'd,
  And stabbed the tyrant on his throne.

This god-like Brutus, whose delight
  Was virtue, which he had ador'd,
Haunted by spectres over-night,
  Fell the next day on his own sword.

If, when his hope of victory lost,
  This noble Roman could exclaim,
Oh, virtue, whom I courted most,
  I find she's but an empty name !

In a degenerate age like this,
  We with more reason may oonclude
That Fortune will attend on Vice,
  Misery on those who dare be good.

JOHN EVELYN, son of SYLVA EVELYN.

THE VILLAGE MAID.

Come, come, dear girl ; come, cease those tears,
  And put thy trust in me ;
Away with all thy foolish fears,
  I'll still be true to thee.
I loved thee in thy childhood, dear,
  When we together play'd ;
Thou wert the fairest of the fair
  To me, my village maid.

As years rolled on, my love for thee
  Stronger and stronger grew,
And dost thou think such love can be
  Dispersed like morning dew?
No, no, I still remember dear
  When we together play'd;
And none with thee my love shall share,
  My sweet, my village maid.

Then take my heart, 'tis all thine own,
  Give me the only prize
I crave : that's thee and thee alone.
  Come, dry those tearful eyes,
And let me see again those smiles,
  The same as when I strayed
O'er hill and dale for many miles
  With thee, my village maid.

JOHN LACY.

MY OLD BLUE COAT.

Old friend, the summer's gone at last,
And soon again the winter's blast.
Will come, old coat, and cannot we,
Be friends as once we used to be ?
'Tis true when summer days were fair,
A coat I had for lighter wear;
Treating thee almost with disdain,
Forgetting I should want again—
          My old blue coat!

But now these summer days are o'er,
The butterfly is seen no more;
The bee that sipp'd from every flower,
The soft, the calm, refreshing shower—
All these are gone, the swallows too
Have for awhile bid us adieu ;
And choking fogs each night proclaim
That shortly I must wear again—
          My old blue coat!

How oft upon a summer's night
I've sat and listened with delight,
To hear the warbling nightingale
Sing in some sweet sequestered vale ;
The bat perchance came flitting by,
And all around, the clear blue sky
Was seen ; but now such joys are o'er,
I feel that I shall want once more—
          My old blue coat!

In flaunting blowse and satin vest,
I thought myself once richly drest ;
And need I tell that thou wert thrust
Aside to slumber in the dust.
But like the tulip when in bloom,
Such summer trappings fade too soon ;
And I must own with truth sincere,
There's nought like thee for useful wear—
                    My old blue coat !

Come forth then from thy dusty cell
And hear what merry hearts can tell ;
Oh, yes. come forth and join with me,
In all the joys of Christmas glee ;
Come forth and hear the jocund song
Pass merrily round the social throng ;
The toast I'll give, whate'er the rest
Of friends may be, I love thee best—
                    My old blue coat !

For 'tis when warmly wrapt in thee
My heart is glad, my mind is free ;
'Tis then my actions I can scan,
And study what becomes a man ;
My faults are many, yet I trust,
Like thee they'll slumber in the dust ;
And may my life hereafter be
To others as thou'st been to me—
                    My old blue coat !

                              J. LACY.

Mr. John Lacy was born at Wroxham, near Norwich, December 19th, 1814. At the tender age of eight years he commenced work in a pottery at Wroxham, leaving home at the same time in consequence of his father's second marriage with a young wife. When fifteen years old he came to Deptford, and singularly enough made his first application for work, unsuccessfully, at the very pottery in Church Street, Deptford, of which he has now been master since 1848. His first engagement in this neighbourhood was errand boy to Mr. Samuel Tooling, of Nelson Street, Greenwich, which he soon quitted for work in a pottery at Norwood.

Mr. Lacy is a self-taught man, the only education he ever received being at the Church Sunday School in his native village. He has always taken a great interest in parish matters, having been thrice elected a member of

the Greenwich Board of Works ; and has been for many
years a Vestryman of St. Paul's, Deptford. He was one
of the founders of the local Philanthropic Society, of
which he is a trustee.

Mr. Lacy is a poet of no mean pretensions, and it is to
be hoped that he will shortly publish a volume of his
lyric poems. Mr. O'Connor, in his recently-published
volume of " Songs for Soldiers," racily and truly describes
him as " potter, poet, and right hearty good fellow."

APRIL.

Herald of Summer, birds, and flowers,
  Joy bringer e'er to me,
April, crowned with sunny showers,
  I'll pipe a lay to thee,
  As erst through copse and lea ;
When life and fire were in my veins,
This harp of mine sung lusty strains
  To thee, through copse and lea.

Through copse and lea, when saffron morn
  Flung off her robe of night,
And, like a child, wayward and wild,
  I sunward took my flight :
  Then 'twas a glorious sight !
To see thee, angered, raise a storm,
To see the sun shine through thy form,
  And make a glorious sight !

The robin and the martin flew
  In joy from tree to tree,
The lark in ether clarioned
  Its glad notes wild and free ;
  And I—I sang to thee
For all to me was bright and fair :
I knew no grief, I felt no care,
  The while I sang to thee.

I mind me well, when blustering March
  Charged all the clouds with gloom ;
They wept their anger out in tears,
  When March went to the tomb,
  When May leapt in thy womb !
Thy travail was refreshing showers ;
It brought us summer, birds, and flowers,
  When May leapt in thy womb.

Herald of summer, birds, and flowers,
   Joy bringer e'er to me,
April, crowned with sunny showers,
   I'll pipe a lay to thee.
   As erst through copse and lea ;
When fire and life were in my veins
This harp of mine sang lusty strains,
   To thee through copse and lea.

Mr. O'Connor, the Irish peasant poet (who recently received an annuity from the Civil List for his poetical works), is a native of the South of Ireland. He is a self-educated man, being well advanced towards manhood before he could even read. His wife belongs to a Deptford family and some of his best poems were written during his long residence here. His best known works are " Songs of a life," " New Irish Melodies," " Songs for Soldiers," " Love is Fair," and " Lives of the Irish Poets.". *The Pall Mall Gazette*, in reviewing his poetry, pronounces him to be " an Irishman with a soul for refinement and delight ;" and he has received cordial words of praise from some of the best of living poets. A memoir of him was published in the *Biograph* for March, 1881.

SUMMER EVE.

When the timid blackbird pipes
From amid the thorny brake ;
When the mavis sweetly warbles
By the green-embosom'd lake ;
When Philomel with plaintive note
Pours forth her ever-varying song ;
When the pale moon in highest heaven
Shines bright the twinkling stars among ;
When the heavy dew distils,
And not a zephyr stirs the air ;—
Then I love to walk abroad,
With my own, my chosen fair.
For fairer than the moon is she,
Her eyes more bright than any star,
Her voice more mellow than the birds,
And sweeter still—still sweeter far.

                      W. T. VENESS.

Mr. Veness belongs to an old Deptford family. He succeeded his father as Sexton and Parish Clerk of St. Paul's, Deptford, in 1840. He married and resided in Hamilton Street before taking orders and proceeding as a missionary clergyman to Berbice, in South America.

LINES ON A FALLEN MULBERRY TREE.

"Desolate Tree! why are thy branches bare?
    What hast thou done
To win strange Winter from the Summer air,—
    Frost from the sun?"—*Sir E. L. Bulwer.*

Thy strength—and thy glory's departed, O Tree,
    And faded thy beauty and bloom,
Then sink to thy rest on the garden's green breast,
    Hoary Mulberry sink to the tomb!

Thou hast weathered the blasts of a century,
    O Tree,
    And smiled at the thunder's dread boom:
Thou hast witnessed uninjured the rush of the
    storm,
    The Autumnal, and Wintry gloom.
Then sink to thy rest on the garden's green breast,
    Hoary Mulberry sink to thy tomb!

Thou hast left thy co-mates of the garden, O Tree
    To associate with what? and with whom?
With relentless decay—and the rude cankerworm
    Which will revel and feast in thy womb;
Then sink to thy rest on the garden's green breast,
    Hoary Mulberry sink to thy tomb!

The hearts—which beat high at thy planting, O
    Tree,
    And gave thee this spot for thy home,
Have long since forgotten to throb in that land
    Where sorrow and sighing's unknown;
Then sink to thy rest on the garden's green breast,
    Hoary Mulberry sink to thy tomb!

The flowers that grew 'neath thy foliage, O Tree,
    Are still fragrant with Summer's perfume;
And the woodlands sweet warblers that sung in
    thy boughs
    Have left thee alone to thy doom;
Then sink to thy rest on the garden's green breast,
    Hoary Mulberry sink to thy tomb!

No more shall the breeze float around thee, O
    Tree.
    Nor the sun thy proud verdure illume,
But still thou shalt not fall unsung, hoary Tree,
    The minstrel thy praise shall attune,
Then sink to thy rest on the garden's green breast,
    Hoary Mulberry sink to thy tomb!

But soon will my rhymes be forgotten, O Tree,
    And die like a zephyr at noon!
And the worms which now feast on thy bowels ere
    long,
    May the heart of thy minstrel consume ;
Then sink to thy rest on the garden's green breast,
    Hoary Mulberry sink to thy tomb!

This, this, is the lot of the wisest, O Tree,
    They are cradled in sorrow and gloom,
And basking awhile in life's noontide ray,
    Like butterflies sink to the tomb ;
Then sink to thy rest on the garden's green breast,
    Hoary Mulberry sink to thy tomb!

B. WALE.

Mr. Wale, a native of Deptford, is, we believe, now a
Baptist minister somewhere in the West of England.

THE HEAVENS.

From the Time's Telescope for 1831.

'Midst dazzling rays! 'midst dazzling rays!
    Of glorious orbs. I wing my flight,
Whose lustre mocks the diamond's blaze,
    With beams unutterably bright.

The glittering stars! the glittering stars!
    Of emerald, topaz, ruby hue ;
That roll along their radiant cars,
    Through heaven's unfathomed depths of blue.

Orion's beams! Orion's beams;
    His star-gemmed belt, and shining blade ;
His isles of light, his silvery streams,
    And gloomy gulphs of mystic shade.

The starry *lyre*! the starry *lyre*!
    Circling with harmony the pole ;
By seraphs swept, the notes aspire,
    And round Heaven's burning *altar* roll

The beaming *Cross*! the beaming *Cross*!
　Dread symbol of the sacred tree ;
Bright stars its hallowed form emboss,
　And sparkle through infinity.

Mysterious ones ! mysterious ones !
　Crowd on the view like spectral gleams
Of wandering or of withering sums,
　Or unformed systems' infant beams.

Each glowing gem ! each glowing gem !
　Which radiates in the stellar train ;
All speak *His* hand that rolleth them,
　Along the vast cerulean plain.

Amazing span ! amazing span !
　Oh, the vast-temple of the skies !
Who shall its deep foundation scan,
　Or to its top-most star arise ?

On Seraph's wing ! on Seraph's wing !
　Through vast creation's field to roam ;
My soul exulting thither brings,
　And finds the universe its home.

But fancy fails ! but fancy fails !
　Though borne by science deep and high ;
The mortal clog of clay prevails,—
　Heaven's mysteries, who would learn—must die.

J. T . BARKER.

"About 50 years ago there was a famous school established in Union Street, Deptford, conducted by Mr. John Theodore Barker, son of the Rev. J. T. Barker, then minister of what was familiarly called "Barker's Chapel, Butt-lane." The fame of this school was known far and wide, and the principal gentry and tradesmen and their wives were at that time educated at this popular school. Mr. Barker gave public lectures on "Botany and Astronomy" in his School Room, to crowded audiences. In the science of "Astronomy," Mr. Barker was highly distinguished. He was editor of *Time's Telescope*, a publication at that day of the highest repute."

HOME.

How sweet is home when holy joys,
  Are like the sunbeam's shining;
When love each honest heart employs,
  The ivy there entwining :

Chorus :

    Where God's sweet gifts, loves's pledges rare,
      In play all round us hover,
    It seems to me the hand of God
      Has gifts for each true lover.

See, every face has got a smile,
  That pure and happy token,
That tells each heart is pure the while,
  And happiness unbroken.   (Chorus.)

See, still unknown to pomp or pride,
  Heart to fond heart is throbbing,
Love there, the ever flowing tide,
  So full of wild sweet sobbing.   (Chorus).

No angry thoughts true joy can kill,
  Love reigns in each pure bosom,
One's pleasure is the other's will,
  For thus true love both blossom.   (Chorus).

O, far from us be grief and tears,
  In love's lists ever sporting ;
And we—we've wedded been for years
  And still are busy courting.   (Chorus).

W. JOHNSON.

Mr. Johnson, son of Richard and Mary Maguinness
was born at Coragoley, Florence Court, Co. Fermanagh,
Ireland, 19th August, 1845. He joined the Police force
24th September, 1866, and has been Inspector in the
Deptford sub-division for some years.

LIST OF SUBSCRIBERS.

W. J. Evelyn, Esq., Wotton, Surrey.
T. W. Boord, Esq., M.P. for Greenwich.
Baron Henry de Worms, M.P.
Rev. H. G. Cundy, D.D., Rector of St. Paul's, Deptford.
  ,, Canon Money, M.A., Vicar of St. John's, ,,
  ,, J. Malcolmson, Vicar of St. Luke's, ,,
  ,, J. C. Wetherell, M.A., Vicar of St. Peter's,
      Brockley.
  ,, H. A. Walker, M.A., Vicar of St. James's, Hatcham.
  ,, R. Gardner Smith, Vicar of All Saints,' ,,
  ,, M. P. Fannan, The Presbytery, High-street.
  ,, J. A. Pearson, M.A., Alvington, Reigate.
  ,, J. P. Kane, M.A., Kennington-park, S.E.
  ,, Henry Wells, Curate of St. Luke's.
  ,, H. S. Brown, Curate of All Saints.
  ,, J. W. Sturdee, Chaplain of St. Barnabas.
  ,, R. Thomas, Curate of St. Paul's.
  ,, J. G. M. Stretton, B.A., St. Cyprian's. Brockley.
  ,, Edward Carroll, Presbytery, High-street.
  ,, S. A. Dougherty, Stainton, Cumberland.
  ,, J. Smith, Manor-road, Brockley.
Mr. E. L. Adams, Southwark-park Brewery.
  ,, Burgess, New-cross.
  ,, Baker, Deptford-bridge.
Messrs. F. Braby and Co., Ida-wharf.
Mr. E. G. G. Bax, Wotton-road.
  ,, G. Bray, Prince-street.
  ,, F. J. Bourke, New-cross Middle Class School.
  ,, Cushion, Edward-street.
  ,, E. H. Cook, Hereford.
  ,, Cole, Warwick-street.
Mrs. Crawshaw, Hosbury.

Mr. Collins, Wootton-road.
„ James Cox, Breakspear-road.
„ James Cobbett, Lee.
„ T. W. Collins, Selborne House, Greenwich.
„ H. J. Collier, Guildford-road, Greenwich.
„ A. J. Dickinson, F.C.S., &c., Neptune Tar Works.
„ F. J. Dickinson, New-cross-road.
Miss E. Denton, Salthouse-lane, Hull.
Mr. Alexander Dickinson, Tyrwhitt-road, St. John's.
„ Eddy, Wellington-place, Deptford.
„ J. C. Eno, Fruit Salt Works, Hatcham.
„ A. G. Fleming, Denham, Bucks.
„ H. G. Fleming, Lee.
„ G. A. Grant, Brockley High School.
„ Grant, Royal Victoria-yard.
Mrs. Garlick, Stanley-street Board School.
Mr. Hugh M. Gordon, The Courtyard, Eltham.
„ G. R. Humphery, Amersham-vale.
„ B. Hills, Regent-street, Deptford.
Miss Ingram.
„ Emma Jelley, Hatcham.
Mr. Johnson, Prince-street.
„ S. Jennings, Deptford-green.
„ Jackson, Steam Navigation Works.
„ F. A. King, 4, Sergeant's Inn, Chancery Lane.
„ Stuart Knill, The Crosslets, Blackheath.
Kent Mineral Waters Co., Dixon-road, New Cross.
Mr. George Kemp, Brockley-road.
„ W. R. Kersey, High-street.
„ John Lacy, The Pottery, Reginald-road.
„ Larkin, Montagu House School.
„ J. Liddiard, New Cross-road.
„ T. W. Marchant, High-street.
„ W. Morris, Kent Water Works.
„ Marshall, Lewisham High-road.
„ T. J. Merritt, Blackheath-road, Greenwich.
„ Mosse, Lewisham.
„ F. Morgan, "White Swan" Hotel.
„ C. F. Miller, Royal Victualling Yard.
Mrs. McKenzie, Liverpool.

Mr. Mowbray, Grove-road.
  ,, Newnham, Church-street.
  ,, Needham, New Cross-road.
  ,, C. P. O'Conor, Plumstead.
  ,, J. J. Pakes, Malpas-road.
  ,, A. J. Potter, Brockley-road.
  ,, E. J. Preston, Tressillian-road, St. John's.
  ,, J. T. Prestige, Wickham-road, Brockley.
  ,, J. T. Prestige, Junr., Breakspear-road, Brockley.
  ,, Sydney Prestige, Wickham-road,   ,,
  ,, Reuben Prestige,   ,,   ,,
  ,, G. W. Paxon, Evelyn Estate Office.
  ,, T. Prior, Reginald-road.
  ,, J. J. Pitt, Evelyn-street.
Mr. B. Roberts, High-street.
  ,, R. Roper, Lewisham High-road.
Mr. W. Gurley Smith, Lewisham High-road.
  ,, J. P. Shelley, The Ferns, Lewisham.
  ,, Job Skudder, Evelyn-street.
  ,, F. Sturdee,   ,,
  ,, Salter, "King's Head," Church-street.
  ,, J. Seaward, Malpas-road.
  ,, J. D., Broadway, Deptford.
  ,, G. Slous, New-cross-road.
Miss J. Stronach, Hull.
Mr. A. Seaman, Endwell-road, Brockley.
  ,, J. Sprunt, New-cross-gate.
  ,, Tavner, Shere-road.
  ,, R. Trickett, Church-street.
  ,, J. Thompson, Peckham.
  ,, J. G. Thomas, High-street.
  ,, G. Townsend, New-cross-road.
Mr. W. Wright, High-street.
  ,, E. T. White, Union-street, Deptford.
Miss Whateley, Hughes' Fields Board School.
  ,, E. Watson, Hatcham.
Mr. Hy. Whelan, 198, Church-street.
  ,, F. T. Wheeler, Breakspear-road, Brockley.
  ,, Wood, "Druid's Head," Church-street.
  ,, E. Wade, Dermody-road, Lewisham.

R. ROPER, Inventor and Patentee of the Self-Launching Bridge Life Raft.

RICHARD ROPER & SON,

143, LEWISHAM HIGH ROAD,

NEW CROSS, S.E.,

Plumbers & Decorators to the Lords Commissioners of the Admiralty.

CONTRACTORS for GENERAL REPAIRS to the WAR OFFICE.

GREENHOUSE, CONSERVATORY & HORTICULTURAL BUILDERS.

PLUMBING, GASFITTING, GLAZING,

BATH, & HOT-WATER WORK.

Bell Hanging and Zinc Work.

CARPENTERS, JOINERS & BLIND MAKERS.

Shop and Office Fitters.

Ships' Cabins Fitted Up and Tastefully Decorated.

ESTIMATES AND COLOURED DESIGNS

SENT TO ALL PARTS OF THE COUNTRY, FOR EVERY DESCRIPTION OF

Plain & Inlaid Graining, Marbling, Decorating, etc.

Having been Highly Commended for Sanitary Arrangements in Houses and on board some of the large Government Troop Ships, we pay special attention to this class of work.

FRENCH AND ENGLISH PAPER HANGINGS.

DADOS FOR STAIRCASES, DRAWING, DINING, AND BILLIARD ROOMS.

GAS FITTINGS, &c.

Experienced Workmen Sent to All Parts of the Country.

People's Co-operative Permanent Building Society.

Woolwich—
BRANCH OFFICE,
No. 6, New-rd.,
Open 2nd Tuesday in every
month from 7 till
8 p.m.

Deptford—
BRANCH OFFICE,
Mechanics'
Institute,
Open Fridays from 8 till
9 p.m.

Chief Office, BLUE STILE, GREENWICH-RD.
OPEN MONDAY EVENINGS FROM 7 TILL 9 O'CLOCK.

Shares, £50 each.   Subscriptions, 5s. Monthly.

ANNUAL INCOME, £60,000.

REGISTERED UNDER THE FRIENDLY SOCIETIES' ACT,
And Incorporated under the New Building Societies' Act, 37 and 38 Vic., Cap. 42.

THE Society was Established in the year 1847, and is Permanent, members can therefore join at any time without having to pay up arrears. There is no liability attached to members. Money may be invested, at a good interest, by periodical instalments, Five per cent. compound interest is added yearly by subscribing shares, and an annual bonus on all shares two years old and upwards. SINGLE DEPOSIT SHARES may be purchased on a 5 or 14 years' scale. Withdrawals paid on giving one month's notice.

Small sums may be invested in the BANK FOR DEPOSITS, and four per cent. Interest (calculated on the monthly balances) allowed on each pound deposited.

NOTE—THIS IS ONE OF THE BEST AND MOST LIBERAL BUILDING SOCIETIES EXTANT FOR BORROWERS.

Money is ADVANCED IMMEDIATELY in large or small sums to members to purchase Freehold or Leasehold property, £10 0s. 0d. per Annum will repay a Loan of £100 in 16 years. The Solicitor's and Surveyor's charges are moderate.

BORROWERS participate in the profits and can redeem their mortgage at any time.

Since the formation of the Society, upwards of £450,000 have been advanced to Borrowers.

As soon as a member redeems his mortgage the Rent of the House will secure to him an ANNUITY FOR LIFE.

RENT PAYERS who give away ONE SIXTH of their income, or ONE DAY'S LABOUR EVERY WEEK to their landlords, are advised to join this Society, and obtain an advance to enable them, by a few years' thrift and industry to abolish the worst of all Taxes, the RENT TAX.   WM. GURLEY SMITH, Secretary.

The Kentish Mercury,

(ESTABLISHED 1833.)

THE GREAT ADVERTISING MEDIUM FOR WEST KENT AND SOUTH LONDON.

The Proprietors have pleasure in announcing a

FURTHER INCREASE IN CIRCULATION,

THE WEEKLY AVERAGE DURING 1881 HAVING REACHED

14,767.

Offices—

GREENWICH, DEPTFORD, WOOLWICH & CITY.

MERRITT & HATCHER, Proprietors.

Sold by all Chemists, price 2/9 and 4/6.

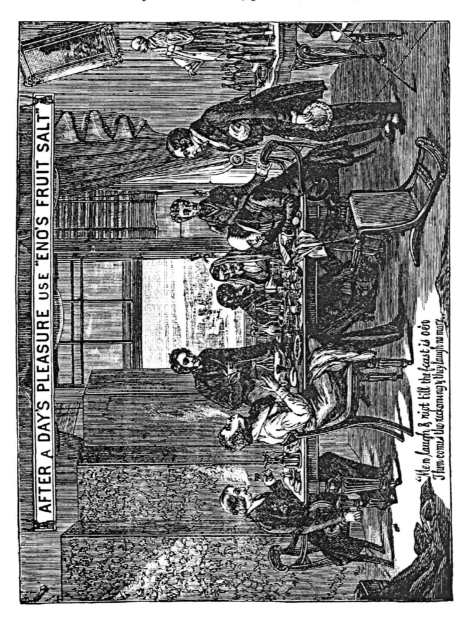

CPSIA information can be obtained at www.ICGtesting.com
Printed in the USA
LVOW072006060612

284955LV00011B/70/P